From the Cab
Stories from a locomotive engineer

From the Cab

Stories from a locomotive engineer

By Doug Riddell

Pentrex

Pasadena, California

Publisher: Michael W. Clayton
Book Editor: Brent Haight
Art Director: Jay Blazek
Editorial Assistance: Andrea O'Brien, James P. Ziegler, Trish Miller
Production Manager: Trish Miller

Copyright © 1999 by Pentrex Media Group, LLC, Pasadena, California

ISBN 1-56342-010-4

Published by
Pentrex Media Group, LLC
P.O. Box 94911
Pasadena, CA 91109
Printed and bound in the United States of America

Library of Congress Cataloging-In-Publication Data

Riddell, Doug 1949 -
    From the Cab: Stories from a locomotive engineer / Doug Riddell
        p.   cm.
    ISBN 1-56342-010-4
    1. Riddell, Doug 1949 -   . 2. Locomotive engineers—United
    States—Biography. I. Title.
HD8039.R322U56 1999
625.1′092–dc21
[B]   99-19470
                                                                      CIP

10   9   8   7   6   5   4   3   2

First Edition

This Book Is Dedicated To

my grandfather, John Everett Beazley,
from whom I learned the love of trains;

my grandmother, Eva Davis Beazley,
from whom I learned the love of God;

my mother, Margaret Beazley Riddell,
from whom I learned the love of family;

my father, Alvin Lanier Riddell,
from whom I learned the love of honor;

my son, Ryan Everett Riddell,
who I hope will benefit from all that I've learned.

Foreward

Actually, I think his grandpa Beazley's Hamilton Railway Special is the perpetrator habitually reminding Doug Riddell to spill the beans on his improbable life of railroading and the absurd characters he's encountered.

For sure, there's a Damon Runyon complexion to a railroad, but extracting the most implausible suspects from the nooks and crannies in which they periodically and alternately practice interpersonal terror and slapstick demands a practical social anthropologist like Riddell. And did I mention his capacity to align words so that a frequently audible "gee whiz" might be sandwiched between raucous guffaws?

An element of Southwest Airlines' success is a written policy to tolerate and encourage individualism and creativity. Then there are railroads. How Riddell has survived a career among the dullard, doctrinaire denizens of railroad corporate offices amazes me. No matter.

Riddell is the first to explain—hell, recognize—the similarity among the symmetry of gymnastics, the training of an operatic tenor, and the discipline of commanding a locomotive.

I've never asked him, but I'm absolutely positive Riddell would confess to being more proud of his locomotive engineer's license than his college degree in communications.

Pull up a chair, a comfortable one, and sit a spell. If there's but a trace of railfan in your flesh, you ain't a goin' nowhere till you meet the chaotic cast of characters comprising Doug Riddell's two-decade obsession with, lust for, and madcap dash across the Seaboard, CSX, and Amtrak.

All aboard,
Frank N. Wilner

Frank Wilner is the author of THE AMTRAK STORY *and* RAILROAD MERGERS: HISTORY, ANALYSIS, INSIGHT.

Acknowledgments

A child grows to reflect the influence of everyone and everything in its environment. Likewise, this book is not merely a product of its author, but ultimately it is a product influenced by many others. Listing each one would eclipse this book in volume, but I wish to thank some very special individuals.

My family is not only my life's foundation, but it has often served as place of a refuge. Special thanks to parents, grandparents, a special aunt and uncle, a brother, and sisters who offer love, direction, and encouragement every day of my life. Cousin Mildred Bowles advised me to insure my success by writing about things with which I am familiar. Jack Stecklein, my father's late cousin, introduced me to the human side of railroading.

Others I'd like to thank publicly are: Richard and Janice Hunt, the late Bob Lewis, Dale Wilson Diacont, the C&O Historical Society, the ACL-SAL Railroads Historical Society, Deborah Koehle, Jan Irwin, Brian Solomon, Carl Swanson, John Gruber, Brent Haight, Andrea O'Brien, James Ziegler, Katie Norton, Trish Miller, Jay Blazek, and Mike Clayton.

None of this would have happened had my wife, Sandra, not urged me to purchase a computer for her use as a classroom teacher. Were it not for her, what you read here and in my monthly "From the Cab" column in RAILNEWS magazine would still be a trash can full of typing paper. Trusting her good judgment, nothing I produce eludes her scrutiny. It must be true that behind every successful man, there's always a wonderful woman telling him "You're doing it the wrong way," because luckily for me, Sandy is usually right.

Contents

Section 1: Gett'n on Track

Section 2: Switch'n Tracks

Section 3: What Track Are We On? Amtrak!

Section 4: Keep'n Track

Section 1

Gett'n on Track

Chapter 1: Oh Boy, They've Hired One of Those Buffs

I'm not really sure what I expected when I parked my 1973 Olds Cutlass in the employee parking lot for my first day of work on Seaboard Coast Line Railroad at Brown Street Yard in Richmond, Virginia. It took a second or two for it to sink in that I didn't have to scan the surroundings for railroad police. There was no need to carefully plan my picture, charge in, shoot, and run. No one was going to question my presence. I was not a visitor. I belonged there. I had a piece of paper signed by Trainmaster W. W. Robertson attesting to the fact that "A. D. Riddell is authorized to ride trains and/or locomotives for the purpose of acquainting himself with the physical characteristics of the road."

At age 27, with a Bachelors Degree in Mass Communications, a 10-year broadcasting career behind me, and a rejection letter from every railway system in the country, on May 18, 1977, I was going to work for the railroad! Well, almost work for the railroad. You see, at that time, you cubbed with an experienced crew for five days (without pay) in order to become qualified to be marked up on the extra board. Once marked up, you established your seniority date when you were called to work your first paid job assignment. (Mine would be May 23, 1977.)

Like a ball and chain attached to the ankle of a convict, the date one first signs the register as a member of the crew forever follows a railroader. Wherever and whenever he goes, it never allows him to escape its influence until the day he casts off that shackle, relinquishes his job to a junior employee, and goes home to await the arrival of his first pension check. Unless of course Father Time or Mother Nature intervenes and overrules the Railroad Retirement Board. My seniority date would determine which days I worked, with whom I worked, when I took vacation, how much vacation I was entitled to, and more. But at that moment, considering everything I had been through for the opportunity to be there, for pay or for gratis, this was the realization of my fondest and earliest childhood dream.

Glancing to the south, at a point where the high iron of the former Seaboard Air Line and Chesapeake & Ohio railroads rose from the floor of Shockoe Valley to embrace the platforms of the abandoned elevated train shed at Richmond's venerable Main Street Station, with its ancient clock tower, I took note of the time. It seems as though I was only at arms length from the touch of bumper-to-bumper motorists rocketing over the James River basin and Richmond's bustling financial district, making their way to the balmy shores of Florida or the towering skyscrapers of Manhattan.

I reached into the pocket of my faded Levis and tugged on the chain that unwillingly yielded a shining gold Hamilton Railway Special—once the most prized possession of John Everett Beazley, my late grandfather, a conductor on the Peninsula Subdivision of the Chesapeake & Ohio Railroad. That priceless timepiece was now the most prized possession of his grandson. Thus, it seemed quite fitting that it should accompany me on this special occasion, following in his footsteps. It concurred with the station's clock. How many times had I seen grandpa smile with satisfaction after consulting that very same watch?

I reached across the front seat and placed a denim Lee railroad hat on my head that featured the Seaboard Coast Line Railroad logo. Along with a pair of Wells Lamont leather work gloves, I grabbed my new, black metal lunch pail with its Thermos bottle tucked under the lid. The last time I carried a lunch box, it featured a painting of Roy Rogers and Trigger on its top, and I was on my way to J. E. B. Stuart Elementary School in the Barton Heights section of Richmond's old north side.

Satisfied that this extra 15 minutes would allow me ample time to get acquainted with my crew, I walked toward the nearest door of the single story, bay windowed, brick yard office, to which a long house trailer had been permanently attached. I paused briefly outside the door, ran my fingers across the smooth glass face of the Hamilton one more time, looked skyward, and said, "I finally made it, grandpa. Wish me luck. Thanks."

It took an extra nudge with my shoulder to open the stubborn door. Losing my balance, I stumbled through the threshold and collided with a chubby, thin-haired fellow in overalls and a denim shirt—my grand entrance onto the stage of railroading.

Attempting to salvage some dignity, I apologized, smiled, and asked him, "Are you conductor Peele?"

"Conductor? Me? Lord no, son. I work for a living. I don't play with them damn boxcars, I inspect and repair them," he laughed. "You're at the wrong end of the building. This is the carman's room. Train and engine crews are down the hall in the lunchroom."

I thanked him for the directions, again apologized for the collision, and walked down the short hallway to an open door, from which emanated laughter and conversation. Around a single laminate-topped table sat a dozen or so men, sipping cups of hot Maxwell House, smoking Pall Malls and Lucky Strikes. The image of these men would forever stay with me. In the years to come, sadly, such scenes of camaraderie would appear only in my memories. Most of these men had 25 to 30 years of service to their credit. Most had been there since 6:30 a.m., although some were not scheduled to begin their tour of duty until 7, 7:30, or 8 a.m. I quickly got the impression that some of them might even show up on their off days. In fact, quite often, retirees showed up for a hot cup of coffee sweetened by memories, stirred with the latest rumors from the sand house. I came to think of it as a breakfast club. For them—almost exclusively former SAL employees—the railroad was still a good place to work, and a distinct pride prevailed. Oh sure, they complained about their job, as all railroad workers do, but it was strictly in-house, among family. The Seaboard Coast Line Railroad was their railroad.

"Have a cup fella?" asked a small, thin, red-faced man, dressed in matching Sears Roebuck gray work clothes with the sleeves rolled midway up his forearms. His tattoos were faded with the years. A stained piece of paper taped to the side of the stainless coffee urn read, "25¢—No Credit!"

"First one's on me. My name's Henry Mason. You must be one of the new hires that's supposed to be showing up this week. We've had a few men step down, and they're running short."

"Better take him up on that coffee, son," joked another. "Railroad men are not the most generous people on earth. I guess that's because as hard as we have to work to earn our money, we're not real anxious to part with it." I later found this to be totally untrue. When someone is out sick, when there's a death in the family, when someone's son needs money to get to Amarillo, Texas, to wrestle in an AAU competition, or for whatever other cause that a fellow railroader needs a helping hand, we almost always dig deep into our pockets. When a case of chocolate almond fund-raising candy bars shows up on the lunchroom table, they're snapped up in a matter of minutes, no matter what high school band or Little League team's name is on the wrapper.

"Thanks," I said, already feeling welcome. "Sugar and cream in mine. Say, where can I store this lunch and my grip?"

"Grip?" remarked another old white-haired railroader, with steel blue eyes, framed by a tanned, weather-beaten face. "You gonna lug that leather bag up and down the switching ladder all day? Hell, son, this is the yard, not the road. We work our tails off putting trains together and tak'n 'em apart here, spotting cars in private sidings, and taking cuts of coal across the river to the paper plant. Those guys on the through freights that stop and pick up here don't know what work is. When we ride the train, it's for vacation. Since all they do is ride the train, they must be on a vacation."

"What all you got in that fancy grip?" inquired another, reaching for the new bag I had purchased the night before. "A rain suit! That'll come in handy, but you won't want to wear it. You'll be doing so much exercising that the cool rain will feel good."

"Yeah," I nodded. "You're probably right, but I had to have something to put my rule book, timetable, and switch keys in."

"Levis Strauss already thought of that, son," snorted the white-haired man, apparently growing a bit hostile as he patted the seat of his faded overalls. "It's called a back pocket. What else?"

"My camera," I announced.

"Camera? You one of them buffs?" he asked, as if he already knew the answer but hoped I would prove him wrong.

"I've always loved trains," I smiled, " and I've always ..."

"Wanted to work for the railroad? I know son." He shook his head and wiped his lips with the back of his hand, as if by doing so he could stop what was coming out next. "Oh god, Rosie, they've hired one of those damn buffs."

"Lord," the other man frowned, squinting out from behind his thick, wire-rimmed specks, "You think his crew will get anything done today, or will they just pose for pictures?"

Before another word could be uttered, the door opened and a tall, stout man with gapping front teeth and precious little hair on the top of his head shouted, "Tater, go double C&O 3 to 4 and put it in 13. Set the Bellwoods in 7 on top of the stuff that's already there. Here's the switch list. By the way, the trainmaster said to tell you that you're gonna have a Mr. A. D. ... looks like Riddle."

"Rid-DELL," I cautiously corrected him as all eyes in the room focused on me.

"Yeah," he agreed, "Riddell. He'll be cubbing with you."

Looking around to see which one the yardmaster was addressing, I felt the table rumble as old white hair stood up, reached out, and snatched the list from the yardmaster. As my eyes met his, his tan reddened two or three shades. Suddenly, there was a loud crash—the sound of my new lunch pail, which had been teetering on the edge of the picnic table, hitting the floor.

"Hope you ain't got a thermos in that lunch pail," Henry Mason said as a couple of the others muffled their laughter.

Closer inspection revealed that not only had the thermos' glass liner shattered, but the lunch pail's contents now floated in apple juice.

"He didn't do it on purpose, kid," offered the bespeckled man called Rosie. "It was right on the edge of the table."

"I know," I sighed. "I guess I'll have to buy lunch."

"Hope you like Cokes and nabs," he said.

Cokes and nabs (peanut butter spread between two cheese crackers—a southern staple). I guess every railroad yard office is the same. I used to stand trackside as a child, mesmerized by the switching operations at C&O's Fulton Yard—just a mile or so away—while my grandfather went inside to pick up his paycheck. For a dime I could extract an eight-ounce cola from the red-and-white machine next to the yard office's screened door, and for a nickel more I could nosh on a pack of peanuts or nabs from the adjacent Tom's vending machine. That was 20 years ago. A Coke and a pack of nabs might have satisfied captain Beazley's seven-year-old grandson, but it wasn't even going to put a dent in the appetite of a 27-year-old brakeman that ol' Taterhead was going to put to the test.

"Preacher," Peele shouted to an elderly pipe smoker. "You've got the 132 today. Make sure it's clean. Mr. Riddell might want to take some pictures of it. Rosie, you and Neely bring him over to the C&O yard. I'll be lining up the switches. Mr. Riddell, you go get on the engine with Mr. Griffith, Mr. Neely, and Mr. Booth."

Stuffing a battered portable radio into one of the pockets of his bibs, our conductor headed out the rear door of the building, down the steps, and across the steep gully to the C&O 17th Street Yard interchange tracks. Shaking his head, I could hear him muttering, "A buff. We ask for help, and they send us a damn buff. God help us."

"You're Riddell from down at Fairmount Baptist Church, aren't you?" brakeman Julian Neely asked.

"How'd you know?" I countered.

"I'm Pat Neely's dad. Your father is my Sunday school teacher," he smiled. I guess people don't look the same wearing their church clothes. I should have recognized him right away. His daughter would someday end up teaching in the same school system as her friend Sandy Trott, who would become my wife.

"I just heard you on WRVA yesterday." He seemed a bit puzzled as he pointed to the radio station on the neighboring hillside. "You gonna quit working on the radio to come out here?" Railroaders have in common that theirs is a well-paying job, but a hard one that most other occupations would certainly take preference over. He and the others

I worked with on the SCL found it hard to believe that the same voice they listened to on the "50-thousand-watt voice of Virginia" could be heard on their two-way saying, "That'll do, SCL engine 132. Stretch 'em out."

"I like that letter you had in the TIMES-DISPATCH the other day," Neely added. "Why would anyone with your education, your voice, and your ability to write want to come out here and work on the railroad?"

Maybe it was the trip home to Richmond from Elmira, New York, I made a couple of months before I was born. Wed just over a year, and just out of the Navy, dad took a job with a typewriter company that sent him to northern New York to become a typewriter repairman and then suddenly reduced the size of its class and laid him off. It was a call from the C&O superintendent in Richmond to the DL&W superintendent in Elmira that enabled my eight-month pregnant mom, and my now unemployed, practically penniless, dad to come home in a Pullman, and then live with my maternal grandparents until I was four years old.

Maybe it was the afternoon walks with my grandmother to Chimborazo Park to watch as C&O's westbound *George Washington* raced down Airport Hill, skirting Fulton Yard in a cloud of blue brake shoe smoke, the horns of its shiny new E8s wailing, as it curved onto the doubletracked James River viaduct. With the yellow and blue LaGrange racehorses reducing to a melodic, 24-cylinder chant, No. 41 strolled haughtily past the cigarette factories on tobacco row, and halted at Main Street Station across the platform from Seaboard's shimmering *Silver Star*. The top half of the rear car's Dutch door would always open as the C&O's flagship train passed the Richmond Gas Works, and its flagman—my grandfather—would wave to us.

Maybe it was the trips to Newport News on the *George Washington*, the *Sportsman*, or the *FFV*. Whether it was standing in the third cab seat of an E8 or FP7 to see out the front windshield, occupying the lap of the engineer at the controls of No. 48's three Budd cars ("Sputniks" the crews called them, since they arrived at about the same time as the Russians put their satellite into orbit, much to the consternation of the railroad's officials), or wandering through curved aisles of the remnants of Robert R. Young's post-WWII Pullman order, there was no other place I'd rather be.

Whatever it was, on that day in May 1977, a love of railroading was bestowed on John Everett Beazley's grandson.

Preacher Booth, Rosie, Neely, and I carefully crossed the double track (former SAL main) that once stretched to Miami but now lay in segments. This first stretch ended 12 miles to the south, where it was unceremoniously joined with hated rival Atlantic Coast Line's doubletrack main at Centralia. The zero milepost sat on the west side of the viaduct at Main Street Station. From there, mileage was measured all the way to Miami. It was just north of there, at Brown Street, that on June 2, 1900, three-year-old John Skelton Williams Jr., son of the road's president, used a miniature silver hammer to drive the golden spike, symbolically marking the beginning of the Seaboard Air Line Railway. Once the racetrack of Seaboard's *Silver* streamliners, it was now designated simply as the East Route of the Collier Subdivision. Four secondary through freights and a number of locals road switchers would use it to interchange with C&O until the merger with that road took place in 1980. Following that consolidation, the line shed almost all of its dual trackage and through trains; and for all practical purposes, it was truncated, as so little traffic used the final two miles between Bellwood and Centralia that crews were obliged to stop and flag road crossings because of rusty rail conditions. Brown Street Yard and C&O's adjacent 17th Street facilities have vanished. The trailer was sold and separated from the old brick yard office, which still stands in a forlorn, weed-covered Shockoe Valley.

On my first morning in 1977, two yard diesels—"butt heads" as they were called by SCL crews—sat beneath the massive Martin Luther King Jr. bridge. Showing its Seaboard switcher-fleet red heritage in places where the SCL black had given way, No. 31 was very obviously former SAL 1406, a 1942 NW2 with the stubby milk can exhaust stacks. Our assigned engine, No. 132, left Electro-Motive Division in purple and silver as ACL No. 650 in 1951, an SW7. Both were battered and worn, and characteristically shuttered and shook as they sat idling in the early morning sun. The small cab interior was painted industrial gray, which had not only peeled profusely during its 20 plus years of shuffling cars in and out of yard tracks, but had acquired quite a collection of graffiti.

Taking a hand signal from Rosie, who stood impatiently at a manual switch stand, the relays popped and rattled as Preacher Booth moved the reverser forward, pulled the bell knob, and opened the throttle. There was just enough room for the short switch engine between the switch and the five aspect dwarf signal that guarded the entrance to the main line. The signal blinked twice and displayed a red over yellow, prompting everyone on the crew to mumble in unison, "Restricting," as if offering up some liturgical homily at vespers.

"Restricting?" I asked Neely.

"Yeah," he grunted. "The 'know nothing' signal. It's little better than a 'stop' signal. It only gives you permission to pass it. There could be a train sitting on the other side of it, but then, we're in the yard, and it's all we need to get over to the C&O yard."

With that said, we backed out on the main line all the way out onto the viaduct that once had tracks entering the train shed of Main Street Station until 1959, when the Seaboard vacated the old French Beaux Arts terminal to begin using James Russell Pope's domed Broad Street Station with Richmond, Fredericksburg & Potomac and ACL. It was no accident that it resembled the Jefferson Memorial and the National Gallery of Art in Washington. He designed both of them as well.

Holding to the single handrail mounted on the side of the engine cowl, Rosie, Neely, and I moved to the front platform of the old SW7 to await the signal allowing us to enter the C&O connection track. Suddenly there was a loud "pop" as the engine's radiator shutters slammed shut. The sound startled me but went almost unnoticed by the two veteran yard brakemen. I rubbed my eyes in disbelief as I swore there was a dark, apparently unused Pennsy-style position light signal next to the SCL's own high-masted, color-light target arrangement.

"What kind of signal is that?" I asked Neely.

"The 'Chinese' signal we called it," he responded. "We used to use it to sign the engineer ahead or to stop before we had radios."

Just as that was said, another restricting signal appeared, and Rosie motioned the engineer to bring the 132 forward into the C&O. After grabbing hold of a cut of coal, we drew back, stopped, shoved forward, and coupled to another cut of cars. Climbing back aboard our engine, yet another restricting signal allowed us to re-enter the Seaboard main, tugging no less than 40 cars up the steep incline, and past the rotting passenger shed, stopping just short of the world-famous triple crossing. It was here that the C&O passed over us and the Southern went beneath us. Every so often, for the benefit of rail-fans or postcard makers, the three railroads would line up special moves so that a train from each would occupy the crossing at the same time.

The clearance above the Seaboard track is only 16 feet, meaning that dome cars, triple-decker automobile carriers, and high-cube boxcars had to be routed over the ACL through Acca Yard and delivered to the C&O by a transfer job called the "Loop Train." This was just one more reason why the old SAL trackage became unsuitable for through traffic. The C&O had already raised its bridge once, creating an awful hump in its long James River viaduct that played havoc with long coal trains slowing to be yarded at Fulton. It also necessitated electronic high load detectors, which emitted an ear-piercing radio alarm when set off by a car, or in some cases thick exhaust, interrupting the beam of light projecting across the tracks at a certain height.

"For a joke, Tater used to hold up a broom that activated the alarm when he passed the high load detector," chuckled Neely.

"You mean that old man has a sense of humor?" I answered in amazement.

"Sure," he nodded. "He's a big practical joker. You just rubbed him the wrong way, being a buff and all educated."

"What have you people got against railfans and people with an education?" I inquired.

"Most of you know more about these engines than we do. You can tell us what model it is, when it was made, who made it, how much horsepower it has, and proba-bly who its mother and father were. All we know is whether or not it runs good, if it has a good heater, and how many cars it'll pull. To us, that's all that's important," Neely told me. "You're gonna end up being a trainmaster, or get some big official job with your education. You'll be our boss someday. After a while, some of the fellows start to resent the fact that people like you will be sitting in an air conditioned office making 10 times what we do, while we're out here chasing butt heads all day long. Shoot, Rosie can't read or write, and can't take promotion, even though he's one of the senior men on the roster."

As we shoved into the switching lead, I got down off of the engine and watched Rosie. He had said little to me all morning. I now understood why. Through those thick glasses he could see the numbers chalked on the sides of each car by conductor Peele telling us which track each would be switched into, and he could recognize the symbols painted on the side that proclaimed ownership of each piece of rolling stock, yet he could not read train orders or waybills.

Rosie reminded me of another railroader—one who could barely read and whose primitive penmanship prompted him to ask his wife to fill out his conductor's promotion examination as he dictated the answers to her: John Everett Beazley, my grandfather. My grandmother got a nice letter from the C&O superintendent upon notification of grand-pa's promotion stating, that she too would likely make a good conductor.

I only saw the family side of my grandfather. Around us, it made little difference that he had gone no further than the second grade. His father felt that a formal education was not the most important thing for a young boy growing up in rural Caroline County, Virginia, who would likely spend his life growing tobacco. But on the railroad, it was different. Once, my grandfather had to attend a disciplinary hearing on a charge of mishandling U.S. mail while working the baggage car on the *George Washington*. In the letter of reprimand, his superintendent assessed him five demerits, noting that the proceedings revealed he had unintentionally miscounted the sacks of mail in his charge, and urged him to be more careful in the future.

Hamlet-bound No. 225 arrived shortly after 11 a.m. and picked up the cut of cars we had assembled on track 13. Number 105 showed up just as we were breaking for lunch and tucked traffic for Rocky Mount and Florida points behind its six black-and-yellow road engines.

Entering the lunchroom, I settled down to the Coke and nabs that would have to make do until I got off work.

"That's not going to hold you 'til quitting time, boy," Peele said as he laid out his feast of potato chips, a sandwich, and coffee. "Do you like potted meat?"

"Sure," I answered.

"Well, here's an extra sandwich. It probably tastes better than the one you had in your lunch pail, and for damn sure, it's got to be a lot drier," he managed to smile. "You worked hard out there today. Probably a lot harder than you had to, but then until you know the ropes, you waste a lot of time and energy. You'll get the hang of it."

"Thanks, Mr. Peele," I said.

Before I knew it, someone else plunked down a bag of potato chips, someone else an apple, and yet another donated a piece of homemade apple pie. Still, when another conductor reached in his locker and took out one of the Seaboard's signature white Lee hats with the "Through the heart of the South" emblem on it, and placed it on my head, that topped it all.

"Wear this for the day, son, instead of the hat you've got on," he said. "To us at Brown Street, SCL means 'Still Coast Line.' We're Seaboard Air Line people, and proud of it."

About 3 p.m., Tater climbed aboard the 132 and gave us the next move. We would set the bright orange former ACL caboose on top of the high cars in number six track to form the afternoon Loop Train, put the engine in the sand track, and call it a day. Tater signed my qualifying paper, Rosie waved as he got into his car, and Neely said, "See you in church." The day had passed quickly, since there were very few times that we stood still. I was tired and took the advice of the old heads, planning to get to bed early.

I had a special respect for Rosie from that day forward, and I would enjoy working with him in the few short years before he retired. Tater I would not get to know as well, for it was just a few weeks after that first day on the job that he entered the hospital, never to come home. Cancer has no respect for retirement plans. Funny, to this day, whenever I think of Rosie and Tater, I visualize them as I saw them a few days later, replete with pinstriped railroad hat, gauntlet gloves, and bib overalls, shoving past the yard office on the lead end of a work train. Peele's snow-white hair blew in the wind as he yelled out to me, "Where's your camera, railfan? Get a shot of this. This is railroading."

I learned a lot that first day cubbing—a lot about railroads, and a lot more about the people who worked on them. As I pass through the barren valley that was once Brown Street Yard at the throttle of Amtrak's Tidewater Virginia trains, only the outline of the brick yard office and the tall light poles hint that this was once a place teaming with round-the-clock railroad activity. But the memories are still there, and they are intangible. While all else may disappear, memories remain forever.

I continue to see Julian Neely until he died, both at church and at Ukrop's Supermarket, where he (and an awful lot of retired railroad men) supplemented their Railroad Retirement checks by toting customers' groceries to their automobiles.

"Someone ought to write a book about the crazy things that happened on the railroad," he would say. "You ought to do it."

Well, Neely, I did.

Chapter 2: The Purple People Greeter

Seaboard Coast Line was but a 10-year-old amalgamation of two bitter rival southeastern railroads when I came to work there as a switchman in May 1977. It was only natural that after cubbing my first day at the former Seaboard Air Line's Brown Street Yard in Richmond, Virginia, my second day should be spent in South Richmond at the former Atlantic Coast Line's Shops Yard. The name on the office door may have declared the existence of a unified railroad, but believe me, there were two operations—almost within sight of each other—as different as night and day. At Shops Yard, the color purple not only showed through on a number of structures and signs, but in the people who worked there as well.

Situated on a bluff, just above the fall line on the south bank of the James River, in what was once the city of Manchester, Shops Yard sat astride the main line of ACL's Civil War era predecessor, Richmond & Petersburg Railroad.

During reconstruction, the railroads were extended, and new lines began appearing with an infusion of capital from northern investors. Through freight service from the north, which since 1888 had been forwarded to ACL from Richmond Fredericksburg & Potomac Railroad over a connection through the cobblestone streets of Richmond at Byrd Street Station (located at 7th and Byrd Streets on the north side of the river), ended almost as soon as it was initiated, when in 1890, a jointly maintained belt line and bridge was constructed to appease the city fathers' demand that steam locomotives be banished from Richmond's main thoroughfares. Skirting the (then) western edge of the city four miles upstream, it connected with ACL two miles south of Manchester, at the community of Clopton. (The belt line was ultimately doubletracked, depressed below street level, and extended further south to its present connection at Falling Creek, FA Tower). At the same time, RF&P and ACL began utilizing joint locomotive servicing and switching facilities in the northwest suburbs at Acca Yard.

Passenger trains were granted a reprieve and continued to use street-running RF&P tracks to access the 1887-built Byrd Street Station, and thus plied the old main line through Shops Yard until the new Broad Street Union Station near Acca Yard opened in 1919. Since all through traffic thereafter used the belt line, RF&P tracks were removed from Richmond's streets, essentially truncating the old ACL main line at Byrd Street.

Little changed until the 1967 merger with SAL made redundant what had historically been an extremely active interchange of coal traffic between ACL and Chesapeake & Ohio Railroad at the latter's downtown 2nd Street Yard, via the same high, spindly, steel viaduct across the river to Byrd Street. The span was torn down almost immediately following the Seaboard/Coast Line merger in favor of a more convenient, side-by-side interchange at SAL's Brown Street Yard from C&O's 17th Street Yard. Had it not been for the abundance of traffic from industrial plants on parallel Jefferson Davis Highway, and interchange from the Southern Railway's adjacent Belle Isle Yard (consisting solely of loads that would not clear Richmond's famed triple railroad crossing on the former SAL), Shops Yard might have been abandoned at the merger's outset.

Oddly enough, the Federal Reserve Bank, which housed CSX's very first head-quarter office suites, now occupies the site of Byrd Street Station. The terminal building, the small ACL yard, and much of C&O's yard trackage in the adjacent Haxall Canal Basin were demolished in the late 1960s to make way for an eight-lane Manchester Bridge, at the north end of which would later be erected CSX's James Center corporate headquarters and office tower complex—the crown jewel of Richmond's business and financial renaissance.

To prim and proper Richmonders residing on the north side of the James, South Richmond was disdainfully referred to as "Scuffletown" or "Dogtown." South side's blue collar residents (still smarting from their annexation by Virginia's capital) nostalgically clung to the name Manchester. Although its courthouse, business district, and no less than three railroad stations were located on east/west thoroughfare Hull Street, South Richmond's character more closely reflected north/south Jefferson Davis Highway (U.S. 1 and 301), a four-lane divided boulevard (the median having once served as the right-of-way of the Richmond-Petersburg electric interurban line). In the area's prime, Jeff Davis Highway was dotted with cigarette factories, round-the-clock diners, country and western honkytonks, and a number of establishments purporting to serve "genuine" Carolina barbecue.

Like the roots of many of its own employees, ACL's heart was in Carolina. Despite its size and prominence, ACL's presence in the capital of the Old Dominion was modest at best, compared to rival SAL's extensive northern terminus. Atlantic Coast Line actually reached but did not enter Richmond, except for the meager Byrd Street facility, until Manchester's inclusion placed Shops Yard inside the city limits. Rocky Mount, North Carolina, served as the road's northernmost classification and marshaling point. From there, it merely forwarded passenger and freight traffic from the south to Acca, where it handed over all of the switching, running repair, and engine servicing chores to RF&P after ACL engines and cabooses were detached from through trains.

Now nothing more than a mere appendage springing from the main line at FA Tower, what remained of the old inner city facility when I pulled up behind the crumbling stucco yard office on that sunny spring morning in 1977 was a lead track with half a dozen switches (some of them out of service), a boarded up three-stall roundhouse, and an abandoned light repair track. Both Cowardin and Semmes avenues vaulted overhead and intersected at right angles opposite the yard office, almost entirely and continuously covering the switching lead in the narrow ravine below. While this helped to shelter switchmen from blowing winds, burning sun, and pouring rain, post storm runoffs from the steep hillsides tended to flood the tracks and linger long after the sun had thoroughly dried everything else.

Only the tops of rails were visible. Crossties in the vicinity of switch frogs and throw bars were the only ones in evidence at Shops. They appeared to have been niggardly distributed in the aftermath of repeated switching derailments, and then only under the most dire of circumstances in order to allow continued use of the yard. Number 5 switch had a mind of its own, more than once sending the "A" end of a boxcar into the correct classification track while the other trundled down the ladder. If good luck prevailed, and the car didn't overturn, with a lot of patience from an "experienced" crew and a bit of gentle coaxing from the drawbar of former ACL GP7, the car could be righted, the switch spiked, and normal operations resumed. On some occasions, however, the Geep itself ended up going two ways at once, causing an "early quit" for the employees who "got on the ground," and an annulled assignment/lost day's pay for their relieving crew.

Shops Yard had what was undoubtedly the most outstanding view of Richmond's skyline from any location. There were no floodlights at the old ACL yard to ruin the panoramic vista at night. Sometimes, at the base of the stairway that ran from the yard office to the switching lead below, I would sit by myself and eat dinner. Though it reminded me of the painstakingly crafted Manhattan skyline model in the Cary Grant film classic, ARSENIC AND OLD LACE, no Hollywood set designer could top the backdrop of concrete, steel, and glass, wrapped in strings of yellow street lights, darting headlights, and twinkling traffic signals that towered above our dark and largely deserted railroad stage. Only the hollow vibrations of cars and trucks passing overhead or the echo of C&O diesel power attempting to accelerate an empty westbound hopper train along its viaduct on the north side of the James River interrupted the solitude and serenity.

Operationally, the Coast Line had weaned itself away from overstaffing much earlier than the Seaboard. Whereas SAL's Brown Street and Hermitage Yards employed an army of yardmasters, clerks, machinists, electricians, herders, and switch tenders, ACL rostered only what was necessary to get by. A merged Seaboard Coast Line still saw a large and varied work force north of the river, even after Hermitage Yard (adjacent to RF&P's Acca facility, with which its duties were combined) was abandoned and razed in 1976; while, in contrast, at Shops an extra stipend was allowed the senior yard conductor each shift, who was accorded the title and duties of "footboard" yardmaster. When required, machinists and/or electricians from Brown Street made house calls at Shops. All of this would eventually adversely affect the former ACL work force.

Seniority and work rights among employees of a merged system are meted out according to the ratio of assignments previously rostered by each railroad. Atlantic Coast Line's token yard presence in the Richmond area meant that the "purple people" (a nickname derived from ACL President Champ Davis' preference in diesel locomotive color schemes) nearly always found themselves in a minority and at a disadvantage. Given their choice of assignments, there was little evidence that anything had changed for the first five years following the nuptials of the two roads. Choosing to stay put on their home turf, there remained a voluntary segregation of work forces that lingered on for many years until the effects of the ACL/SAL merger and a slowing economy began to take hold. The dwindling amount of work, the combining of road and yard seniority rosters, and the appearance of post merger hirees (without prior right protection, affiliations, or allegiances) eventually diluted the ranks of both sides.

Faced with the prospect of working side by side with the hated Seaboard men across the James River at Brown Street, a number of prior righted ACL yard men opted to take road freight assignments between Acca and Rocky Mount when the number of yard jobs at Shops was severely pared back in the late 1970s. Though time mellowed the resolve of many, until it was abandoned, bulldozed, and built over, Shops Yard represented the final bastion of the former ACL in Richmond. Until it was finally leveled by the wrecking ball in the late 1980s, the old stucco yard office stood on the hillside, a purple-and-white Alamo, signifying defiance of the inevitable.

Entering the yard office for the first time, I was immediately struck by the spartan furnishings. On the brown linoleum floor sat an ancient Arcola space heater, two worn oak desks, and a half dozen chairs. On opposite ends of the structure were a small office and the employee locker rooms. While there was an abundance of metal lockers, few were in use, as very few people worked here anymore.

"Who the hell are you?" growled a tall, stocky, gray-haired man in matching tan work clothes. "What's your business here?"

"Doug Riddell," I responded, rolling my eyes upward to determine if I had worn the white "Through the heart of the South" SAL trademark hat that morning by mistake. "I'm supposed to be cubbing with the 6:30 a.m. job here."

"You a new hire, or one of them damn Seaboard bastards?" he questioned, as his eyebrows furrowed and his lips parted to reveal a gritty picket fence of tobacco-stained teeth.

"Just turned in my A-3 [written rule book questionnaire] to Trainmaster Walker day before yesterday," I proudly announced.

"And where did that Seaboard sonofabitch send you yesterday? Brown Street?" he continued as his face began to redden while he flicked the ashes from the tip of his non-filtered cigarette to the floor. "He always does."

"Well," I said, attempting to be diplomatic, "everyone's got to start somewhere."

"Just remember that they started you at the bottom of the barrel so you could work your way up," he said as if gaining some degree of satisfaction with his put down. "We work here. Forget everything you might have picked up over on the other side of the river. We do it just the opposite here on the Coast Line." With that said, and without ever introducing himself to me, he grunted, shook his head, and walked back into the small office, from which two or three other people snickered as the old man babbled under his breath. Two of them emerged shortly, walked past me without speaking, headed out the door and down the steps to the switching lead, where the throaty moan and the harmonic whine of a former ACL Geep resonated off the overhead bridge, scattering a congregation of pigeons feasting on spilled grain.

"Gawddamn, son, you ain't gonna learn anything sitting in this office. The work's out there," he shouted, heading for the restroom. "I can see now that you ain't one of them self-starters. You'd have made a good Seaboard man."

"No one's even spoken to me. How am I supposed to know what to do?" I countered. "Is there a radio for me to use?"

"Radio?" he erupted. "There's one on the engine, one in the office, and two in that top desk drawer, and that's where they stay! We don't use them over here. If you can't use hand signals, you don't belong here. The less the officials know about what you're doing and where you're at, the better off you are. Now, leave that fancy grip here on the desk and get your lazy butt out there with the yard crew before I call Walker and tell him to either fire you or send you back over to that Seaboard leper colony at Brown Street."

Climbing up into the cab of the black and yellow GP7, I quickly discovered how cramped it was. Though essentially bathed in dark industrial green today, the interior had been painted over scores of times since its initial date in the paint shop at LaGrange, as evidenced by the pallet of colors that showed through the profusely chipped walls. The two brakemen had taken their seats on the fireman's side, and the engineer, of course, occupied his own. The Mars oscillating headlights (which remained on either end of this unit and its counterparts until they were removed, first from the long end, then from the short hood, in the early 1980s) immediately disclosed No. 745's identity as former ACL locomotive No. 157. Years later, unlike many of its brethren, it would not be a candidate for conversion to a Tampa rebuilt GP16, and instead would be sold for scrap the same year I took leave from SCL to work for Amtrak.

I took the initiative, since it seemed that the two yard brakemen were content to sit there and ignore me all day, "Hi, I'm Doug Riddell. I'll be cubbing with you."

Finally showing some sign of life, the two brakemen managed a forced smile, extended their hands, and grunted their names, first and middle initials followed by their surname.

The engineer was somewhat friendlier, "Sparky Walters. Glad to meet you, Doug. Whatever you do today, just remember, the most important thing is not to get hurt. It's hard not to."

"Who's the conductor?" I inquired.

"You met him in the yard office, remember?" one of the brakemen offered.

"I thought he was the yardmaster," I replied, obviously confused.

"He's both. He's what we call a footboard yardmaster," the other informed me, apparently sensing that it was permissible to speak.

The old man, whose name I still did not know, climbed aboard the grimy locomotive, stared at me briefly, and began giving orders. "The loop train's stuff is in No. 6. Set the cab in No. 7. Come back and get the first three cars, and we'll go work Phillip Morris and Overmeyer." The two brakemen headed out the door, and before I could ask the old man what I should do, he barked again. "I assume you came here to be a brakeman. Unless you're planning on learning to be an engineer, you better get down on the ground with them. That's where the work is."

I began wondering if I hadn't made a mistake.

Yard assignments fall into two categories: drill and industrial jobs. The drill crew switches or "drills" cars on a lead, and in some cases over a hump, in a classification yard. The industrial crew places cars at or collects them from sidings belonging to the railroad's customers. Since mainline trains no longer used the five miles of the old ACL main line which connected this yard to the outside world, Shops served as a set off and gathering point for the Loop Train—a transfer train—which arrived late each evening, delivering the day's inbound shipment. While its crew took supper, other yard crews assembled the outbound consist for the train's departure with the traffic for Acca and Brown Street. As individual yard crews came on duty throughout the next day, each would switch out the cars destined for industries in their particular sector, like vultures picking apart a carcass, until by the end of the day nothing remained.

Because both Shops and Brown Street sat near the floor of the James River Basin, the loop train had to assault near 2 percent grades at some points at either end of its circuitous journey to connect them. Since available yard power was used for this move, an assemblage of aging NW2s, SW7s, and an occasional Geep pulled the short train with a caboose on the trailing end. It could be witnessed each night storming up the hills from Brown Street to Acca on the former SAL and from Clopton to Meadow, across the high, vaulted James River viaduct, and then into Acca on the former ACL—sparks flying, sand blowing, and radiators overheating.

The entire five miles from Shops to FA Tower on the old ACL were considered a "yard" for contractual and operational purposes. Midway between them at Clopton, where the original, singletrack belt line formed a wye at its connection with the old ACL, a small, five-track switching yard had been built. Used primarily for storage, it was employed by crews serving adjacent industries to arrange and turn cars for placement. Of particular note was the David M. Lea Manufacturing Company at Hopkins Road, where a small steam engine (now the property of the Old Dominion Chapter of the National Railway Historical Society) worked as a plant switcher into the late 1960s or early 1970s.

No longer plied by freight or passenger trains, even the northbound and southbound main lines were littered with standing freight cars and were used as yard tracks. Of course, it was still necessary for a clerk to list each car on the property daily, which at Shops meant walking the nearly five miles each way, which brings to mind one very memorable story in my later days as an engineer, working one of the afternoon jobs there.

The listing clerk, Brenda, could hold her own in a shouting match with the saltiest mouths on the railroad. Heading back up the main line toward the yard office, our crew spied her and asked if she would like a ride. Grateful, she climbed aboard.

Immediately behind the engineer's seat is the handbrake wheel, which piqued Brenda's curiosity as a relatively new employee.

"That's the steering wheel," I said, suppressing outright laughter. "Would you like to drive?"

"Sure," she responded. "But is it okay?"

"Just don't tell anyone," I warned her.

For the next 10 minutes, Brenda diligently maneuvered the "steering wheel" at the crew's direction, until we arrived at the yard office.

"Now remember," I repeated, "don't tell anyone."

Back on the same job the next afternoon, we encountered Brenda again and stopped to ask if she would like a ride. Without hesitating, she dropped her clipboard, hopped up the steps into the cab, and pointed her finger in my face.

"You sonofabitch," she screamed. "All day long I couldn't understand why people were laughing and giggling when I walked by after I told them that you let me steer the engine last night. Someone finally told me that an engine doesn't even have a steering wheel. That was a handbrake wheel!"

"Why do you think I told you not to tell anyone?" I responded. A good sport, and a practical joker in her own right, Brenda paid me back in spades many times over during the years we worked together before she finally took a buyout, left the railroad, got married, and raised a family.

As we drifted south toward Clopton to do our work that first day, we crossed Hull Street, where the oldest remaining (at that time) ACL structure, South Richmond Station, stood. Long since abandoned, the purple ACL herald still remained just below the apex of its roof. So dilapidated was it that the thousands of silk screened posters applied to its walls over the years, touting everything from prize fights to rock concerts, seemed to be the only thing preventing its outright collapse. A tower that controlled the crossing gates once sat on the opposite side of Hull Street, but it disappeared when automatic ones were installed. Most people had forgotten.

But our conductor, Willford Strickler, remembered. (I would learn his name—not necessarily the one appearing here in print—later that day from my trainmaster). He grew up not far from that old station when Manchester was a thriving community of modest brick and frame homes, long before it had been reduced to a burned out, run down neighborhood—the red-haired step-child of the city of Richmond. He had sat in the gateman's tower as a child and witnessed ACL's high-drivered Pacifics on the point of a New York-bound express slowing for the big curve at Bainbridge Street, which would take them past Shops Yard and across the James to halt at Byrd Street Station. He also remembered when Shops Yard had a roundhouse and a riptrack teaming with blacksmiths, laborers, hostlers, and carmen. Retirement was nearing, and he had begun to quietly wonder if he would continue to outpace the wave of change that threatened to come crashing down and wash away the last vestiges of his old railroad before his last day on the job, or whether he would have to drive across the river to Brown Street and work side by side with the "Seaboard bastards" he so despised.

Things hadn't always been so bad. In fact, just prior to the merger, traffic had increased so dramatically that a number of new brakemen had been hired—some of whom had to be pressed into service as yard conductors well before the usual two-year service requirement. One fellow, who had been hired less than six weeks earlier, was called to be the conductor on an early morning yard job at Shops. While not disastrous, his initiation into the fraternity of "Captain of the Cars" was quite comical.

Willford remembered, because as "yardmaster" he had ordered the green conductor to spot a single-door, 50-foot boxcar at the Phillip Morris plant. Atlantic Coast Line (and later SAL) not only served the cigarette manufacturing plants of most of America's major tobacco companies along Jeff Davis Highway, but their vast processing and storage facilities as well. Each year at market time, the number of jobs at Shops would double just to handle the tobacco traffic. When one of them called for a switch, the yardmaster would immediately radio the nearest yard crew to service their need—even if it meant dropping everything else being done at the time to do so.

An hour passed, and another call came from the shipping clerk at Phillip Morris. No yard crew had appeared, and the loading dock was becoming cluttered. What was going on? Strickler radioed the yard job.

"How are you coming with that single-door 50-foot box?" he asked.

"I'm still looking," answered the rookie conductor.

"There must be 30 or 40 of them just outside the plant gate," the increasingly agitated old purple man retorted. "It doesn't have to be spotless, but they need it badly."

"Oh, there are plenty of clean 50-foot boxcars out here all right," the greenhorn noted, "but all of them have two doors."

Willford Strickler, obviously puzzled, then told him, "The sheet from the listing clerk doesn't even show a double-door 50-foot box on the yard."

"That's funny," the new man answered. "Every one I've seen has two doors—one on each side."

I learned a lot that first eight-hour shift I worked at Shops Yard in 1977. What I gleaned about being a brakeman I did so only by asking questions, because it seemed no one but our engineer wanted to volunteer information. I learned the proper way to apply a hand brake only after I almost fell off the end of a boxcar attempting to do so. I found out that you open the angle cock of a railroad car's brake system very slowly in order to prevent it from going into emergency—or "dumping," as we call it—causing the highly charged air hose, with its deadly glad hand coupler, to flail about (in my case, wrapping itself around my arm, almost breaking it, and just missing my head. Almost 20 years later, my wrist still hurts at times from this mistake.)

What I discovered about my future coworkers was gained by observation. They answered all of my questions without ever having been asked. This was not the happy, joking, coffee klatch brotherhood on which I had intruded the previous day at Brown Street Yard—and with good reason. Though with some of them I forged lasting friendships, a few remain distant to this day.

"All you need to do is watch us," one of the brakemen sneered. "We do it right over on this side of the James."

While evidently suspicious of strangers and newcomers, the old ACL men had a good working relationship that often continued beyond the end of their shifts. One old engineer I greatly miss, for whom I later fired, and who allowed me a great deal of throttle time running passenger trains, was Walter Powell. Walter undoubtedly picked up the phrase "Ol' Hoss" from the television series Bonanza and used it to address everyone he spoke to. The phrase became his nickname. Diving into the station at Petersburg, Virginia, one night on the Silver Meteor in an attempt to make up some lost time, Walter looked at me and issued a stern warning, "Ol' Hoss, that heavy braking is going to get you in trouble one of these days."

Walter (Ol Hoss) unfortunately was said to bear a striking resemblance to a different famous TV personality—Fred Flintstone. Everyone on the railroad has a nickname—some are flattering, but most tend to be less than complimentary. He hated it when someone would jokingly refer to him using the cartoon character's name. After working the graveyard shift on Friday night as a young fireman, Ol' Hoss and the rest of the crew were to meet at his engineer's apartment (a fellow nicknamed "Preacher") to help him and his wife move to a new apartment.

Arriving at Preacher's home after the others had already left with the first truckload, Ol' Hoss rang the doorbell, and the lady of the house, whom he had not met before, greeted him. "I'm Preacher's fireman. I came over to help you move."

"Come in. Have a seat and a cup of coffee while you wait for them," she smiled. "It's nice to finally meet you, Mr. Flintstone." Undoubtedly, the relationship between engineer and fireman suffered somewhat after that encounter.

As our shift drew to a close, we began to assemble the cars we had collected in track number six, on top of the caboose, for that evening's Loop Train. Whereas at Brown Street cars were shoved into tracks, coupled, and uncoupled with the air brake system employed because the yard was built on a sleep incline, at Shops, cars were allowed to roll into tracks toward the river. It was important, I was told, that the bottom car in each track had a good, tight hand brake. Otherwise, it might roll downgrade, out onto what was then left of the old steel bridge—a mere seven carlengths at the end of number five track. Once, an unmanned GP7 errantly crossed the James on it, passed through 2nd Street Yard, moved out onto the C&O's main line, and was only stopped by a brave and skillful crew from their moving train on an adjacent passing siding some 60 miles upriver. A disgruntled employee or trespasser was thought to have caused the runaway, though no one was ever charged.

"I guess we'll see you out here again," Willford Strickler grunted as he opened the door to his old pickup truck. "There's not that much work left here, so they'll probably be calling you mostly for assignments at Brown Street."

"Maybe so," I shrugged, "but I'll look forward to working with you again [like a toothache, I thought], and thanks for all the help."

It only took five minutes to get to trainmaster Walker's office in the old Seaboard freight station at 15th and Franklin streets, next to Main Street Station and just south of Brown Street Yard. Unlike the stucco yard office at Shops, the name "Seaboard" was chiseled into a long white stone mounted over the front entrance. The thought occurred to me that to report to their supervisors in the offices of their former arch enemy must have been the ultimate insult for the Coast Line men.

Walker's secretary informed me that he would be tied up for a few minutes because he was meeting with some employees who had gotten into trouble. I took a seat. When the door opened, two men—the two brakemen I had worked with at Shops—walked out, papers in hand, heads hung low. They had just been given 60 days for failing to apply sufficient hand brakes to a cut of cars in the tracks, allowing two boxcars to get loose, which then rolled off the end of the high steel bridge and fell onto the Southern Railway yard below, nearly toppling into the roaring waters of the James River. As they headed for the door, their eyes caught mine, but then quickly darted back down to the floor. As a fellow railroader and later as a union representative, I would see that look repeated on the faces of men and women with whom I worked side by side, and whom I would represent at disciplinary hearings. Aside from fear of death or injury, it is the worst fear that working railroaders constantly live with: making one mistake—large or small—and paying dearly for it.

I would return to Shops Yard to work with those two men, as well as Willford Strickler, countless times before they retired. And yes, Strickler made his last day at Shops the day the yard was slated to be closed. I imagine that for once, as he piled into his old pickup truck and turned into the narrow alley entrance way, a smile of satisfaction beamed across his rugged old face. He had beaten them. He never had to work with those

"Seaboard bastards" at Brown Street. The day he pulled the pin, the old ACL in Richmond died in body and soul. Some years later, when I learned of his passing in the RICHMOND TIMES-DISPATCH, it came as little surprise that among all of his life's accomplishments listed in his obituary, the proudest was that "Willford Strickler was retired from the Atlantic Coast Line Railroad."

Chapter 3: A Cast of Characters

A PASSENGER TRAIN JOURNAL reader once suggested that I submit a script to the TV networks for a situation comedy about my experiences on the railroad, because after reading my columns, he was convinced that there was certainly "a cast of characters" from which to pick and choose. Looking back on my railroad career, I would definitely have to agree, although while their tales do provide the basis for some interesting short stories, I'm not sure that the material would sustain a weekly television series.

Of course, every situation comedy is the result of a creative spark, usually from the interactions between the cast and an unusual central character in reaction to an often overworked gimmick.

Imagine, if you will, a college educated television and radio announcer giving up his profession to become a railroad brakeman and, later, an engineer. No, that idea would probably never fly in Hollywood. But there have been those who have done just the opposite—celebrities who began as humble railroaders. In his youth, Michael Gross, star of TV's *Family Ties*, worked as a fireman on commuter trains into Chicago. He once shared the cab of an F40 with me on the way to Pittsburgh when I was the engineer of Amtrak's *Capitol Limited*. After he told me he still remembered how to cool down an overheated E9 (by jamming open the radiator shutters with a fusee and blocking in the radiator fan relays to bypass a faulty thermostat), I knew he was for real. I gave him my official *Capitol Limited* hat as a memento, which I'm sure occupies a place of honor in the Gross household.

Does anyone remember working with a brash young brakeman on the Santa Fe named Don Imus? I'm sure I have left out other notables who also belonged to the fraternity of the flanged wheel.

In my own case, I actually juggled two jobs—the railroad and the radio station—for almost a year before I had to finally choose between them. During the day, I was a yard brakeman for the Seaboard Coast Line Railroad in Richmond. At night, I sat in the glass-windowed studios of WRVA AM (a 50,000-watt NBC affiliate, heard across the country) on a hillside immediately overlooking Richmond's Main Street Station and the very rail yards I'd worked in only hours earlier. Thinking back, I don't know how I managed it.

How and why my dual careers ended is legend with my coworkers. Whenever there is an old-timers' gathering, or when it's mentioned to new hires that I used to be on radio and television, someone will inevitably laugh heartily and say, "You ought to hear the one about the helicopter and the day Doug had to quit the radio station." In truth, I continued performing both jobs for some months after the incident, but it makes good copy, good sense, and after all (as I like to joke with my family about some of my columns) it's just good use of poetic license.

WRVA was (and remains to this day) a Richmond institution. Top-rated morning personality Alden Aaroe coaxed Virginians out of bed for nearly 50 years—a record unparalleled anywhere in the business—until cancer silenced him in 1993. Always the innovator, the radio station began broadcasting morning and evening rush-hour traffic reports from a helicopter in the 1950s. In the summer of 1976, in addition to my duties as host of the evening 6 to 10 p.m. show and as the station's commercial production director, I began substituting for the regular "trafficopter" reporter, Tim Timberlake, our 10 a.m. to noon personality.

In May 1977, I began working for the railroad. Being a good railfan, I took along my trusty Canon FTb whenever I was airborne (and once or twice, a Sears 8mm movie camera). I can assure you, few buffs could come up with the camera angles, or witness the sights to which I was privy from my gyrating perch in the sky. Add to this the fact that I flew out of Byrd Airport's Hawthorne Aviation hanger, located next to the C&O main line, and I was figuratively and literally as close to railfan heaven as anyone is going to be.

Our pilot, the late Willie Windham, was in the Army's first vertical flight class. He flew experimental helicopters in WWII, Sikorskys in Korea, and Hueys in Vietnam. When he was at the stick of our classic 2-place Bell 47 chopper (the bubble type featured on M*A*S*H), you knew you were in good hands. Since he was addicted to, and chain-smoked pack after pack of unfiltered Lucky Strike red dots, Willie and I soared through the otherwise clear blue sky of central Virginia enveloped in a hazy white cloud of tar and nicotine, alerting motorists to potential snarls and backups in Richmond's gridlock business district and on its ever expanding system of expressways, which served as arteries channeling the lifeblood out of the rapidly decaying downtown core—a sad fact of life in most medium- and large-sized cities.

Out of concern that something might happen to him while we were airborne, Willie taught Tim and me some of the basics of helicopter flight. (Amazingly, years later I was to discover the same principals of balancing propulsion and retardation would come in handy when I began learning to handle freight and passenger trains.) In return for his insight, I taught Willie what I knew about railroading after I took the job with SCL. Soon, he too began to see a pattern and could readily predict that within 10 minutes of the Amtrak *Silver Star*'s departure from the Staples Mill Road Station at Greendale, it would be crossing the James River and begin interrupting homeward bound motorists at the crossings at Jahnke and Broad Rock Roads. The clouds of gray smoke from the stacks of black-and-yellow SCL GE U33Bs at Acca Yard meant that within 10 minutes traffic would be halted where a long, descending east-route train would cross Hermitage and Brook roads and eventually foul 7th and Hospital Streets.

Many of Richmond's traffic tie-ups in fact resulted from long, slow-moving freight trains that blocked so many of the city's main thoroughfares at grade, especially during rush hours. Southern Railroad's daily local freight, returning from the small paper mill town of West Point, swaggered into "Dodge" for its daily showdown with motorists in the heart of the business district at peak afternoon rush hour. While it may have thrilled ardent railfans to see a pair of green or black and gold Alco RS-3s in charge of a seemingly endless string of empty pulp wood racks, chip hoppers, and loaded boxcars, trailed by a bright red bay-window caboose, it elicited quite a different reaction from the stockbrokers, bankers, and secretaries whose retreat to the Chesterfield County suburbs across the James River was abruptly cut off at the north end of the 14th Street Bridge. The late Howard Bloom took it all in stride. A trafficopter predecessor, who was killed when his chopper (manned by a substitute pilot) lost its tail rotor and crashed into a building on W. 31st Street, Howard used to chuckle when he spied the lowly local approaching the world-famous triple railroad crossing at 17th and Dock streets (C&O/SAL/SOU). In his deep, resonant radio voice he'd calmly announce, "Well folks, pull up a chair and sit a spell, the 5:15's right on time."

There was quite understandably a great deal of friction between the city fathers and the railroads over this touchy subject, fueled by irate commuters who frequently flocked to the convening of City Council, demanding that something be done about the problem. They found an ally in one council member from the East End, who had to regularly cross both C&O and Seaboard tracks on Hospital Street before climbing 7th Street Hill to reach City Hall. If it wasn't a through freight, he'd be blocked by a yard engine or a passenger train. The angrier he got, the hotter he became, and the higher on the railroad's pecking order he would call to vent his frustrations.

I had just qualified for through freight service as a brakeman in early summer of 1977 when Willie and I hovered over the former Seaboard Air Line's Brown Street Yard in Shockoe Valley, in the shadows of Richmond's downtown business district, during Alden's morning show.

"He don't seem to be moving. Look at that backup on Brook Road." Willie pointed to a stalled northbound SCL freight train. Taking another drag on his Lucky, flicking the ashes out of the open cockpit door and down onto the general population below, he exhaled and added, "He couldn't have picked a worse time, just before eight o'clock. I'll try to get closer and see what's going on. Maybe he's struck a car at a crossing or something. I'll call the police. They might need help."

Another voice crackled in my headset. "You've got a report for Shoney's [restaurant] coming up after this 30-second Curles Neck Dairy spot. Keep it fairly short; John's [Harding, our news director] heavy at eight o'clock, and he wants to come back to you for a quickie after the lead story. It appears that there's some train tying up everything coming in from the North Side and East End," Alden Aaroe added. "You got anything on it? Oops, stand by."

"We're one minute away from the eight o'clock news with John Harding, but first, let's check on your morning commute downtown with Al Douglas [my air name] in the WRVA trafficopter," Aaroe's thousands of faithful listeners heard him announce. "This report is brought to you by Shoney's Big Boy Restaurants. What's going on, Al?"

On cue, my mouth went into gear before my brain was engaged. "Well Alden, our listeners can forget using 7th or Hospital streets inbound from the East End. It looks like the engineer on No. 120 has jerked that train into three pieces, and it's strung out from

Brown Street Yard all the way up the hill to Hermitage, blocking the crossings at 2nd, St. John, and Brook roads as well. You can hang it up for at least the next hour, 'cause by the time those boys finish tot'n knuckles [coupler parts] it'll be lunch time. You'd be wise to consider an alternate route this morning inbound from the East End and North Side. This is Al Douglas from the WRVA trafficopter, now this from Shoney's."

Willie turned away from the sun as we headed upriver to check out the series of bridges that connect Richmond with its south side. Inbound traffic was normal for a major population attempting to move across a wide river basin over seven bridges—jammed. I noted the major backups and listed them on the writing pad strapped to my knee.

"A disabled freight train is giving rush-hour commuters a real headache this morning. Here's more from Al Douglas in the WRVA trafficopter," John Harding said.

"When a train separates," I explained as a good, knowledgeable railfan, "the brakes go into emergency, and the train is stalled until it can be recoupled, the air lines charged up, and the brakes released. It's going to take a while to put this SCL freight train back together again and get it out of the way of motorists coming in from the North Side and East End, so use I-95 or I-64 as an alternate route. The backup at the toll booths may be a real pain, but believe me, they're nothing compared to what you have in store for you if you're waiting for that train to move."

Rush hour lasted for just an hour in the morning and evening in 1970's Richmond, Virginia. I made three or four more reports, and then Willie turned the bird into the sun as we chased an eastbound C&O coal train up the hill to the airport. We were preparing to land when ground control came on the air.

"Doug," Alden called out, "when you put down at Hawthorne, call a Mr. Robertson at this number. He says it's vitally important."

As I copied the phone number down, I scratched my head and wondered who Mr. Robertson was. The name was familiar; a listener or a client, probably.

"Is he someone with an ad agency that wants me to do some voice work?" I asked Aaroe.

"Didn't say. Just said it was urgent."

Just as the yellow steel caboose of the C&O coal train passed under the road's signature cantilever signal bridge at Charles City Road, the occupant of the cupola waved to us, while Willie spotted the Bell-47 perfectly on the rubber tire equipped transfer wagon on which it would be moved inside the hanger. Before removing his headset, the old warrior killed the engine, reached inside his jacket pocket, tapped out the only unfiltered Lucky that remained, ignited it with his worn Zippo lighter, drew a deep lung full of smoke, exhaled, nodded his head with satisfaction, and proclaimed, "Mission accomplished. I was just about out of smokes. I was scared they'd hold us up there to watch that damn train."

I rushed into the Hawthorne Aviation office to use the phone. The classic old Hawthorne hanger with its rounded-arch roof has appeared in many movies, most notably substituting for Dallas' old airport terminal in the feature film LOVE FIELD, as well as A WOMAN CALLED JACKIE and the TV mini-series KENNEDY. As airports have expanded, old hangers of this type have become extinct.

As the rotary dial clicked, I scanned my memory, trying to come up with a clue that would lead to the identity of this mystery man named Robertson. When the voice on the other end answered, I was left with no doubt.

"Seaboard Coast Line Railroad, Robertson speaking," a gravely voice spoke.

"Doug Riddell, Mr. Roberston," I answered cautiously, "May I help you?"

"You damn sure can, son," my trainmaster responded in an instantly agitated tone. "You know, it's bad enough we have to take all of that crap about blocked crossings from the radio station, but we shouldn't have to take it from one of our own employees! This is the same Riddell who just came to work for us as a brakeman, isn't it?"

"Yes, Sir," I gulped, startled and afraid I was the same Riddell who was about to be fired.

"Being a big time radio personality, I assume you already know the mayor of Richmond?" he asked stormily.

"Yes, sir," I responded, my throat going totally dry.

"Well, I was just introduced to him and spent 15 minutes on the phone apologizing to him for the traffic jam this morning caused by one of our freight trains, No. 120. I think you identified it on the radio. The mayor was caught up in the traffic on Hospital Street, listening to the eight o'clock news on WRVA, when you talked about one of our trains being 'in emergency.' He thought there was some kind of hazardous material spill or danger to the public, called the president of the railroad in Jacksonville from his car phone, and chewed on his butt for a while, until the president explained that it was just a railroad term and that there was no impending disaster of any kind."

"Oh," I said.

"Well, Jacksonville called the division superintendent in Rocky Mount, who called the superintendent of terminals in Richmond, who called me. Do you know what it's like to have just sat down at your desk with a fresh cup of coffee and a doughnut on a beautiful, warm, sun shiny morning like this, and have your ear torn off by your boss because he's had his talked off by his boss?" Robertson asked. "The coffee's gone cold, the doughnut's stale, and I really don't have the stomach for them any more."

"Well," I answered slowly, tugging at my shirt collar as I chose my next few words carefully, "I think I'm beginning to get the picture pretty well, sir."

"You know, Mr. Riddell," I heard his old wooden office chair creak in the background, "I don't have anything to do with your choice of careers, but if I were you, I'd damn sure decide right now whether I wanted to work for the railroad or stay in broadcasting. The next time you identify one of our freight trains by number on the air as a cause of a traffic jam, or in any other way embarrass this company, I'll make that decision for you!" When he hung up, the click was deafening.

As it turned out, a few months later, when the offer was made by the radio station for me to become the regular trafficopter reporter and midday air personality on WRVA, I was forced to make that decision. I left broadcasting and never looked back.

"You're a damn fool," my program director told me when I announced my choice. "We're going to pay you $175 a week plus talent! This is the most visible job in broadcasting in this city outside of Alden Aaroe's show. Do you know how many people would kill for this opportunity you're turning down?" (A 24-hour round trip to Florence, South Carolina, as an Amtrak trainman paid $180 at that time.)

Oddly enough, with the exception of an occasional reunion at some of the radio stations I once worked, and an invitation by PASSENGER TRAIN JOURNAL reader and NBC cameraman Jan Kassoff to attend a dress rehearsal for *Saturday Night Live*, I've never been back in a broadcast studio, although I have since had one very memorable encounter with a helicopter.

Firing Amtrak's northbound *Palmetto* for SCL engineer Rob Yancey one day in the early 1980s, I was at the throttle of a roaring F40 when we left Rocky Mount, North Carolina, heading for Richmond. Something on the track ahead caught my attention as we rounded a long curve north of the small community of Battleboro. The doubletrack main line dropped through a swamp at that point over a series of wooden trestles, where it was customary for us to check the accuracy of the engine's speedometer between mile posts 112 and 111.

"Good God!" shouted Rob, jumping from the fireman's seat. "Shoot'em! Shoot'em! There's a helicopter on the tracks."

Shoot'em is railroad slang, at least on the railroad for which I worked, meaning apply the emergency brakes. Depending upon the section of the country where a railroader is employed, the common expression may be "put 'em in emergency, dump'em, big hole'em," or something else, but the meaning and the tone leave no doubt that there is a life-threatening situation requiring immediate action to stop the train. When the brake valve is moved into the emergency position, all of the air is exhausted at one time, resulting in a loud noise that sounds like a cannon—thus the origin of the expression "shoot'em" on SCL.

The odor of the train's wheels being flattened as they burnished the surface of the rail head added a horrifying element to an already frightening predicament. That smell permeated the cab of our train while Rob and I watched in horror as we lurched and bucked toward the ancient, yellow, Korean War Sikorsky helicopter that sat on the nearest wooden trestle, blocking our path. It would have seemed a natural reaction to ask what a helicopter was doing perched on the railroad tracks, but we were too afraid to say much of anything. Our thoughts were more directed to how we were going to survive this imminent collision that would likely derail our train and pour the locomotive, baggage car, seven coaches, hundreds of passengers, and crew of nine into a snake-infested swamp as I pulled the horn handle repeatedly to get the attention of the pilot.

Just as it seemed that my wife was going to get to collect on my Travelers life insurance policy, the big yellow bird jerked, lifted, and cleared our train. Drawing closer, I could see that a large chain had been suspended from the chopper, wrapped around a number of huge tree trunks. The force of the quick lift-off broke the chain and spilled the logs into the marsh below, forcing the workman collecting the wood to dive into the water with them.

"Emergency! Emergency! Emergency!" I screamed into the radio. "This is No. 90, and we've put the train into emergency to avoid hitting a helicopter at milepost 110."

"SCL north-end dispatcher Rocky Mount to No. 90," Lee Horace Joyner's concerned, high-pitched southern drawl boomed, "I've got you protected in both directions. Is everyone okay?"

"We're all right on the engine," I panted. "I'll check with the train crew. We missed him. He took off at the last second."

"I thought you said you almost hit ... well, it sounded like you said you almost hit a helicopter?" Joyner asked. "What kind of helicopter?"

"A big yellow one," I responded.

"Would you repeat that please?" Lee Horace asked.

"A big yellow one, like the ones the Army flew in Korea," I told him.

"You were in Korea?" he seemed confused. "You don't look that old."

"No," I said, "It's the type they show in those Korean War movies."

"You know they're gonna drug test you if anyone hears that you put a train in emergency to avoid hitting a big yellow Korean War helicopter on a bridge in the middle of a swamp, don't you?" he responded, semi-seriously. "Then they're gonna put you in a straightjacket and send you over to Dorthea Dix Hospital in Raleigh."

"SCL roadmaster to the north-end dispatcher," came another voice. "I believe Mr. Riddell is referring to some people that asked for permission to log for ash wood in that area; but they were given strict instructions not to foul the right-of-way until they called the railroad and had someone from the roadway department on hand to flag for them. I'll take care of this. Mr. Riddell is not hallucinating. He did see a big yellow Sikorsky helicopter."

I saw it many times after that incident sitting beside the hanger at the old Rocky Mount airport, right across from the Hardee's hamburger headquarters building on North Church Street. Other than to have it removed from the property when the airfield was converted into an athletic playing field, it never flew again. The railroad pulled the contractor's permit to log on SCL's right-of-way because of the near miss.

Rob Yancey and Lee Horace retired shortly thereafter. Alden Aaroe, Willie Windham, and trainmaster Robertson have passed away, but both stories about me and those helicopters never die down. Twenty years later, I was sitting in the crew room at the Richmond Amtrak Station, preparing for my daily run to Washington, when the CSX yard crew working an adjacent industry walked through the door to use the telephone to call the yardmaster at Acca. The conductor was Dean Polly, with whom I had worked one of my first days on the railroad at Brown Street. The remainder of the crew was originally from C&O and RF&P.

"See that fella there," Polly laughed and pointed to me, almost swallowing a big wad of chewing tobacco. "He used to be a big radio celebrity before he came out here to work, but he had to quit broadcasting when he started railroading from the WRVA trafficopter. Ain't that right, Ry-dell?"

Sure, Polly. Why should they think anything different than everyone else who's heard the story, really.

Chapter 4: Hit the Road, Jack

The first few weeks on the railroad we new hires must have looked a lot like newborn pups with huge feet. We tried so hard to stand up tall like everyone else, to become a part of this big new world of flanged wheels and steel rails, only to end up tripping, falling, and managing to look totally awkward and helpless in the process. It became a matter of pride for us to attempt to pull our own weight and not burden an experienced crew. But no matter how hard we tried, the fact remained: A green recruit anywhere was still a green recruit.

In the locker room before going on duty or during a meal break, there was the usual rash of sophomoric practical jokes and hazing—a rite of passage that comes with initiation into the fraternity of railroading. Out on the property, however, it was all business. With millions of dollars of freight tucked into thousands of boxes of steel wobbling eerily down the iron ladders and into the maze of classification tracks, in the noonday sun or pitch black darkness, awareness of the danger and responsibility that comes with the territory was the first order of business (something that stays with you until the day you look at the crew clerk and say, "Mark me off and don't call me anymore. I'm retired.").

I've been told countless times, "I'd love to work for the railroad. I've watched railroaders. I could do what they do. They make all that money, have all those benefits, and it's all for nothing more than sitting up on an engine or a caboose and riding."

When I hear that, it's all I can do to hold my tongue. I spent a few evenings doing radio talk shows, and it became second nature for me to come back hard and strong with a knockout jab, cutting off an offending old autocrat. I'd punch up another flashing telephone line, grin through the glass at the laughing studio engineer, and invite the next caller to vent his or her frustrations on the air. One night, a faulty transfer switch on the phone kept disconnecting callers just as they were about to speak. I offered apologies in advance and warned listeners every few minutes throughout the program about the technical difficulties. Everything went fine until as we were about to go off the air, one caller (lost in space, evidently) began chewing me out as soon as he hit the airwaves.

"Mister Riddell," he snorted. "Have you no manners? Since you've been on this evening, I've counted 14 people you've hung up on!"

"You're wrong, sir," I angrily countered just before I hit the transfer button, "You make a total of 15 (click). Hello, next caller, this is Open Line; you're on the air." (Of course, the next day I had to go see the station's general manager to be reminded that "that type of unchivalrous behavior is frowned upon down here in Dixie, sir.")

Pouncing on uninformed non-railroaders might make me feel a little better, but it would likely leave them more convinced that their instincts were not only correct, but that in addition to being lazy and overpaid, railroaders are rude. My 20 years experience makes me strongly disagree with that misconception, but I can understand why outsiders might think that way. Someone who can perform his or her craft flawlessly makes it look easier than it is. A good brakeman or engineer is a lot like a skilled gymnast or talented artist who accomplishes the extraordinary as if it were commonplace. Most people have the opportunity to compete in athletics or audition for community theater and can thus relate to the difficulty involved. But very few have the opportunity to hold the reins of 20,000 horses while attempting to keep two miles of freight train together at 70 mph.

You won't see many brakemen getting up onto the side of a moving boxcar any more, but I used to stare in awe at men three times my age who could carry on a conversation with me one second, and the next second, catch a grab iron on a train passing by at 15 to 20 mph, all the while continuing the conversation without missing a beat. A good number of them, now retired, suffer with hip or knee replacements and crippling arthritis. Most railroads now recognize just how dangerous this is, and how costly it can be in a court of law when an employee loses a foot, a leg, or their life attempting to catch a grab iron.

As a part of my job requirements at SCL in 1977, I was expected to be able to get up and down off of a moving piece of equipment at 15 mph. After a couple of years, I thought I was pretty much adept at this feat until one night at Rocky Mount, North Carolina, preparing to board the *Auto Train* for a crew change on the fly. The engineer, Raymond Weaver, nearing age 70, caught up on the leading end of the old red, white, and purple U36B with ease but had to stop the train so that I, a young buck of 29, wouldn't be left behind. One of the truly great gentlemen of railroading that I would have the privilege of meeting, Raymond didn't chide me for not catching up, but instead made me feel that I had done the right thing by not attempting something unsafe. Now that's class.

As I learned my first day on the job, you don't just take a cut of cars and drop them into their assigned tracks when working a yard assignment. You'd be there all day. An experienced yard conductor (or foremen as they are called on most railroads) can scan a switch list, plan a series of moves, and turn a duke's mixture of rolling stock into a fully blocked and classified freight train in no time at all. They know all the shortcuts.

The same goes for the conductor of mainline or branchline locals. A lot of men avoid the stop-and-go way freights like the plague. It's hard work, rain or shine, winter or summer. I love the name B&O crews out of Cumberland, Maryland, accord their workhorse: the Dirty Shirt. That pretty much says it all. Some conductors almost made working the locals a pleasure. Two that came to Amtrak with me come to mind immediately: Wayne Dixon and Jimmy Boone. They got SCL's Richmond to Rocky Mount local over the road quicker than many of their counterparts could move a through freight. You would frequently find them with their head in the phone box (and their butt out in the rain as the old joke goes), promising the train dispatcher that they would not delay any glass window jobs (passenger trains) or hotshot piggybacks if allowed to hold the main line and go to the next siding where there was work to be performed. It took a lot of nerve and a great deal of faith in their engineer, but on the SCL, we took a great deal of pride in doing a good job. There was an unspoken edict to which we adhered that said you never stuck a passenger train, no matter how fast you had to run to get out of its way.

Late one afternoon, my engineer on the Roanoke Rapids to Raleigh, North Carolina, local was informed by the dispatcher that he could not take us all the way into the yard until No. 81, the *Silver Star*, passed us.

"I can only take you to the end of double track at Crabtree Creek," the train dispatcher told him, "but he's already by Henderson, and you're just out of Franklinton [about 20 miles]. I can't take a chance you'll stick him, Ed."

It was said that Ed knew only two throttle positions: No. 8 and dearly beloved. He was extremely fast, but he was extremely good, too. He ripped the throttle wide open and sang out, "Yippee Ka-aye, ride 'em cowboy!" Those two GP7s roared, whipping the 20 or so cars in our consist around the curves at Wake Forest and Neuse while I gripped the arm rests for dear life. Why was I not surprised that the distant signal to Crabtree Creek shown green as we thundered by it, clattered over the Norfolk Southern diamond at Edgerton, and pulled into Raleigh Yard? Yes, the *Silver Star* caught up with us, but not until after we had cut off from the train, chocked the engine wheels at Johnson Street roundhouse (across from the passenger station), and were signing the register book before heading home. The phone rang, and Ed answered.

"You have engine trouble or something, Ed?" the dispatcher laughed. "Right toward the end, we were beginning to bet he'd catch you. Good run!"

Although there was (and probably still is) a great deal of intramural rivalry between yards crews and road freight crews, there is a healthy respect by both for the job the other does. Frequently, road men address yard trainmen and engineers as "yard birds." Of course, as one yard brakeman put it, "If that name means having to eat home-cooked meals three times a day and sleeping in my own bed every night, you can call me the bluebird of happiness as far as I'm concerned. I won't complain." That usually ends the bantering.

Most outsiders have no idea the price railroaders pay for the few minutes they sit in a warm locomotive cab or caboose instead of hanging on the side of a boxcar whose grab irons and stirrups are coated three inches thick with ice, or marching two miles toward the rear of a freight train in a snake-infested swamp during a drenching rain. I was certainly in for a rude awakening when I got the call to make a qualifying trip on the road.

Two weeks on the railroad (in the yard), and I was already chomping at the bit to grab up onto a caboose, climb into the cupola, stick my head out the window, and wave to everyone I saw and yell, "Hey, look at me!"

"Heck," yard brakeman Julian Neely laughed, "they run short of people all the time. Just last night they called me for 289" (the notorious all-night, every-siding local from Acca to Raleigh).

"Them road men can have that life," chimed in Dean Polly, a relatively new employee but already confirmed yard brakeman. "I ain't living out of no suitcase. I ain't been on the road, and I ain't going if they call me."

Railroad men looked forward to Sunday, not necessarily for religious reasons, but to see if they would be furloughed, retained, or recalled. Although SCL trainmen were then assigned to either the road or the yard for a period of 30 days, at which time they could elect to swap, when there was a manpower shortage, anyone could be used—regularly assigned brakemen by choice, extra board employees by directive. Yard employees were guaranteed five days work each week, thus the railroad regulated the number of them so assigned. On the road extra board, however, the number of unassigned workers was adjusted each week by the union representative according to the total number of miles the board worked the previous week in anticipation of the requirements for the following week. A yard man might work three days one week and draw full pay, while his road counterpart might not work at all and get no paycheck.

My grandfather was hired by the Chesapeake & Ohio Railroad in 1929, just weeks before the stock market crashed. After establishing his seniority, he was cut off for nearly 10 years, until the onset of World War II began seriously challenging the ability of Chessie's road to keep traffic moving into and out of the embarkation port of Hampton Roads. To pay rent on the two bedroom walk-up flat that served as home for him, my grandmother, and their three daughters, he worked as the janitor at Highland Park School, gutted hogs and dressed chickens down on 17th Street in Richmond's produce market district, and occasionally received a call to work for the railroad. He always answered that call, because failure to do so would have jeopardized his seniority in the event that he was ever called back to work permanently. Even in the 1950s with almost 30 years on the roster, and because so much of C&O's traffic was coal, he could expect to be cut off when the miners went on vacation or on strike.

Seaboard Coast Line hauled some coal, but it was primarily a passenger and merchandise freight railroad. Before my time (and long before air conditioning and Walt Disney World turned the Sunshine state into a year-round playground), it was the lull in Florida's tourist season that forced layoffs in the trainmen's and engineer's ranks. I've been lucky. Only once was I furloughed at Richmond, and then for only a week. Because my seniority district covered the states of Virginia and North Carolina, I actually stood for a regular through freight assignment in Portsmouth, just 80 miles away.

I began railroading at the end of an era where you were taken under the tutelage of experienced employees. Though by accident, I believe that having been hired to work in the yard helped to make me a better employee, because I learned the basics in a setting where there was time to discuss what was being done and to question why. Today's mega-merged systems send new hires away to school for weeks, where, isolated from home and family and insulated from disgruntled senior workers, they can be taught fundamentals the way the railroad wishes them to be taught. Quite possibly, separation from the familiar also serves to let the new hire come to grips with the reality that he or she will spend a great deal of his or her life away from home and family.

"Ry-dell," crew clerk Dickie McGraw mispronounced my name, shouting, as if it were necessary to do so in SCL's small, two-person manpower nerve center at RF&P

Railroad's Acca Transportation Center, as our yard crew awaited the completion of a brake test for our transfer run to Brown Street, "I could have used you on No. 111 last night, but you're not road qualified."

"What do I have to do to become road qualified?" I anxiously asked.

"Just make a trip to Rocky Mount," he answered. "Ride the head end going down, and the cab coming back. When you get through tonight, call me. You'll be five or six times out with only one job showing. You won't even miss your turn in the yard."

"Does it pay?" I inquired.

"No, but it'll pay off for you if you get furloughed," Dickie laughed.

McGraw set me up to ride No. 105 from Richmond to Rocky Mount and return on the first thing smoking. Although freight schedules in the timetable are not especially representative of the actual departure time of most freight trains, No. 105, the workhorse of the north end through freight pool, was almost always called out first. Most pool crews standing first out hoped that the *Piggyback Special*, No. 175, would be early enough that they would catch it instead. By contract, if your train made two or more stops en route to pick up or set out, you were entitled to be paid at the local freight rate, as opposed to through freight. For the dollar or two difference, most people would just as soon be on one of the hotshots and let some one else have the money.

Trains like Nos. 105, 111, 214, and 289 had a reputation that they all too often lived up to. They seemed to stay in trouble, and trouble seemed to follow them. To begin with, they operated over the East Route of SCL's Collier Subdivision, which not only meant that they had to handle traffic for the C&O connection at Brown Street and the highly industrialized Hopewell Branch at Bellwood, Virginia, but whenever there was a restricted load which mandated a lower speed, or the necessity to stop while other trains passed with caution, they were always placed behind the engines of the "through locals," as they were termed.

As if to add insult to injury, since little was expected of them (in terms of over-the-road performance), those trains were usually assigned the oldest and poorest power. Quite often, while their engine crews were inking the register book, the shop forces at RF&P's Bryan Park engine terminal would be in the process of swapping out the best engine in No. 105's already weak line up with one deemed not acceptable for the *Piggyback Special* No. 175 or hotshot Jacksonville freight expediter No. 109.

Not wishing to stick their neck out on a bad gamble, train dispatchers would hold No. 105 and its brethren until the parade had completely passed them by. Since No. 105 was the first scheduled southbound through freight of the day, unless RF&P delayed it between Potomac Yard and Acca, the first out pool crew was often the first to leave Richmond and the last to arrive at Rocky Mount. That's when Murphy's Law kicked in, and a bad trip grew even worse. Because you had to have eight hours off duty after completion of the run before you could work again, you might be run around by one or more rested crews for your return trip. Since they saved the best for last, as the old saying goes, you were almost assuredly going to be called for No. 120—No. 105's northbound counterpart.

"Ry-dell," McGraw nonchalantly announced, "You're called for No. 105, on duty at 11 a.m."

"Where do I show up for work?" I asked.

"Here at the yard office," McGraw informed me. "You'll ride the cab with conductor Freddie Bailey."

I remembered my grandfather's steel C&O caboose. He took me over to the cab track at Fulton once and let me get on board. There was a stove and high-back black leather seats in a restaurant-style booth configuration at one end, bunk beds at the other. He had a carpet on the floor and pictures on the wall. It was clean and homey, but then he lived in that cab: He slept, ate, and did his work in it.

I arrived the next morning at 10:30. If I had expected to see such accommodations 20 years later, I was to be bitterly disappointed. The era of assigned caboose cars on SCL had long passed, with the exception of those entrusted to the care of road switcher or local freight conductors for 30-day stretches. Through freight cabs were tacked on at Potomac Yard and ran through to Miami, Birmingham, or wherever. Built from 40-foot boxcars, SCL's spartan M-5 cabs, which lacked cushioned underframes, dominated the rear end of most trains on the road. The only seats were in the cupola— high-back walkovers that could be reversed so the cab did not have to be turned. The hinged cover of the equipment bins served as a table, and the captain sat on a leather-topped wooden bench using a Masonite lapboard (when one could be found) on which to write.

By contrast, it would later turn out to be a real treat to catch a trip on a former SAL 5700-series wide-cupola cab. Manufactured by International, they rode like Cadillacs with their cushioned underframe and draft gear. Most kept their booths, their SAL lettering, emblems, and safety slogans (A man at rest is at his best/Hold tight 'til footing's right) to the very end.

Former ACL road conductor Bailey, along with our former SAL yard brakeman, and I watched the random collection of tank cars, boxcars, hoppers, flats, and gondolas roll by. They carefully checked each against the waybills and switch list (something now taken for granted by a generation used to surfing a computer-generated paper trail). Sure enough, on the rear was a dingy former ACL M-5 caboose, which, after boarding on the fly, we discovered lacked a lap board, sufficient ice, or drinking water.

"That'll do SCL 105," Bailey's West Virginia accent sang out. "We've got to have this cab supplied before we can go anywhere."

"Can't you get it at Brown Street?" asked the RF&P yardmaster. "Amtrak No. 89 is getting ready to leave the station, and you're in the middle of AY interlocking, blocking him."

"Look, Gene," Bailey warned. "It's hot out here, this thing is filthy, and the toilet smells. I've got to spend the next 12 hours on this damn thing while you're sitting up there in a nice clean office with air conditioning. I have the right to demand a new cab altogether. I'm only asking for ice and a lapboard. You know they won't have the proper supplies at Brown Street. You just want to get me out of the yard."

"Okay, I'll have the car inspectors bring you what you need," the exasperated yardmaster acquiesced. "Just pull clear of the signal so I can run some trains, will you please?"

Just then, like rolling thunder, the slack rammed in, the caboose jumped what seemed to be two feet in the air, and everything that wasn't nailed down became airborne in a hail of dust and dirt. I found myself flat on my face on the floor. Holding onto some of the black grab irons that seemed to be distributed throughout every nook and cranny of the cab's mint-green interior walls and ceiling, both Jim, the flagman, and Bailey stared at me.

"Are we still on the tracks?" I asked.

"On the tracks?" answered the flagman, as if puzzled by my question.

"Son, you had better learn that on a caboose you hold onto something every second unless you want to get hurt," Bailey spoke authoritatively.

"That's normal, captain," Jim laughed, "especially with that old Coast Line hogger up there."

From what I had gleaned of the animosity that existed between former employees of the two merged systems, I fully expected Bailey to counter with a protest of some kind to defend the honor of his former railroad, but evidently, in this case, he concurred, like it or not. The blue truck with our supplies arrived quickly. Our conductor gave the go ahead to the engineer, and braced himself against the equipment cabinet below the cupola Jim and I occupied for what would come next.

WHAM! I had not included the word "fear" in my railroad vocabulary. In my railfan world, the cupola of a caboose was envisioned to be a perch from which to get the best view of the realm. Riding in the caboose was to be thrilling, exciting—like an amusement park ride. I suddenly found myself afraid to let go of anything that appeared to be solidly anchored to the floor. I held onto the arm rests of the chair like I was readying myself for the dentist to extract my teeth. I'm sure the impressions of my thumbs and fingers remained in the arm rests' paint long after the old orange M-5 went to the bone yard. Until I could acclimate myself to the comings and goings of freight train slack, a cab ride became a terrifying prospect, especially in the dark when I could not see the terrain and predict when the next wrenching earthquake was likely to take place, and instead had to rely on the crashing sound of this metallic tidal wave that was just as deadly as the Atlantic Ocean's pounding surf and undertow at Myrtle Beach. Forget about the children's railroad primers which nostalgically describe it as "the conductor's business office." It became clear that a cabin car, a crummy, or a van (as Europeans call it) was little more than the bobbed tail end of a whip that cracked constantly.

"That old sonofabitch is gonna jerk this thing in two before we even get out of the yard," Bailey screamed. "SLACK OUT, SCL 105!"

"You're supposed to let the engineer know when the slack is in so he can reduce the throttle and keep from getting a knuckle or draw head," flagman Jim explained to me. "Only this guy is so bad that he defies the law of gravity."

So that was the duty of the flagman on a caboose: calling the slack—letting the man at the throttle know that he did not kill you when it ran in, and informing him that you survived the whiplash when it came out. No wonder crew members in the cupola of a caboose were sitting down with their feet braced up against the forward bulkhead and their backs arched against the high seat back when they passed by me as I spent my pre-railroad free time fanning. I began to understand that they weren't reclining in those high-back seats for comfort. It was evasive action, taken to prevent injury.

It was slack that ended the career and eventually contributed to the death of my grandfather. With five new C&O EMD GP9 road switchers on the head end of an empty coal train descending the nearly 1 percent grade into Richmond's Fulton Yard, the two feet of play between each of the 220 coal hoppers compressed in a matter of seconds after the air brakes unexpectedly went into emergency, catching John Everett Beazley off guard as he prepared to alight from his caboose. He was found by coworkers writhing in pain, laying beside the track with a broken back.

Bedridden most of the next year, worried that he would lose everything he had worked so hard and so long for, he applied for Railroad Retirement and received a relatively small settlement from the railroad for his pain and suffering just before he developed pneumonia and died one day prior to the arrival of his first monthly pension check. I then understood why he called the otherwise comfortable caboose he occupied a "skull buster," and why he (and after his death, my family) so vehemently opposed my plans to work for the railroad someday.

"It's not like you're a coal miner," I was reminded every time I broached the subject of railroad employment. The reference was made to generations of mountain folk who had little choice but to follow in their forefathers' footsteps and later lead their own offspring by the hand into jagged shafts thrust into the crust of the earth, there to die suffocating from black lung, gas explosions, or cave-ins. (Visiting my grandmother's brother, Frank Davis, in Robson, West Virginia, many years ago, some coal miners learned that my grandfather was a railroad conductor, and told him that they wouldn't have his job—it was too dangerous!) "You can get an education, be a doctor or lawyer, make something of yourself. Your grandfather is probably turning over in his grave to think that, after all the suffering he went through, you would want to go to work for the railroad. He loved you. He wanted you to have better."

For the first time, I stopped and thought about it. This was the reason why my grandfather so often limped into the house in the middle of the night, hanging his worn felt fedora on a branch of the hat tree in the foyer, laying his black work jacket with the leather elbow patches on the kitchen table, groaning in agony while bathing himself in liniment or pressing a towel filled with ice to his swollen forehead. Why then did he take his grandson to the rail yard with him on paydays, or to work with him when he worked a passenger train? Because he loved him, I guess, and because John Beazley knew that in spite of anything he could say, his grandson, Douglas, would be a railroader someday.

I'm sure my lack of color and the uneasiness with which I walked was apparent as I stumbled over the rough ballast following my conductor into the yard office after we stopped to make our first pickup at Brown Street Yard. At that moment, I'd have loved to climb up on an old butt head (yard engine) and switch cars for eight hours, just to stay off of that caboose.

"Well, look whose a big road man now," came the familiar voice of conductor Garland Elam. "Moving on up to bigger and better things, eh?"

"I've got to get qualified for the road," I said, leaning on the yardmaster's desk for support, still shaky from the short cab ride from Acca.

"Don't let 'em teach you any bad habits," Elam smiled. "And be careful. It's real easy to get hurt out there on the road."

Brake test completed, we departed Brown Street. We didn't have to stop at Bellwood that day. We had a set-out and a pickup at Collier Yard, the Norfolk &Western interchange at Petersburg, Virginia, about 30 miles to the south. After climbing out of the James River basin, our speed increased to the degree that we were keeping pace with motorists on a parallel stretch of I-95 near the huge Phillip Morris cigarette manufacturing plant and blasting through the Chesterfield County suburbs. Freddie began sorting the waybills and making up a switch list for the Collier set-out just as we crested the hill and rounded the curve at Bellwood. Evidently, while slowing down for our entrance onto the former ACL main line at Centralia, the slack had eased in without notice.

WHAM!

I was thrown back up against the high back seat by a violent wave of slack.

"Sorry sonofabitch!" screamed Freddie as he, the bench, the lapboard, and the waybills went flying past us down the aisle below the cupola, from the front of the cab to the rear, landing up against the closed door. Reaching for the radio, he picked it up and began chewing on our engineer. "If you can't run a freight train, go back in the yard. You're killing us back here!"

I used the few moments when calm prevailed to familiarize myself with the railroad's timetables. I had both a Rocky Mount and a Raleigh Division timetable, because at that time there were two separate operating divisions headquartered in those two Tar Heel cities—effectively the old Coast Line and the old Seaboard. Both shared the same (former ACL) trackage from Collier Yard to Richmond. The maps on the backs of both orange covers had already begun to shrink, as two fiercely competitive railroads were gradually merged into one. I kept a copy of each timetable under which I worked. When I flip through them now, I am amazed at how much of the railroad—over which I used to be qualified—no longer exists. Since timetables were put out about every six months, it is possible to document when certain branches were abandoned.

Passing through south-side Virginia in 1977, at Jarrett we rumbled over the rusting diamond that once clattered with the passage of the six-axle coal hoppers of Henry Huttelston Roger's Virginian Railway. A two-aspect signal with a "C" marker (stop and check if red was displayed) guarded the junction that now saw no traffic eastbound toward tidewater Virginia, since the VGN was swallowed up by coal-toting rival N&W in the late 1950s. Ten miles to the south, at Emporia, we thundered over an interlocking, where a trio of Alcos (a notch nosed T-6 switcher lettered for N&W and two RS-11s bearing the letters NF&D), awaited their turn to burble west over the Norfolk, Franklin & Danville (former Atlantic & Danville) Railroad.

"Clear board at Emporia," drawled the electronically transmitted voice of the phantom engineer I had yet to meet, but whose hand I had felt.

"Clear board," our flagman responded. Turning to me, he explained there was an open agency both here and at Enfield, North Carolina, which meant that we were subject to receive orders on the fly from the operator. Both were closed within the next six months, but on this day I stuck my head out the cupola window, observed the semaphore arm straight up, and waved at the operator, Mr. Wheeler. The cab shook violently again as the steel wheels battled with the hard surface of the railroad crossing at grade somewhere between 60 and 70 mph, and the slack ran out as we passed over the Meherrin River.

Highway 301 parallels the old ACL along much of its route from Virginia to Florida, and adjacent to a long, sweeping curve (State Line Curve) just south of Emporia. The pavement change was noticeable near a sign proudly welcoming everyone to North Carolina, "variety vacation land." On the reverse side, the commonwealth of Virginia welcomed those headed north with a reminder that radar detectors were illegal and subjected the owner to a fine and confiscation.

Nearing the Roanoke River, we slowed down and crossed over to the other mainline track at Garysburg to wait for the southbound *Auto Train* to pass us. Mars light wagging and stack exhaust billowing, No. 3 roared by us.

"Well, I guess we didn't stick him too badly," Freddie Bailey said.

"Why didn't the dispatcher cross us over earlier? I saw lots of crossovers," I noted.

"The dispatcher can only cross you over at an interlocking that he controls," Bailey explained. "From Collier to Garysburg (a distance of roughly 50 miles) is Rule D-251 territory. It's like a dark, two-lane road with no passing allowed. You must stay to the right side of the road. Didn't you notice that there were signals only on one side of the track? The dispatcher knows you're somewhere between Collier and Garysburg, but not your exact location. Those are all hand-operated crossovers, over which the dispatcher has no control."

I began to find out just how much I didn't know about railroading. When I lived in Raleigh, I used to visit the dispatching center and watch as three men routed movements between Hamlet and Richmond on the former SAL with the flip of a lever and the push of a button. A singletrack railroad with passing sidings, the SAL had opted for CTC (Centralized Traffic Control) over most of its Richmond to Miami main line beginning during World War II, while Atlantic Coast Line advertised itself as the only doubletrack railroad to Florida. It was during Tom Rice's rein in Jacksonville that the economies of single track and CTC were examined and employed. Much of the old ACL south of Rocky Mount was already converted to a solitary strand, and the Petersburg to Rocky Mount line was eventually single tracked in 1986.

There was good reason for a three-mile stretch of CTC to exist at this point on the fall line, separating North Carolina's undulating Piedmont from its flat, marshy coastal plain. It was at Weldon, on the south bank, that the former SAL's Portsmouth to Raleigh line (the long barrel) crossed the Roanoke River and shared a bilevel passenger station with the ACL prior to Amtrak. Seaboard Coast Line derived much of its profits from the many textile and paper mills served by the former SAL yard at nearby Roanoke Rapids. Since bridges are highly taxed and expensive to maintain, a connection between the former SAL and ACL was hastily constructed after the merger, thus eliminating the need for the SAL span, which was dismantled in due time. At one time, ACL's bridge had a gauntlet track—two overlapping tracks on the single-width span, which separated at both ends without the benefit of a switch.

Passing Weldon Yard, our flagman pointed out the no longer used Armstrong (hand operated) turntable as well as one of ACL's single story brick towers. Though CTC had rendered them useless, except to house operators to hand up clearance cards and orders during signal outages for track work or in an emergency (such as a derailment), many remained into the 1990s, but face eventual demolition since they represent an unnecessary tax liability.

"You must have brought us good luck," Bailey laughed in a moment free from scribing switch lists or sorting waybills. "We got by Bellwood and Weldon without having to stop. We're not that far behind No. 175 and No. 409. If we can get into the yard and get off duty, we might even hold our turn going back. We'll probably stand for No. 176, the northbound *Piggyback Special*. Of course you are just qualifying, so you can jump on the first thing headed for Richmond."

That sounded good. We had been on duty over nine hours and had gone less than 130 miles when the six black-and-yellow General Electric U-boats that spirited us over the Collier and North End subdivisions followed the iron pathway lined up for us by the yardmaster through "Charlie Baker's" crossovers and into the receiving yard, just south of the passenger station at Rocky Mount. I pulled out my Canon FTb and took some shots of the decaying Emerson Shops. Years later, I was amazed to discover that the old ACL twin water towers were still standing in those black and white prints.

"Yardmaster says there's a 'juice train' called for 9 p.m.," conductor Bailey informed me. "That ought to give you just enough time to grab a bite to eat and get back here to meet the crew. We get off here at the wash room. The carryall picks us up and takes us to the yard office. We'll actually get there before the head end of the train passes it."

The train had slowed to 5 mph, a speed that would allow the head brakeman to line the switches for our train to head into a track in the south yard, where traffic for eastern North Carolina would be taken off and blocks of cars for points in South Carolina and Georgia would be added by a waiting yard crew.

"I appreciate the pointers, Freddie," I said. "Your help too, Jim."

"Just remember to hold onto something every minute you're on a cab, and you should be all right," they sang in unison.

"Stay marked up and we'll catch you again soon, and then we'll find out just how much you learned," the flagman nodded.

At that moment, a dark green Chevy Suburban that had apparently survived a demolition derby screeched to a halt. A tall, lanky fellow with a crumpled, faded, Madras rain hat, and wearing a plaid shirt, across which was suspended an old blue tie, jumped out and opened the rear doors of the vehicle.

"Chief [dispatcher] says get your rest," he uttered with raised eyebrows, as if he had been made privy to the meaning of life. "They're gonna run an extra off the yard—a Pot Yard train, I understand—on your rest."

"Yeh," Bailey shrugged. "Pot Yard cars on the head and on the rear, Weldons, Colliers, Bellwoods, and Brown streets in the middle. I know, they do it to me every time. Anything to keep me from catching No. 176. It'll be a solid Pot Yard train after I get off of it in Richmond, I'm sure."

We all laughed as we climbed into the dusty carriage that would transport us to the long frame yard office with the three story spire that housed the yardmaster and the operator at CO Tower.

"Ry-dell," Bailey lectured me. "Just remember, the railroad never lies to you; they just have a very liberal interpretation of the truth."

Arriving at the yard office, we signed in and awaited the arrival of the head brakeman and the engineer to be transported to the railroad YMCA. Patronized by SCL, whose employees (a majority of the town's population) were its membership, it served as a social nucleus and health club for Rocky Mount residents, as well as an out-of-town home for crews from Richmond, Portsmouth, Wilmington, and Hamlet. I would come to know it well in the next nine years, but not this trip. No, I would be treated to some famous North Carolina barbecue, hush puppies, and sweetened ice tea before climbing aboard the engines of the Tropicana orange juice train for my return to Richmond.

"Hi," I introduced myself to the engineer, "I'm Doug Riddell. I'll be riding to Richmond with you to learn the road."

"Where's my two tickets to the movie?" Vernon Collier laughed.

"What?" I was puzzled.

"You're the guy on the WRVA radio I was listening to once who was giving away two tickets to the movies if anyone could answer your quiz," he said. "I knew the answer to the question, but someone else called in before I could get through."

Now I remembered. I was still working for the big Richmond radio station ("Don't quit your day job, son; if they don't lay you off, they'll find a way to fire you," I was urged). Vernon had called me and identified himself as an SCL locomotive engineer. We talked trains over the phone for a few minutes while I did my show. To this day, whenever I see Vernon (now retired), he keeps ribbing me about those tickets. Over the next few years, I would fire for him and learn a lot from him about running a freight train.

Seaboard Coast Line saw to it that three of its best GE diesels were assigned to the juice train every trip when it left Bradenton, Florida. Although it was only 60 cars long, it was undoubtedly the toughest train to handle on the road, because the processed, packaged Florida gold inside each white refrigerated car sloshed incessantly. It was like trying to pull a suitcase with a rubber band. It had to be coaxed carefully to prevent it from being torn in two. Vernon Collier, one of the very best engineers I've ever worked with, made it all seem like child's play. Years later, as its engineer, I once stood beside the juice train's diesels at Rocky Mount, exchanging information with my inbound counterpart, when the train actually separated while it was standing still because of slack resulting from the turbulent liquid.

Arriving back at Acca Yard, only three hours after departing Rocky Mount, I felt as if I was going to experience jet lag compared to the torturous trip down on No. 105. I had now been on the head end and the rear end of my first freight trains, and I had acquired a new respect for the men who manned them.

"Crew clerk at Acca calling brakeman Ry-dell on the inbound juice train," came the familiar voice of swing crew clerk J. P. Brown. (Smoking his trademark pipe, and always wearing his New York Yankees baseball cap, J. P., it seemed, showed up at all hours of the day or night, anywhere in the Richmond/Petersburg area to work—crew clerk, yard clerk, operator, carryall driver.) "You stand first out for a yard job in the morning. Better get your rest."

No one was going to have to sing me a lullaby that night. A good railroader man learns early on to sleep hard and sleep fast. I was tired, but railroading was new and exciting—every aspect of it—and I'd be ready to go when the phone rang.

Chapter 5: On the Road Again (and Again)

Have you ever been a newcomer to a situation and found yourself totally baffled by the way things are done? I did when I went to work for the railroad. I had not only exited the relatively sedate, clean, comfortable, Mondays through Fridays, broadcast studio life I had known since college, but I was about to be swept up into a 24-hour-a-day, seven-day-a-week cyclone of rules, regulations, discipline, union agreements, strikes, and grievances.

When my name was first listed on the brakeman's seniority roster after I was hired by the Seaboard Coast Line Railroad in 1977, the initials "NP" appeared beside my name: It indicated that I was a "non-protected" employee. No, here we're talking about job protection for those employees who worked for either the Atlantic Coast Line Railroad or the Seaboard Air Line Railroad prior to the amalgamation of those two systems to form the Seaboard Coast Line Railroad in 1967.

Since I was hired after the merger, I was not a beneficiary of special dispensation (protection) accorded employees who were hired before it. In exchange for the presumed loss of jobs or forced relocation that is the byproduct of most large business consolidations, railroad union representatives had worked out an agreement between the employees they represented and the new railroad, clearly spelling out, among other things, how the smaller, leaner employment pie would be divided, who would have rights to partake of it, and for how long. Once satisfactory assurances were made that employees left without jobs would be properly compensated, and that remaining employees would not suffer a loss in wages or otherwise be placed in a worse position to earn a living, the unions dropped further opposition to the merger.

Twenty years ago, all of this mumbo jumbo about prior rights and merger guarantees was Greek to me. Twenty years later, I've been through one major consolidation (the one which formed CSX) and the establishment of an independent Amtrak work force (which combined seniority rosters of employees from many different railroads). Today, as a railroad employee, I make it my business to stay informed about such matters. In this day of mega-mergers and corporate downsizing, it is necessary for every employee to remain informed.

With the exception of a few immediate facility consolidations and physical connections at strategic locations, SAL and ACL remained pretty much two separate railroads in Virginia and North Carolina for almost 10 years, despite the bright yellow and black logos and locomotives that quickly blanketed the southeastern United States proclaiming "the new railroad is here." While swift and sweeping changes might have netted even more substantial savings than those that were realized by this very successful union, they would have been more than offset by severance and relocation liabilities incurred by uprooting so many people. Changes in traffic patterns, line abandonments, and terminal closings seemed to progress and quicken at about the same pace as the slow, plodding process of attrition eliminated protected employees.

Prior to the merger, all work on the former ACL north of Rocky Mount, North Carolina, belonged to the Richmond manpower supply point. As part of the merger contract, it was agreed that trainmen and conductors would be deadheaded to Rocky Mount to protect any northbound work terminated there until such time as no protected employees remained to claim those assignments, or until the rights to the work were waived. This included through freight service to Portsmouth, Virginia, as well as local freight runs to Ahoskie, North Carolina, and Jarrett, Virginia. In order to be legally rested to work the following day, it was necessary to send these employees to Rocky Mount the night before (under pay) to be lodged at the YMCA, when there were actually extra board employees living within sight of the yard office at Rocky Mount, who could not be used for those assignments unless there was no one available at Richmond. Worse still, after having worked the assignment for the day or for a round trip, there was no guarantee that you would be sent back to Richmond. If you were not notified that you were released before going off duty, it was back to the YMCA to get rest for tomorrow. That also meant enduring yet another day of working with the rest of the regular crew (most of whom were good, hard-working, God-fearing people who lived in Rocky Mount, but who welcomed outsiders with slightly less enthusiasm than they would have greeted the arrival of their mother-in-law for a month-long visit).

To me—then a new hire—this arrangement was absurd. To older employees who had been furloughed many times during their years on the railroad, this was money in the bank, insurance, something to fall back on if things turned bad. They knew too well that very often a job at an outlying point that no one else wanted meant the difference between the ability to put food on the table and having to ask for a handout.

"Never give up anything," I was constantly warned by the old heads. "Never!"

My mother recounted that my grandfather often stood for nothing other than a passenger flagman's job on C&O trains Nos. 47/48, the Tidewater Virginia section of the *Sportsman*, between Newport News and Richmond. Richmond men had first claim to the jobs on that train, although they worked out of Newport News. Their only time at home with their families was the short daily layover in Richmond.

"He'd get home at 10 o'clock in the morning, after we'd gone to school," she told me, "and he would have to be back on duty at 4 o'clock in the afternoon, before we got home. We never got to see him except on weekends or school holidays."

Hardly a month into my railroading career, I was no longer able to hold a position on the yard switchman's extra list at Richmond. I was cut off, but I was also offered the opportunity to be placed on the road trainman's extra board (which, since I was relatively young and single at the time, suited me just fine). I wasn't crazy about the idea of being beaten to death by slack on the caboose at the end of some 200-car freight train, but, as I was to learn, being on the road encompassed a variety of tasks besides the traditional passenger, through freight, and local freight assignments I associated with railroading.

For instance, railroads are constantly maintaining their tracks, especially during summer months, so it was not unusual to be called late Sunday night or early Monday morning for a work train. There were trains that distributed crossties, set out welded rail, and dumped ballast. Others operated the Jordan ditchers or Drott cranes to clear the right-of-way. Most dreaded was the dusk to dawn, 3 mph Speno rail grinder. Because of the heavy equipment involved, the high noise level, and the concentrated mass of humanity on work trains, it could easily become a very dangerous place.

Seabord Coast Line, like many railroads by 1977, had adopted a 10-hour, four-day week for its larger, system track gangs. This allowed the laborers (many of whom hailed from points as far away as Georgia and the Carolinas) an extended weekend to travel home, to be with their families, and return to the work site. By working two four-day weeks back-to-back, the gangs could work eight days straight and have six days off. (But believe me, after watching the sheer physical work those men performed in everything from 100 degree heat to two feet of drifting snow, I can assure you that it probably takes six days to recover from eight continuous days in maintenance-of-way service.)

After the work train left the terminal on Monday, unless a senior trainman or engineer made a seniority move onto the job to displace you, the same crew remained with the train until it came back into the terminal on Thursday or Friday. There have been times when I prayed that someone with more seniority than I had would spot my block in the crew dispatcher's window, realize that a junior man was working a "regular" job, and pull me.

Work trains, at least those engaged with large gangs, had their own kitchen car and a cook. You don't feed a burger and fries to a huge, strapping gandy dancer who has been hoisting 39-foot sections of 132-pound rail in the midday heat. Some of the most delicious meals I've ever enjoyed were prepared over pressed wood logs, served on paper plates, eaten with plastic utensils in the shade of trackside trees, and washed down with Styrofoam cups filled with sweetened iced tea. Since the food came out of their funds, the roadway people always charged the train crew a dollar or two for lunch, but we paid it gladly and always felt that it was a bargain—a privilege, really. During that short time when we sat around breaking bread together, there were no engineers, no conductors, no foremen, no laborers—we were not White, Black, Asian, or Hispanic. We were railroaders.

In the 10 years I spent on SCL and CSX before I moved to Amtrak, I was only called a few times to work a wreck train. Since there was a provision in the Hours of Service Law that exempted covered workers from the 12-hour maximum allowable tour of duty to clear the line following a wreck, you didn't know when you would be back or how long you would work when you got to the scene of the derailment.

In addition to the obvious danger from jagged and twisted pieces of what used to be locomotives, rolling stock, and rails, there was always the possible presence of spilled or leaking hazardous materials. Railroads do a commendable job of educating their employees, as well as local emergency authorities in online communities, on handling hazmats, as we refer to them.

I was at a local restaurant, entertaining my cousin Jack Stecklein (a retired

Pennsy/Conrail engineer) and his wife Elanore on their way to Florida from their home in Philadelphia, when my pager went off in early January 1978.

"A. D. Riddell," Plug Stegall's familiar voice rang out in panic, "they done piled 'em up at State Line Curve. You're on duty right now. Get here as quickly as you can. You'll be the flagman to take the RF&P wrecker south to Trego and await further instructions."

It would be the next to last time I would see a steam derrick work. Within a matter of months, the Richmond, Fredericksburg & Potomac Railroad disposed of its ancient steam-powered wrecker. (The last time I photographed one working was when C&O's steamer rerailed an engine at Fulton Yard, in Richmond, a couple of years later.)

This was my first derailment. A northbound SCL freight had come off the rails in the big sweeping curve on the Virginia/North Carolina border, creating an open field where, only seconds before, a thick forest had been. It was as if God himself had wiped the landscape clean and tossed the wreckage of 35 or 40 mixed freight cars into a smoldering heap for good measure. Frost-covered sections of panel rail were stacked beside the right-of-way like pieces of HO gauge track on the shelf at Bob's Hobby Shop.

Moving among the wreckage, the wreckmaster, Ashley Bullock, was in complete control. From the moment his phone rang, the pressure was on him to clear the line and get traffic moving. Like the E. F. Hutton of his specialized line of work, when he spoke, everyone listened, and what he said was law. He was the ace, the closer, the specialist, who sat on the bench most days until he was called in from the bullpen with little or no warm-up to perform miracles for the SCL team. His wreck train with its diesel-powered derrick, tool car, equipment cars, kitchen car, dorm, and fire fighting equipment stood ready at the north end of Rocky Mount Yard, parked in its own specially equipped track across from the engine servicing facility. Within minutes of being informed of an emergency, a crew could be dispatched, a locomotive coupled to it, the train turned on the wye if necessary, and the Rocky Mount wrecker could be on its way.

So vast was the destruction at State Line Curve that the Hamlet wrecker was brought up from that pivotal junction on the former SAL Railroad. Within 12 hours, one tenuous strand of panel rail rejoined the north and south ends of the former ACL.

Besides the friendly competition between the former ACL and former SAL wrecker crews to see who could clear the most the quickest, there was a competition between the cooks on their respective kitchen cars. They evidently tried to outdo each other. The Rocky Mount wrecker cook came up with a mouthwatering North Carolina barbecue, while a hardy beef stew was whipped up in the Hamlet galley. They baked fresh bread as well as cakes, pies, and cobblers for dessert. During my stay there, I sampled the fares of both, many times.

Today, railroads call in a heavy equipment specialist that simply bulldozes the wreck site and restores the main line as quickly as possible. Scrap dealers are then contacted to haul the metal away, and salvagers eagerly tote saleable commodities to their stores. It's all very cut and dried—very efficient I'm sure, but I'm glad I had the opportunity to watch the old RF&P steam derrick in action. There was a thunderous roar, a sky filled with smoke and steam vapor, all surrounded by an atmosphere of urgency and camaraderie—a long-gone part of railroading that I'll always remember. While the track forces had camp cars in which to stay, the work train's crew usually managed to get a ride back home each night, if the tie-up point was within reasonable proximity of the terminal. If not, we were taken to a motel. Back then, in 1977, we were given a $6 daily lodging allowance, plus $4 for meals. Needless to say, since that wasn't enough for a suite at the Plaza or a thick, juicy steak from Blackie's House of Beef, we had to settle for considerably less. Usually, we would double up with another crew member and split the cost of a room in some cheap, cinder block palace on the side of the highway. At points where no such luxury accommodations existed, we often slept on the cab. (You kept the door tightly locked and the windows securely closed, because there were always intruders who assumed that a darkened caboose was an unoccupied treasure trove, making it a prime target for pilfering or vandalism.)

Once, at Henderson, North Carolina (where all of the lodging facilities are located miles out of town on Interstate 85), brakeman Henry Crump was stopped by a sheriff's deputy as he walked the streets at night after the rest of the crew (all of whom lived nearby in Raleigh) had gone home, leaving him to fend for himself until the next morning. Explaining to the constable that he had no place to stay, nor any means of getting to a restaurant for food, Henry was allowed to sleep in a cell at the local jail. After the authorities contacted the railroad the following morning, confirming both the brakeman's story and his identity, a directive was issued by the superintendent insuring that in the future someone would always be available to transport crew members to a lodging facility, thus preventing any recurrence of such an embarrassing situation.

The uncertainty of the job's duration made being called for work trains even worse. When the crew clerk notified you that you were being called for "one or more days," you didn't know if you'd be back in town that night, the next night, or at the end of the week. Your best bet was to take along several changes of clothes; a grip filled with Vienna sausages, Spam, and sardines; and a wallet full of cash.

Such Monday morning surprises were socially crippling, if not totally devastating. I discovered that a lot of young ladies, knowing that I worked for the railroad, were fairly understanding when I called them at work at the last minute to cancel a date scheduled for that night. Some weren't. Two or three times of having to excuse myself from keeping a date for dinner and a movie, however, was usually sufficient to kill whatever chance I had for a future date. Being called for a work train, or for a local or through freight at an outlying point was like the proverbial two-edged sword: it meant steady work, but it also meant you most likely were going to be stuck out of town.

"Riddell," second trick crew clerk Johnnie Lee spoke when I answered the phone. "Deadhead on No. 83 to Rocky Mount to be the brakeman on the Ahoskie Local for one or more round trips. You're on duty at 10 p.m. to depart at 10:30 p.m. It goes on duty tomorrow at 12:15 p.m."

"The what local?" I asked.

"Ahoskie," he repeated, as if he had answered the same question by new brakemen many times before. "It works from Rocky Mount, up to Weldon, over toward Portsmouth, goes south at Boykins, and ends up in Ahoskie. It signs up at 4 p.m. the following day in Ahoskie and returns to Rocky Mount. They'll let you know if you've been relieved. If not, go back to the YMCA, get your rest, and make another trip."

"Where do I stay in ... what did you call it ... Ahoskie?" I asked.

"That's up to you," he answered as if he had other things to do. "The crew usually comes back to Rocky Mount by automobile for the night—drives back to Ahoskie the next afternoon. You can stay at the YMCA, but you'll have to pay for your room, since the layover is technically in Ahoskie. That's what most of the fellas do."

That night, the *Silver Meteor*'s warm steam heat felt especially comfortable because of the crisp Virginia fall weather. There seemed the very good possibility of an early frost. As the backdrop of the Old Dominion changed casually and unnoticeably into the Tar Heel State in the darkness outside my Heritage Fleet coach's plexiglass window, I pulled out the powder blue Rocky Mount Division timetable No. 5 and glanced at the map on the back cover.

Ahoskie was on the once-thriving, former ACL East End Subdivision main line between Rocky Mount, North Carolina, and Portsmouth, Virginia. (Southern Railway at one time also had trackage rights to the busy Hampton Roads port, taking the old ACL right-of-way further south of Rocky Mount at Selma. Were it not for the fact that an obvious gap existed between Tarboro and Kelford, North Carolina, it would have been a straight shot of only 58 miles. Owing to a number of bridge condemnations, however—chief among them the Chowan River span at Tunis—SCL opted to use the former SAL's parallel Portsmouth Subdivision from Weldon, North Carolina. While bits and pieces of the old ACL remained, they were accessible solely via the former SAL.

From Rocky Mount, we would travel north to Weldon (on the doubletracked former ACL) and northeast into Virginia, where at Boykins we turned south to Kelford, North Carolina (on the former SAL). There we would take the old ACL to Ahoskie—116 miles. After leaving Weldon, it was strictly dark territory. Railroading was done the old-fashioned way—timetable, train orders, and a reliable pocket watch. The former SAL from Weldon to Portsmouth was heavily traveled by a number of through freights, locals, and road switchers. It was an exceptionally well-maintained line consisting of continuous welded rail set in heavy ballast. From Boykins on, however, only our train and its opposite direction twin meandered through the thick woods and marshy swamps over aging ties and jointed steel on ballast that was often totally obscured by vegetation.

Of course, being a workhorse way freight, the Ahoskie Local (Nos. 493-494 in the timetable) delivered cuts of local traffic to Weldon and Boykins, picking up anything there destined for points in eastern North Carolina. Between Boykins and Ahoskie, there seemed to be an endless array of manufacturing plants, farm cooperatives, and wood yards at the ends of rusting, weed-hidden spur tracks, reaching out like long, slender fingers from the slightly better maintained rails of the Lewiston and Ahoskie subdivisions. From these tracks, locals collected their bounty for forwarding to destinations far and wide. This was railroading as it used to be, before the big boys opted to throw the baby out with the bath water—abandoning localities it once vowed to serve (in exchange for generous land grants, in many instances) to concentrate on mainline unit train and intermodal long hauls.

I guess it probably meant nothing to the clerks in the billing department at Jacksonville, Florida, but if they could have seen the look of satisfaction on the face of the crusty old farmer at Severn, North Carolina, on my first trip, when we spotted a flat-car laden with a huge, green and yellow John Deere combine in the house track, they would surely have shared his excitement. After examining his investment for any damage in shipping, and after determining that the crates of supplies were all accounted for, he stuck his pipe in his mouth, smiled, nodded his head, and gave the thumbs up to the lady (his wife, I assumed) in the cab of a mud-coated Ford F-150 pickup truck.

"Gives you a good feeling, doesn't it," I told my engineer, who glanced at his pocket watch while opening up the throttle as we trundled south.

"What does?" he asked, tugging on the horn chord of the lead GP7.

"Helping people like that old farmer," I answered.

"Shit," he frowned and shook his head. "I hate to destroy your big-city notions about Ma and Pa Kettle there, but that old codger probably has two more of those things, a couple thousand shares of stock in this railroad, and owns half of Northampton County. I'll bet he's only driving that old heap 'cause his Mercedes is in the shop. Farm'n is big business. I've been out here on this damn local for 30 years, 12 and 16 hours a day to feed and clothe three young'uns and keep a roof over my head. I'll never have half of what he has."

After that failed attempt at making meaningful conversation, I tried unsuccessfully to lose myself in the shallow recesses of the old Geep's cramped cab. Avoiding any similar social discussions, I stared out of my window, watching the clearly defined silhouette of our train dance across tobacco barns, silos, and farm houses. The temperature began to plunge as the sun's rays faded and the shadows lengthened. The two old former ACL Geeps tugged the collection of loaded wood racks, empty phosphate tanks, and lime-filled boxcars out of the woodlands and into the open to where an assortment of small stores, grain elevators, and a service station surrounded an intersection with a single traffic light suspended high above it from a cable. The sign on the neat, well-kept, former SAL wooden freight depot proclaimed this to be Conway, North Carolina—the former ACL (and today a spunoff short line) serves a town of the same name in South Carolina, near Myrtle Beach.

"We're picking up orders," I yelled out to the engineer, noting the position of the semaphore blade planted beside the station's bay window.

"I guess he's going to change the meeting point with 493," he moaned, as if greatly displeased. "Whatcha got for us, Doc?" the hogger said, pressing the transmit button on the engine radio.

"The switcher was late getting back from Tunis, so 493 got a late start," crackled the voice with the thick Dixie drawl on the speaker. "They want you to pull past the connection track at Kelford and let him get by you there."

Despite the fact that, per the rules, northward or eastward trains were superior to southward or westward trains of the same class, it was standard operating procedure, by train order, for 494 to take the siding at Rich Square to meet 493. Though I would spend hours in that siding on subsequent trips, that day (luckily) would not be like that. After switching the mill at Conway, we headed down the old SAL branch, where we would cross the former ACL Portsmouth main, await the passage of our westbound counterpart, then run the last leg of our journey east to Ahoskie.

As we dropped through a swampy marsh at Potecasi, the brakes suddenly went into emergency.

"Shit," our hogger exclaimed. "I'll bet we're on the ground in the creek again. They ought to fix this dad-blamed track. It'd be cheaper than calling out the wrecker every two months."

"Everything's okay, 494," called the conductor over the radio. "You can go ahead."

"What happened?" the engineer asked.

"Just you don't worry about it," laughed the conductor. "All I'll tell you is that we're gonna have turtle soup for supper at Kelford."

"That damn fool pulled the air on us to stop and pick up a turtle," muttered the exasperated hoghead.

"Isn't that a bit dangerous, I mean, with the condition of the track and everything?" I added.

"Dangerous hell!" he snorted. "He knows I don't like turtle soup!"

The conductor and his flagman just happened to be two brothers from a nearby town. A couple of avid outdoorsmen, they would rather spend a day in a duck blind with their hunting buddies guzzling lukewarm beer than be treated to a night on the town with a centerfold sipping chilled champagne. Once, while deadheading to Ahoskie to work with them in their four wheel drive Jeep, we suddenly left the highway, headed into the trees, and sped through the swamp.

"Deer! Deer!" one of them squealed with excitement as the other gripped the steering wheel, reached across the back seat, and grabbed a pump action shot gun.

"Have we really got time for this?" I asked. "I mean, we're on duty in 30 minutes."

"There's all the time in the world for railroad'n, Bo," one brother grinned.

"But deer season is never long enough," laughed the other.

We didn't get the deer, but we did get to work on time.

"SCL 493 passing you with engine 743, displaying no signals," I heard the engineer of the westbound Ahoskie Local announce as the flanges of his two Geeps and 20 or so cars squealed around the connection track and headed north toward Conway, and eventually home (for them, at least) to Rocky Mount, as we sat waiting at Kelford. No signals meant that he had no green flags in the brackets on the front of the locomotive or classification lights lit to indicate a following section. "Fred's Oldsmobile is at the station, and the keys are in the desk drawer. Tell Eddie not to show up with that damn little Volkswagen, or we won't let him be part of the car pool any more. Five people just can't fit in that foreign tin can, and we usually have a fireman."

The crew going on duty at Ahoskie commuted from Rocky Mount in a crew member's automobile each day. Upon reaching this small eastern Carolina crossroads on the train, the other side of the job drove it back to Rocky Mount. Each rider deposited four dollars in the glove compartment each way for gas. At 40 dollars a day, three or four times a month, these guys had created a cottage industry. Sometimes there were heated arguments between the crew members who wanted their car to be used for the round trip.

Me? I was just glad to get to Ahoskie and yard the train on what had been the old ACL main line (now nothing more than two deteriorating streaks of rust that went from no place in particular to nowhere at all). Built just prior to the merger, the small, attractive brick freight depot was barely used after the line was closed to through traffic, though its semaphore still stood guard over the main line. A road switcher crew would commandeer our engines in the morning to do local siding work and assemble the outbound train.

With a soda and a Moon Pie to feast upon, purchased from the Shell station at the junction of routes 13 and 42, I eased into the back seat of the big, roomy Olds 98 that awaited us at the station door, as promised. We'd be back tomorrow afternoon—hopefully not in Eddie's Volkswagen, or after chasing some buck through the woodlands of eastern North Carolina. As the miles passed and the conversations between the regulars centered around railroad gossip about people and places with which I was totally unfamiliar, I sat quietly and prayed that a message would be waiting for me at the front desk of the Rocky Mount YMCA, informing me that after my return trip on the Ahoskie Local the next night, I would be freed from captivity to deadhead home to Richmond on the *Silver Meteor*.

Chapter 6: Good Humor Man's Sunday Go to Meeting Clothes

I took some ribbing when I showed up at work with an old 8 x 10 black and white glossy, taken by friend and CSX engineer Dale W. Diacont. In it, a much slimmer, 28-year-old Doug Riddell appeared in his new Amtrak trainman's uniform, checking watches with conductor Whitey Jones as they awaited the *Silver Star* at the old Seaboard Air Line station in Raleigh, North Carolina. Many of my junior coworkers knew me only as an engineer.

"You were a trainman? I'm just amazed that you actually fit into a uniform," one insulting rookie ticket puncher cajoled. "Look at that hair and those sideburns. Where are the bell bottoms and tie-dyed shirt?"

For years, surrounded by men as much as 40 years my senior, I considered myself one of the young bloods. Suddenly, with 18 years spent in perpetual motion on a web of steel stretching along the Atlantic Seaboard from the rural South to the Rust Belt, I find myself sitting down to crew briefings with men and women whose birthdays barely eclipse my own seniority date. Thanks to Mother Nature, Father Time, and employee buyouts, I am now Mister Riddell, No. 25 on the Amtrak Zone 5 Engineer's Seniority Roster, one of the old heads. ("Mister Riddell is my father," I tell them.)

At home, I took my old uniform from the closet, the one I keep in the gray, zippered suit bag with my grandfather's classic black Chesapeake & Ohio outfit. I'm too embarrassed to try on my uniform some 18 years later. It is smaller than my grandfather's, and his is now too tight to even consider buttoning. It used to dwarf me. Both literally and figuratively, I never thought I would fill it. I was lucky enough to have one of the original Amtrak monkey suits with the arrow-shaped hash marks and stripes on the cuffs, as well as one of the later, more conservative versions in navy blue with simple red stitching. The former I kept. The latter I sold to another conductor upon entering engine service. Grandpa's C&O uniform coat seemingly weighed a ton and bore the tag "Pettibone Brothers, Cincinnati, Ohio." The Amtrak original, made of much lighter material, was from Huntley Career Fashions and came with a blue tie and two pinstriped shirts, one red and one blue. I wish I had the leatherette belt and pouch that were threaded through the red stitched loops around its coat waist, but I'm eternally thankful to former Atlantic Coast Line conductor Henry Hall for just giving me the uniform.

"Here," Henry said when I broke for him in freight service on Seaboard Coast Line between Rocky Mount and Hamlet, North Carolina, in 1977. "You look about the same size as me, and I'm gonna retire on the *Auto Train*. I'll never have to wear an Amtrak uniform on that train. I use a toothbrush and laundry soap to keep those hash marks clean," Henry added. "You can bet that they went to some hotshot Paris designer who's never been on a train to come up with these. Who in their right mind would put white stripes on the cuffs of a railroad conductor's uniform coat? Those green surge suits we wore on the SCL—they were uniforms."

I recall scanning the glass window at the crew clerk's office in June 1977, finally locating my name with 10 others on an orange wooden block on the road trainmen's extra board. I'd been on the railroad a scant three weeks and had already been furloughed as a yard brakeman. That suited me just fine. I was single, and the call of the high iron beckoned.

"Riddell," called out Richmond crew clerk Johnnie Lee. "Here's a passenger uniform requisition form and a headend pass for you. Trainmaster wants you to get qualified for passenger service. Get over to the tailor shop in Carytown, around the corner from the Byrd Theater, and get yourself fitted. Then make a trip to Florence on No. 89 and come back on No. 84. Wear a shirt and tie. Work flagging down and baggage coming back."

I couldn't help but feel excitement, knowing I truly was about to follow in my grandfather's footsteps in my own uniform. It made no difference to me that some of the old-timers claimed it looked like the Sunday go to meeting clothes of the Good Humor man. It was a passenger conductor's uniform. While not as dignified as the one that John Everett Beazley strode the isles of the *George Washington* wearing, I was sure that he would be bursting with pride at the sight of of his grandson putting it on.

I tore out of the parking lot of the Richmond, Fredericksburg & Potomac Acca Transportation Center and raced down the boulevard as hard as my white 1970 Mustang would gallop. One of the most beautiful, tree-lined avenues in the world, the boulevard is fronted by marble-columned repositories of our city's history, art, and culture.

Had I not been in such a hurry, I would have stopped for a ham and Swiss on rye at the New York Deli or browsed through some of the small shops lining Cary Street, where the wealthy dowagers of Windsor Farms and the bohemians of the Fan District rubbed shoulders—each shaking their heads at the other in passing. I fumbled for pocket change to feed the ravenous parking meter in front of what was once Bob's Hobby Center, where my childhood fantasies of railroading took form and motion in HO scale. There was never a decal, a detail item, or a minute fact about engines or rolling stock that Bob Smith could not immediately produce from a long balsa wood tray or off the top of his head. Today, my son Ryan and I often stop to check out the latest releases in video, print, and miniature.

Around the corner, the small tailor shop sat on a sidestreet linking Carytown with the busy downtown freeway, bisecting a middle-class neighborhood in a state of rapid decline. A windowless gray brick building, it was hidden by the dark shadows of the bustling commercial district's neon lights, and by huge elms whose roots upended concrete sidewalk sections uncontested.

The ringing of the brass bell attached to the top of the clothier's shop door apparently startled the small bespeckled man from whose narrow shoulders dangled a worn yellow tape measure.

"What may I help you with?" he inquired in a thick European tongue. His rolled up shirt sleeves revealed numbers tattooed on one of his forearms.

"I would have remembered you had you brought something in, so you are not here to pick something up, right?" he asked with a furrowed brow as he visually began to size me up.

He needed to say nothing more. As the awful significance of those numerals registered in my head, I wondered how many times the opening of that door and the sudden, unannounced coming of strangers had triggered the same cautious reaction within him.

"Since you have nothing in your hands, you are obviously here to order something," he nodded in the affirmative, while simultaneously wringing his hands. He stopped and pointed at me, "You are a size 40, I can see."

Now it was me who was startled. I remembered reading in the local paper of the youth shorn from this man in a concentration camp; of his later years of service to his community; and of his tested but unbending faith. It also explained his amazing ability, or rather instinct, to instantly identify a visitor as someone there to avail themselves of his talents, or someone entering his shop to rob him of the little not already taken from him.

"I need an Amtrak uniform," I answered as I pulled the multi-colored form from my coat pocket, his eyes never losing sight of my hands.

"Ah! I shall measure you and take your order, but only after I have received payment will you get your uniform," he grumbled. "There on the wall hang uniforms that I have never been paid for by your Amtrak. They send me more orders but never any money."

In the dimly lit shop I could make out the names of coworkers embroidered in red on the left front breast pockets of the brass-buttoned uniform coats.

"I'll go to my supervisor and attempt to find out what the problem is, but please take my order so I'll have a uniform to wear," I pleaded. "I can get by with some blue slacks and a white shirt during the spring and summer, but I'll have to have a uniform coat in the fall and winter."

"We shall see," he said, shaking his head as if he had heard it all before.

With only 90 minutes before the scheduled afternoon departure of No. 89, the less-than-year-old *Palmetto*, I hurried home to dress; gather my shaving kit, toiletries, and a change of clothes; cash a check; and dash for the station. When the railroad calls, you have two hours to completely rearrange your life, cancel social engagements, provide for child care, and make apologies.

I had no idea who I would be working with. Mergers were never meant to benefit employees and frequently resulted in terms that pitted one worker against another, turned neighbor against neighbor, and in some cases alienated members of the same family. Following the amalgamation that created SCL, Richmond was as divided as postwar Berlin. Terminal consolidation with RF&P, relatively short mileage in their seniority district, and a quick drive up the Interstate from North Carolina combined to initially put former ACL Richmonders at a severe disadvantage. Amtrak's non-renewal of secondary passenger trains such as the *Palmland* and the *Everglades* in 1971 was the nail in the coffin for many of their hopes of ever working in passenger service again. Worse yet, for others it meant a one-way ticket to "Palookaville"—exile to some outlying point, with the choice between a lengthy daily commute back and forth, or five nights a week in some run-down rooming house. It goes without saying that there were a lot of unhappy people; and there still are.

With that in mind, you can imagine how relieved I was to recognize the face and friendly smile of Bob Lewis, who had commuted to work from his Raleigh home on the *Silver Star* that morning. All the crew members were former SAL Virginia Division men. Jim Grim was the baggage man. Dick Clifton took me under his wing explaining the duties of a flagman on a passenger train as the short station stop ended and my first qualifying trip began.

My indoctrination into Passenger Train Public Relations 101 lasted little over 24 hours but yielded much in terms of what I learned about human nature. To be sure, the Amfleet equipment and motive power for the daylight New York to Savannah *Palmetto* was relatively new, properly functioning, and attractive in 1977. The aging steam-heated Heritage Fleet consist of the *Silver Meteor* was clean and comfortable. The on-time performance for both was flawless.

But the idealistic railfan turned railroader quickly discovered that a friendly smile and helpful attitude was unfortunately wasted on some passengers. I met a new, impatient generation of travelers who had become accustomed to rocketing from one Holiday Inn to another on the Interstate, slowing down only in the drive-thru at McDonald's. In their all-consuming haste, mere travel was something to be endured rather than enjoyed.

The smiling models that graced pre-NRPC railroad industry public relations brochures and early Amtrak advertisements—well-behaved children, ladies in hats, and men in suits—were nowhere to be found. Archie and Edith claimed seats previously reserved by Ozzie and Harriet. The Simpsons of Springfield now reigned supreme in the depot abdicated by the Cleavers of Mayfield. By the time I stepped down on the long concrete platform at Florence, South Carolina, my whole perspective on passenger trains, the people who rode them, and the employees who worked them had radically changed.

We registered at the five-story Heart of Downtown Motel while bantering with other crews who were watching television or playing cards in the lobby. Showing its age, with its restaurant long ago vacated, the motel was constructed as a fashionable, chain operated motor inn. Located near the intersection of what had been two major north/south and east/west highways, its owners put it up for sale as they and their competitors rushed to the western outskirts of the railroad town and the teaming off-ramps of recently completed I-95. After haggling with Nancy, the manager, over which rooms assigned had color TVs or functioning window unit air conditioners, we piled into someone's old rust bucket and headed down Irby Street to look for cheap eats.

Appetites satisfied, we returned to the motel lobby, where the crew members for the northbound *Silver Meteor* had taken their 8:30 p.m. wake-up calls and were checking out. The flagman, Kelly Harrelson, was one of the few former ACLers living in Richmond able to hold a passenger job. Conductor Bob Hall and baggagemaster Irving Rose, both former ACL men from Rocky Mount, put hundreds of miles on their pickup trucks weekly, sharing the drive back and forth on I-95 to Richmond in order to work their jobs. (The customary 300-mile runs between Richmond and Florence, South Carolina, and the 372-mile runs to Columbia, South Carolina, fly in the face of the vaunted 100 mile basic day/featherbedding horror tales dispensed by railroads at contract time to convince the public that all unionized railroaders are overpaid, underworked, and unproductive.)

Unlike today's Amtrak-employed onboard crews where everyone is required to wear a uniform and do almost anything, SCL's baggagemasters wore whatever was comfortable (within reason) and neither sold nor collected tickets. Near retirement age, Rose wore a plaid shirt and cotton pants.

"You must be the crew for No. 84," I said as I stuck out my hand. "I'm Doug Riddell, and I'll be riding with you to qualify in the baggage car tonight."

Peering over the top of his horn-rimmed glasses, Hall cordially returned the gesture and introduced himself, as did Rose.

"How long you been out here on the railroad Mister ... eh ... how did you pronounce it, Riddle?" Hall asked, slightly embarrassed.

"Rid-DELL," I said, emphasizing the last syllable. "Don't feel bad. Most people don't even come close. And to answer your question, only three weeks."

"Just as long as they spell it right on the paycheck, right?" he laughed.

"Well, welcome aboard Mr. Riddell," smiled Rose. "Come along and I'll show you the ropes. We have to stack everything in route classification, write up every bag we put on, show where each piece is put off, and account for all mail and express we handle."

"I see," I nodded in concurrence. "That's a lot to remember."

"The most important thing," he chuckled, "is to put in for the extra dollar for handling express or U.S. Mail." We both laughed.

The crew room at the old Florence station was illuminated by a single fluorescent fixture dangling from the high ceiling. I was amazed to find old purple ACL public timetables and seat checks from the 1950s in scores of unused lockers. I delved through this veritable treasure trove, only stopping to accompany conductor Hall to get our orders from the operator at FC in the modern brick SCL Florence Division freight offices.

The older, balding gentleman in the office and his diagram board looked vaguely familiar for some reason. I couldn't figure out why. I arrived here before on the *Champion*, met by my vacationing family in nearby Myrtle Beach, but I came nowhere near the office. Yet I felt I had been there before.

Of course! THE RAILROAD SCENE by author/photographer William D. Middleton, who spent a similar hot, humid June night at Florence exactly 20 years before, capturing in black and white time exposures the nocturnal images of the mighty purple and silver fleet streaking in and out of this important former ACL junction. Could it be? I opened the book and compared the track layout on the panel. A lot of tracks were covered up by black electrician's tape, and this was not RA tower, but FC.

"Excuse me, sir, but is your name Guyton?" I asked the man.

"Do you want me or my son, the Amtrak ticket agent?" he responded.

"L. S. Guyton, operator at RA tower—the man in this picture?"

"Picture?" he said, appearing quite puzzled as he glanced at the volume.

"Good Lord," he grinned. "I had hair then. I remember him taking my picture. That was years ago. This is the same board—a lot less tracks. They brought it here when old RA tower, out by the wye, closed. How 'bout that."

Overcome with pride that he had been featured in the book, I got him to autograph it right by his picture. "Thank you for showing this to me," he said.

The trip home was fairly uneventful until Richmond. Walking through the lounge car, I stopped to see if the elderly man, sleeping with his head on the table, was also supposed to get off. He did get off at Richmond, in a sense. He had died somewhere en route. I called for help.

"It's a waste of your time," grumbled the obviously half-a-sleep and totally inebriated little old lady with a harsh New Jersey accent, seated across from him in the rare glass-roofed former SAL sleeper/lounge *Palm Beach*. "Don't even bother talking to him. I've been speaking to him for the last hour and a half, and he has just sat there being rude and ignoring me. People on the train are just not as friendly as they used to be, if you know what I mean, conductor."

Chapter 7: It's All in How You Say It

"That damn thing is just a noose around your neck! A ball and chain attached to your leg, boy!" A blistering assessment of the use of two-way radios on the railroad and a verse from the gospel according to the late Jesse James Rideout—one of three colorful brothers from the town of Wise, North Carolina, who hired out on the old Virginia Division of Seaboard Air Line Railroad. (They were thus affectionately known as the three wise men.) "When you speak, you're telling everyone your business. It'll get your job if you're not careful." The dispensing of wisdom from the elder statesmen of railroading is sometimes wasted on the young, but I clung to each and every word. I not only accepted it for the simple truth it represented, but often marveled at the manner of men so gifted in their evaluations of the obvious. Jesse was not alone in his feelings. He, like others who earned their seniority amid the scent of kerosene in a cloud of coal dust, abhorred and mistrusted radios for a long time.

When they were first introduced, the few rules that directly addressed this assault on traditional railroading by the forces of technology dealt more with assigning responsibility to the employee for the proper care and safe return of his radio than what (or what not) to say. Today, however, radio transmissions are strictly regulated by the Federal Communications Commission and the Federal Railroad Administration. Railroads hold employees accountable and pass along penalties for improper radio use assessed by those two government regulatory bodies and have even added their own rules. Thus, over the years, many railroaders have fulfilled Jesse's prophecies.

Because railroad communication in general has never been an exact science, the stories that come to mind—both those that I personally experienced and those I have been told—are often humorous and frequently elicit a smile or chuckle when remembered and shared.

While the diesel locomotive may have dethroned steam as king of the road, the evolution of electronic communication has revolutionized every aspect of the railroad industry from finance to transportation. During the period after radios were first placed into general use, the relationship between a railroad employee and his radio was like that of a first time father with a newborn child: While you were sure you were going to love it, you were never sure of what was going to happen when you held it in your hands.

No matter which manufacturer produced early radio models, the rough treatment and rugged requirements of railroad work soon took their toll. It became clear that if a radio was to survive the railroad, it had to be well made. This was especially true of the suitcase-sized models that found themselves clamped onto a mounting bracket inside the nose of a speeding E8. What punishment was not inflicted by vibration was dealt to it by heat from the lack of ventilation. Sometimes you could actually resurrect one from the dead by unplugging it and laying it out on the walkway of a Geep, where it would cool down and later resume transmitting.

To be sure, even some Indian Summer steam locomotives had been equipped with two-way radio communication to wayside stations, putting them in touch with tower operators and train dispatchers. It also enabled them to communicate with passing trains, as well as the rear of their own, when comparably equipped. Though most people tend to dote on the tail sign that read *Broadway Limited*, there was an induction antenna on the roof of *Mountain View* that carried the markers of Pennsy's signature streamliner. Still, for a long time, the day-to-day chores of making up trains in stations, spotting platforms in the hinterlands, and giving the engineer the highball were accomplished by hand signals.

In addition to the backup hose (or conductor's valve) and communication cord on passenger trains, there was an entire litany of hand signals given with lanterns, fusees, and flags. When you realize just how comparatively primitive these methods were by today's standards, you wonder how anything was ever accomplished. But then, walking through the Smithsonian's Air and Space Museum (as I sometimes do on layover in Washington, D.C.), the sight of the Wright brothers' fragile bi-winged craft only a few paces away from a space capsule that has actually orbited the moon makes their first flight across the windswept sand dunes of Kitty Hawk seem all the more incredible.

The reluctance of the old-timers to fully embrace the use of the radio probably stemmed from their fear that junior employees would become so reliant on them that with that black plastic box in their hand, everything would come to a screeching halt if electronic communication failed. Just as many of the progeny of America's immigrant population forsake their forefathers' native tongue for English, many of today's newest railroaders are less than fluent in the language of hand signals, although the rules clearly state that the failure or interruption of radio communication does not relieve an employee of the safe and orderly operation of his or her train.

Backing our empty *Carolinian* equipment around the wye track at Arrowwood Junction after arrival at Charlotte, North Carolina, some months ago, I had just shoved clear of the main line and was awaiting the signal to continue back when our green flagman began giving me the sign to "go ahead." Since this made no sense, I did nothing. To comply would have meant running over a derailer and through a switch. I refused to move until our conductor made sure that the new hire understood why. When I later questioned the flagman on the way to our hotel, she explained, "When we were being trained in Washington, we moved our lantern up and down when we wanted the movement to come toward us." When I explained that any movement signal was relative to the direction of the locomotive, she seemed confused. When I explained that a "back-up" signal required a circular hand motion, she smiled and said, "Oh!"

Before concluding that today's railroaders are just not cut from as good a bolt of cloth as the old-timers, remember, this was a relatively new employee, and every railroader was a "new hire" at one time. For instance, when the late Seaboard conductor Bob

Lewis was told to help train a new brakeman on an empty troop train returning to Raleigh from the busy World War II demarcation port of Hampton Roads one night on the non-signaled Portsmouth, Virginia, Subdivision, he simply told his charge to "Do everything I do." They had hooped up an order at Boykins, Virginia, to pull by and back in the siding at Seaboard, Virginia—a small town near the state line, proudly named for the railroad that served it. Backing into the siding to meet another train loaded with servicemen, Bob lined the switch and was swinging his lantern to give the circular back-up sign, when the handle snapped off and the globe flew into the woods. The cubbing brakie did just as Bob told him, making the circular motion twice and letting his own lantern fly. Hurriedly grabbing a fusee, Bob then frantically taught him the hand signal to get the engineer to stop the other train.

It's not only new hires that misinterpret hand signals. At Newport News, Virginia, on the C&O prior to radio, an old hogger slowly rounded a curve in the foggy midnight darkness with a long cut of cars being shoved onto a car float to be transported across Hampton Roads to the small yard at Norfolk. Following what seemed like eternity after having been signed down to a stop, the engineer saw the up and down motion of what he mistook for a brakeman's lantern. After moving only a few car lengths, the brakes went into emergency. Minutes later, the conductor excitedly clamored aboard the locomotive to inform him that they had shoved two cars into the James River, and he wanted to know why he moved the train while the rest of the crew had gone inside the station restaurant. As it turned out, the engineer had missed the "cut off" signal to take supper and had moved ahead on the authority of a bobbing channel buoy with a broken lens, according to local railroad lore.

Even the fusee itself (more commonly called a highway flare by non-railroaders) has undergone change. Although it still comes in varying sizes and colors in order to burn for different lengths of time and for completely different meanings, those manufactured with metal spikes at one end—enabling them to stand upright in wooden cross ties when dropped from moving trains—are generally no longer used for obvious safety reasons. Until I made my first working trip over C&O in 1980, following the merger which formed CSX, I'd never seen a green fusee burning. Fusees—especially those tossed at speed—often extinguish themselves upon hitting the ballast, usually necessitating the lighting of two or three to accomplish the intended task. Modern radio communication has virtually eliminated their usefulness in mainline railroading, except for flagging highway crossings and to thaw frozen switch points or passenger car piping. Railroad officials use them predominantly for testing the ability of engineers to stop their trains to comply with flagging rules. Many a lump has formed in my throat as I reacted to what appeared to be a burning red fusee between rails, only to discover it was an illusion created by a crumpled Coca Cola can gleaming in the noonday sun.

Fuses were used for just about everything, and not always as they were intended. Once, after acknowledging a proceed radio transmission from the section foreman directing rail replacement near Battleboro, North Carolina, I had just notched out to number eight on the F40 powering the northbound *Carolinian*, when a lighted red fusee was thrown from the window of the work train's caboose, landing in the middle of the mainline track immediately in front of me. Thoroughly indoctrinated to assume that this was a sign of immanent danger, I stopped my train as quickly as possible. As it turned out, the newly promoted work train conductor, wishing to toast his career advancement with an expensive Cuban cigar but lacking a match at that unfortunate moment, lit a fusee instead, and thoughtlessly tossed the remainder. For delaying and endangering a passenger train, he was given 10 days in the street, a stern tongue lashing by the division superintendent, and a "safety award" cigarette lighter to prevent the possibility of any such recurrence.

I first marked up on the railroad when the old heads (as they will forever be called by each new generation of railroaders) had just been handed their very first Motorola portables. Portable? They must have weighed two tons (or so it seemed) and were about as portable as a telephone booth. Toted using a shoulder strap, they were roughly the size of a construction worker's lunch pail and were even nicknamed "lunch bucket" radios by employees who used them on Union Pacific. Its handle doubled as a cradle to hold the telephone receiver handset into which you spoke and with which you listened. Programmed to send and receive only one or two channels, they were powered by either two lantern batteries or 16 D cells. Their two-foot-long antenna frequently broke off, rendering the radio useless. The dangling handset's cord often wrapped around switch stands, arms, and feet, causing them to be more dangerous than useful. The late Seaboard conductor Red Hunnicutt often told me that as a young man, he spent many a night seated in the round-end observation car of the *Silver Meteor* with one of those cumbersome radios. "The first ones were about the size of briefcases," he recalled.

Likewise, one of my most frightening experiences involved having a radio at the rear of a passenger train. With but a few months of railroad service in 1977, before it was required of engine crews to announce the indication of each wayside signal on the radio, I was called as the flagman on the *Palmetto* between Richmond and Florence. Soon after reporting, I learned that our baggage man had just come from a severe reprimand by the trainmaster for his misuse of the radio the previous trip, so our conductor handed the brand-new, hand-held WABCO portable to me. "You keep the damn thing," he growled. "It's no good for anything but getting people in trouble." Northbound the next afternoon, crossing the Roanoke River on the high, singletrack span at Weldon, North Carolina, I overheard my engineer, P. W. Wright, excitedly conversing with the engineer of southbound piggyback train No. 175. It became immediately clear that both of us had signals permitting movement onto the bridge at the same time! A head-on collision!

Proving that there is absolutely no substitute for wisdom gained through experience, former Atlantic Coast Line engineer veteran Jimmy Pippin on No. 175, knowing that the northbound *Palmetto* No. 90 was due, had slowed his train on the steep downgrade with the dynamic brake. When he popped around the curve and saw us on the bridge, he was able to stop his train, although many engineers running on a clear signal would have been flying. To this day, he has my utmost admiration and respect. (Thanks, Jimmy.)

Within 30 minutes, the area was crawling with railroad officials and government investigators. The signal had been miswired 48 hours earlier. When SCL Road Foreman of Engines John Smith questioned me as to what action I had taken—knowing that I was positioned near an emergency brake valve on the rear of the train with a radio—I truthfully answered that weighing the possible consequence of pulling that handle on the high, shaky viaduct and sending the whole train crashing into the river below, "I started praying!" Apparently dumbfounded by my answer, he stared at me for a second, shook his head, laughed, and said, "Get out of here." Nothing more was ever said to me, although every crewman who had passed that location on a caboose the preceding 48 hours had to submit a written statement.

Certainly less dramatic, though nonetheless unforgettable, was the morning that the northbound *Silver Star* made its customary servicing stop in front of the classic circular waiting room of the passenger depot at Hamlet, North Carolina. Shorn of its multiple tracks and "subway" platform accesses, this heart of SAL still saw a flurry of activity upon arrival of the town's sole remaining streamliner. Porters and passengers immediately jumped train and raced into the Terminal Hotel—recognizable to moviegoers as the setting for Dustin Hoffman's Dutch Schultz in BILLY BATHGATE—to buy up cartons of brand-name cigarettes, which at $1.85 constituted a bargain, even then. Laborers and machinists watered and tended to the train, and everyone switched to the more practical "yard" radio channel. In the dining room of business car No. 310, positioned on the rear of No. 82 this particular day, imagine the reaction as a radio transmission from a brakeman in nearby Yard A blared out over the scrambled eggs, country ham, grits, and red eye gravy, "Hell! Stop the movement. Hold on a second, dammit. I'm all screwed up." Grabbing the radio handset, the startled vice president of Seaboard Coast Line Railroad identified himself and demanded the offending party immediately reciprocate, to which came the reply: "I may be all screwed up, but I ain't that screwed up!"

It was not always the transmit button becoming stuck that provided the laughs. Many times it was the lack of transmission altogether that sparked a lively episode. In 1979, I found myself firing for Johnny Barnes on the *Palmetto* between Rocky Mount and Florence, down the old ACL South End Subdivision. Though still an hour away from our destination, I was already looking forward to freshening up at the Heart of Downtown Motel and walking the two blocks to the Highway 301 Drive In for a helping of fried chicken and barbecue before taking the *Meteor* back north four hours later. Because it paid 172 miles down and 172 back in just under 12 hours, it was understandably one of the most desirable passenger assignments.

We overtook train No. 175 with its five U36Bs struggling to lift its two-mile-long string of piggyback flats and autoracks out of Fayetteville in the unrelenting August heat. As we both crested the oddly desert-like North Carolina sand hills at Natal Hill before dropping into the tight curves of Hope Mills, No. 175's engineer, Harvard Gardner, called us to announce that a trespasser was riding on the rear, sitting on the coupler, grasping the backup hose. "I'll take care of him," confidently announced flagman Kelly Harrelson. Passing the defect detector at Parkton, just eight miles further south, neither he nor conductor Brooks Bowen answered repeated calls from us on the engine radio to confirm its indication of "no defects."

Short in stature, Johnny Barnes was a ball of energy. As we raced further south, our plaintive calls still unanswered, he became as nervous as the proverbial cat on a hot tin roof. "Riddell," Johnny shouted. "Something's wrong back there. Anyone who'd ride the rear of this thing holding on to the backup hose has to be crazy or desperate. We don't know what could be happening. Take off that railroad hat and gloves. Try to look as much like a passenger as possible and go back through the baggage car to see if you can help." I did as ordered but returned shortly, when after struggling to get through the P30CH without being sucked into the radiator fans, I found baggage man Ronnie Rideout had locked the door. Just as Johnny was about to stop the train, Harrelson came on the radio and asked us to have the "bulls" (railroad police) waiting at Florence.

"Whatcha got going on back there, Kelly?" he asked.

"I don't know. Some kind of damn foreigner—Iranian, or something. Don't speak English. Everything's okay," he assured us.

At the Heart of Downtown in Florence, Johnny jumped from the ancient but well-kept Chevy II that transported us to and from work, restaurants, and shopping malls while on layover, and raced up to the front desk, inquiring of a jovial Brooks Bowen as to what had transpired and why he was laughing. "At 80 miles an hour," howled Brooks, "My flag-man opens up the rear door, looks this poor, shaking fellow in the face, and says, 'Got a ticket, Bub?'" At the railroad picnic two years ago, just weeks before he answered life's last call, I asked Kelly if he really said that.

"Of course I did," he smiled. "We were always taught to be polite to the public."

Through the years, it has been borne out that the frequency and degree of trouble you can get into with a radio increases proportionately with your proximity to a large terminal. For instance, a fellow engineer, Dale Diacont (then working as a fireman), was once at the throttle of his train in the Richmond area, briefly relieving his engineer, when suddenly, radio communication with the train's conductor was overridden by static, causing the young fireman to ask, "Paul. Paul. Is that you, Paul?"

"Who is Paul?" demanded a rather agitated voice emanating from the engine radio's speaker.

The engineer sneered (in an answer intended solely for the ears of his fireman), "He was an apostle in the Bible, you idiot."

Before he could be stopped, the young fireman pressed the transmit button on the handset and parroted the stunned engineer. "He was an apostle. Don't you ever read the Bible?" As it turned out, the man on the other end of the conversation, SCL Superintendent of Terminals Bill Hobbs, read his Bible regularly. He not only knew who Paul was, but also recognized the source of the remark, got into his automobile along with Trainmaster Jim Benz, met the train, climbed aboard the locomotive, and lectured the crew on proper radio usage. "You're good at writing letters, Doug," Dale said over the telephone. "How about helping me write an apology to the superintendent?"

Of course, you don't expect an audience when you're more than 60 miles away from anything and anybody, but life is full of little surprises, as I embarrassingly found out one morning when I blasted past the defect detector at Emporia, Virginia, on No. 4, the northbound *Auto Train.* Long before the age of articulated piggyback "spine cars," with their odd numbers of axles, you always received an even axle count announced by the "talking" hotbox detectors. (One memorable exception was the night I transported a former New Haven FL9, with its two-axle lead truck and three-axle trailing truck, on its way to rebuilding, in a freight train.) When, in its post-train analysis this particular morning, the obviously malfunctioning detector announced, "Total axles, one, three, one," I called the conductor and jokingly told him, "We'd better stop and look for that axle we've apparently lost." From out of the blue crackled a familiar voice, "SCL Mobile One, Superintendent Wilkes, to train No. 4, Mr. Riddell. I don't think that will be necessary, but President Sanborn and I are on our way to Richmond on I-95, and would be more than willing to offer any assistance we can if you think you have a genuine emergency of any kind. Otherwise, I'd suggest you not delay that train."

"Yes sir, Mr. Wilkes," I answered. Of course, I declined their offer of help.

Railroads of the 21st century may employ atomic power to move trains or lasers to signal them, but as long as there are human beings involved somewhere in the process, there will always be a story—albeit a humorous one. It's all in how you say it.

Chapter 8: The Picnic

"I wouldn't let my own mother ride this train without a ticket!"

As I looked at the old retired conductor with whom I once worked during my early days as a trainman on Seaboard Coast Line, I laughed and shook my head. I couldn't help but think of that utterance and the circumstances that led to it back in 1979. When I saw him at the 1995 old-timers picnic, he had changed very little.

The incident occurred while I was attending engineer's training school in Rocky Mount, North Carolina, after my new bride of six months—totally disenchanted with the railroad and with this small tobacco market town—had packed her bags and moved back to Richmond. I didn't have that luxury. Committed to stay there for 18 months, my only alternative was to quit the railroad, and considering all I'd gone through for this chance of a lifetime, I refused to do that. She'd just have to understand that, in the long run, it was best for both of us.

The wage I earned while in school was about half what I had earned as a trainman. I managed to afford an upstairs room in a large house on Franklin Street, a two-block walk down Hammond Street from the old Atlantic Coast Line passenger station, which housed the Rocky Mount Division's headquarters. I shared a bathroom and kitchen privileges with two old winos and another engineer trainee from the Richmond area, Larry Hull, who later gave up his engineer's rights and is now the senior Virginia Railway Express conductor. Our landlord—a refugee from Brooklyn, his wife, and kids—treated us like family. Every Sunday night, I'd board the *Meteor* at Richmond for Rocky Mount with a week's worth of groceries, clean linens, and $20. Some nights after class, Larry and I would scour the streets looking for enough glass soft drink bottles to exchange for money to buy food. My bitter memories of that time and that town are quite possibly distorted by poverty and loneliness, which only amplified the pressure on me to study. Short of passing through town on the way to Myrtle Beach, I've never been back to visit, although I should have at least written my host family. Both winos died by the bottle: one from alcoholism, the other after being struck over the head with a long neck beer in a Saturday night barroom brawl.

Getting home on Friday afternoons was the bane of my existence. Every three weeks I would catch the northbound *Palmetto* manned by this now-retired conductor. If No. 90 was on time, I had just enough time to ease out of the rear door of our round-end observation car turned classroom, dash around the rear of the standing passenger train, and hop aboard as the brakes released. Usually this was simple, but every third Friday, I found it nearly impossible to board the train without a confrontation.

"You got a ticket to ride this train?" he asked. Keep in mind that I flagged for this man, worked the baggage car for him, rode in his car (I had to pay him), and sat at the same restaurant table with him on layovers. "What have you got against stopping in at the ticket office and getting a ticket?" he inquired. "You have a pass. Just get them to cut you a ticket."

"They aren't open when I go to class in the morning," I explained, "and they let me out of class just in time to catch your train."

"Don't try it again, or I'll wire the superintendent and have you brought up on charges," he responded.

The superintendent? Now maybe that's the ticket. I went directly to the office of the Road Foreman of Engines and explained the situation. He had a very simple solution. He issued me a permit stating that I had permission to ride the engine or train—any train—for the purpose of learning the road. It was signed by the division superintendent.

"That should take care of any problem that might arise," he laughed.

Unfortunately, we had both underestimated the resolve of this diehard grump. I had no problem with anyone for the next three weeks, but when Mr. Niceguy's turn in the passenger rotation came up again on Friday, I walked up to him and handed him my permit, only to have him scowl at me and snort, "How many times have I told you that you have to get a ticket to ride my train?"

"But this says ..."

"This isn't a ticket, and I don't give a damn if it's a copy of the Declaration of Independence signed by John Hancock, authenticated by the King of England." He reiterated, "My mother doesn't ride this train without a ticket!"

Dejected, defeated, and destroyed, I lowered my head, turned, and was heading for the Trailways bus terminal, where my union card and a sob story would get me on the next thing smoking for Richmond, when I heard the old geezer grumble, "You got any other way of getting home?"

"No sir," I answered.

"Come on, get on board, and wait for me in the lounge car," he frowned.

As I was climbing aboard, I heard him addressing someone else, "I don't care who you are. You of all people should know you don't ride my train without a ticket."

You can imagine my surprise as I glanced out of the lounge car window to discover that the old fellow was addressing—you guessed it—the road foreman! I sat down at the table where the captain was set up to do his work as we pulled away from Rocky Mount. It wasn't long thereafter when he entered the car, sat his pipe down on the table, looked me sternly in the eye, and lectured, "It's okay if you ride with me from now on, son, as long as you don't let anyone know I didn't make you get a ticket. They'll think I'm getting soft in my old age. Pretty soon, they'll all expect the same thing, just like that new road foreman."

"You didn't let him get on?" I asked in total disbelief.

"He didn't have a ticket either," grinned the former ACL conductor. "I think that Seaboard engineer let him get on the locomotive. That's his engine. This is my train."

Sixteen years later, he was sitting across the table from that same Seaboard engineer and the road foreman, laughing and reminiscing as if they had fought on the same side in the Civil War. I started to walk over and tell him that he wouldn't be fed unless he produced a ticket. Nah!

At another time, during the annual State Fair of Virginia, I got an emergency call to get to Acca Yard as quickly as possible to deadhead to Rocky Mount to work the *Silver Meteor* back north. The fireman, my best friend, had been badly injured when the door of the *Palmetto's* F40 slammed on his fingers as he exited the engine room prior to No. 89's arrival in Rocky Mount.

"They're holding No. 87 right here at the yard office for you," crew clerk "Plug" Stegall excitedly shouted into the receiver.

"But Plug, I live right across from the fair grounds," I warned. "I'm not sure how long it will take me to get through the traffic on Laburnum Avenue."

"That's all right," he said. "The train will be here."

I hopped in my car and got there in only 20 minutes, much to my surprise. While the turbochargers whistled on the *Meteor's* two SDP40Fs, I put my Mustang into park and hustled into the caller's office.

"Just get on board," Plug motioned, interrupting another phone call.

The door of baggage/dorm No. 1426 (one of the converted Army Hospital Corps cars which had replaced aging, pre-World War II Budd equipment) was open, and I noticed the baggage man waiting for me to board. Handing up my grip to the old man dressed in poplin work tans and a baseball hat, I was startled when he looked at me and asked, "Did they give you any transportation?"

"What?" I asked in total befuddlement.

"A ticket," he said, exasperatingly. "Do you have a ticket?"

"Look," I fumed. "This is an emergency. They're holding the *Meteor* at the yard for a half hour for me to get on, and you want a ticket?"

"Everyone's supposed to have one," he shrugged, "and you know who's the conductor!"

"Well, call the clerk, have them take me to the passenger station, and I'll pick one up," I cracked. "Just let me get your correct initials, so that when they fire you, I'll know the right name has been removed from the roster."

"Get on board. I guess it'll be all right." He said no more.

I wouldn't miss the old-timers outing for all the money in the world. I treasure the cool, crisp, fall Saturday afternoon each year when the unmistakable aroma of Doug Saul's genuine Rocky Mount barbecue drifts out across Richmond's Bryan Park (located, quite appropriately, adjacent to the former Richmond, Fredericksburg & Potomac Acca Yard) to the delight of hundreds of retirees from RF&P, Seaboard, ACL, and Southern Railway, as well as those of us who still toil for CSX, Norfolk Southern, and Amtrak. Along with our families, we gather in and around the large, open log shelter with its huge stone hearth to enjoy that traditionally spicy delicacy along with southern fried chicken, Brunswick stew, hush puppies, and boiled potatoes washed down with gallons of sweetened iced tea. Homemade pies, cakes, and brownies, lovingly baked by wives who once waited patiently for the return of their husbands from such places as Washington, Raleigh, and Keysville, are quickly snatched up by hands that were once just as adept at hooping up onion-skin flimsies at the drop of an order board. They are devoured with no less gusto than coffee, Spam, and beans cooked on the stove of a local's caboose sitting in some remote pass track in the darkness of a winter night. Just as sure as both my wife and I swear that we are on a diet and refuse to gorge ourselves, no matter how tantalizing the fare, we "dig in" and "pig out."

Scanning the crowd, I note that there are still many present who worked during the heyday of steam, but never as many as the previous year. Dwindling also are the numbers of those who guided the purple and silver E6-led *Champion* or punched tickets aboard Southern's quaint local to Danville. Comparisons are busily made between today's mega-merged transportation conglomerates and the days of real railroading. While the children and grandchildren of railroaders gather up pens, pencils, and key chains emblazoned with the logos of the Brotherhood of Locomotive Engineers, United Transportation Union, Operation Red Block, and Operation Lifesaver, you can't help but notice the faces of the senior attendees, pensively glancing across the parking lot with the approach of each and every car. For some of them there is the joy of seeing former crew mates emerging from aging but well kept Fleetwoods and Crown Victorias. For others, however, after the final rounds of the horseshoe tossing competition have drawn to a close, with trophies awarded and door prizes handed out, there is a sadness in the realization that some coworkers didn't make it back this year, won't be here the next, or ever again. The thought occurs that they, themselves, may soon be among the missing.

There's a bonding among railroaders forced by seniority, circumstance, and luck. In many instances, it's a life paralleling your own, which begins in your late teens and lasts until retirement. It often transcends marriages, divorces, children, measles, mumps, puberty, college, grandchildren, and frequently widowhood. The generation of railroaders who sired today's baby boomers worked under a 16-hours-per-day Federal Hours of Service Law, seven days a week. Paid vacations came in the autumn of their career. Personal days and bereavement leave were negotiated after their retirement. When they wanted off, it was without pay. For some, there is satisfaction in having paved the way for this new crop of railroaders, but for others, there is resentment at having been deprived of recently attained benefits.

I spied Amtrak Conductor Jimmy Boone Sr., with whom I've worked almost 18 years now, and thought of another day, another place, in which those same words, "You're not riding my train without a ticket," got the best of an old head conductor who initially threw down the gauntlet but lived to regret his challenge. In the waning days of Raleigh's prominence as a division headquarter and crew base on SCL, the sole remaining through freight runs to Richmond on the former Seaboard Air Line's Norlina Subdivision were trains No. 289/214 between the capitol cities of the Old North State and the Old Dominion. All other traffic was now run through Hamlet to Pembroke, North Carolina, and from there over the former ACL. While home terminated in Raleigh for the convenience of the few remaining SAL employees, it was protected off of the Richmond extra board, requiring a deadhead down on No. 85, the *Champion* (just prior to its discontinuance), and a deadhead back to Richmond on No. 82, the *Silver Star*, if we reached Raleigh in time to yard No. 289 and hop aboard the northbound Florida streamliner.

On one trip, after having worked every siding from Hermitage to Henderson, Jimmy and I jumped off No. 289's engines at the Johnson Street roundhouse and were preparing to hop aboard the *Star's* rear car, when the conductor, an old SAL Raleigh man, embittered by the trend that threatened outright abandonment of his hometown by the railroad, stopped us and asked for our tickets.

"Come on. You know us. We've just got off 289 and have to deadhead to Richmond," Jimmy complained. "If we go get a ticket, we'll miss the train."

"I guess you'll just miss it then," the old man laughed as he gave the engineer the highball.

Riding the bus to Richmond, we discussed ways of getting even. Little did either of us realize that our chance was just up the road a piece, for it was only days later that this old man would take an assignment on the *Palmetto*, requiring him to deadhead on No. 82 to Richmond. Everyone on the railroad has a nickname derived from his initials. The old man's was N. B., "No Brains," and on his first deadhead trip to Richmond, for which he showed up at the last minute and for which he had not acquired a ticket, the conductor on the *Silver Star* was none other than—you guessed it again—Jimmy Boone. With no ticket, No Brains had no choice but to drive to Richmond. Revenge does have its rewards.

One face I knew I would not see at this year's picnic was that of the engineer I most often found myself firing for—much to both of our dismays. A heart attack had taken him quickly and silently two months earlier. It wasn't just me. Harwood (not his real name) hated firemen—all firemen.

"Fireboy," he railed as I threw my grip under my seat on the C&O U23B that we would both occupy from Richmond's Fulton Yard to Portsmouth, Virginia, and on the return trip the next day. "Do you like to run trains?"

"Sure," I responded. "I need the experience."

"Then you better mark up with someone else, because you're never going to touch the throttle on any engine on my train," he laughed.

"That's fine with me," I retorted. "If you want to sit there and work yourself to death for 12 hours while they cut your salary and pay me handsomely to watch you, that's your business." The brakeman's brief laugh was promptly stifled by the leer from the red-faced hoghead.

Entering the lobby of the Rocky Mount YMCA some months following that episode, after my first trip as a passenger engineer on the southbound *Silver Meteor*, I spied our most senior engineer, John Cutchin, who was about to take the *Meteor* north to Richmond at 2 a.m. Also in the lobby, about to be transported to the yard for a 12-hour battle with an underpowered, 200-car through freight, was my least favorite engineer, Harwood.

"What did you come in on?" asked Cutchin.

"No. 87," I boasted. "Rob Yancy took off a trip."

"They should call the senior freight engineer," Harwood angrily denounced me. "Here I am with 30 years service getting a call in the middle of the night to work No. 120, and they call you—just out of school—to run a passenger train. I was earning my seniority with a hickory handle when you were in diapers."

Before I could answer him, John Cutchin, who had nearly 50 years of road service seniority, most of it firing Seaboard's workhorse, seven-days-a-week road switchers in steam, spoke up.

"What? Did they have hickory handle brooms on those diesel yard engines you fired, Harwood?" he roared. "When did you ever fire a steam locomotive?"

An embarrassed Harwood momentarily groped for an answer, finally blurting out that he had once been cut off Seaboard and hostled some of C&O's few remaining steam engines in the early 1950s.

"Well, I've spent most of my life living in some cheap rooming house, working jobs at outlying points 16 hours a day, away from my family for weeks at a time, while you sat with your feet propped up on the seat of a diesel yard engine before going home to eat homecooked meals and sleep in your own bed every night," Cutchin ranted. "When the merger came, they gave you road rights—something you never earned or worked for. And you have the nerve to jump on this boy because he worked what they called him for?" Harwood quickly walked outside and sat on one of the cement benches where weary railroaders passed much of their life away awaiting the call to go home again.

Just before I left CSX for Amtrak in 1986, I was cut back to firing, and as fate would have it—you guessed it—I was paired up with Harwood; but this time, there was something different about him. No, he wasn't glad to see me, though I noted far less hostility as we signed the register sheet. Off to the side, our conductor, Sparky Schaff, confided to me that Harwood's wife was terminally ill.

"He'd like to quit to stay home with her. He's hoping the railroad will offer a buy-out of senior employees so he can retire and still retain his hospitalization. Otherwise, he just can't," sighed the usually jovial conductor. "I'm glad we've got you back on the job. He cries a lot, and his mind is not on the job. I know he's never treated you right, and you're not the best of friends, but try really hard to help him."

Sparky was right. It wasn't easy to be kind to someone who breathed hatred. His current circumstances led to confrontation with everyone. At one point, I even found myself pulling a brakeman off to the side and aggressively suggesting that he get off Harwood's case.

However, climbing on the engine at Portsmouth at 3 a.m., barely able to lift his swollen, bloodshot eyes off the floor, he looked at me and said, "Fireboy, do you think you can handle this train?"

"Sure, Harwood," I said. "Thanks."

The trip was an easy one. The old engineer sat with his eyes glued to the passing farmlands. He said nothing until we were getting off the engines at Fulton.

"You run a good train, fireboy," he whispered softly, clearing this throat. "You go on. I'll get the handbrake."

Entering the old brick yard office, Sparky asked, "Who ran the train today?"

"The fireman," Harwood answered. "Why? What was wrong?"

"Nothing. Smoothest trip we've had in months. Just kidd'n," the conductor laughed. "Seriously, you ought to let him run more often."

"Look who's been teaching me," I injected, trying to salvage the situation and keep the old man from bursting his pop valve.

I never ran for Harwood again. As I headed down the splintery wooden steps to the parking lot below, I watched as the old man's Pontiac Catalina headed down the gravel road toward town. He didn't look up. His thoughts were elsewhere. He marked off the next trip, and within days a buyout was offered. A few months later, his wife passed away. I left for Amtrak and, other than at the annual picnics, managed to run into him only once at a Sears store. I introduced him to my son Ryan and explained to him how much I learned firing for Mr. Harwood.

Years later, I slipped up behind him at the retiree's gathering and tapped him on the shoulder. Turning, he smiled, stuck out his hand, and shook mine until he recognized me. Then, the warm smile turned to an icy scowl, the handshake was quickly broken, and Harwood retreated to another group of coworkers to commiserate.

As I said, railroaders are thrown together by seniority, circumstances, and luck. Sometimes for the good, sometimes for the bad, and sometimes just for barbecue, sweetened iced tea, and memories.

Section 2

Switch'n Tracks

Chapter 9: Have You Considered Engine Service?

Doug Riddell, the conductor of a train? No. It just doesn't sound right, does it? Certainly not for a man whose monthly column in RailNews magazine (originally in Passenger Train Journal) is called "From the Cab." For many years, I have been identified as an Amtrak locomotive engineer—not a conductor.

Admittedly, when I began to work for the railroad, I had no intention of ever becoming an engineer. I dismissed the idea entirely, repeatedly resisted it, and actually passed up several earlier opportunities to go into engine service. Who said that all little boys growing up in post–World War II America wanted to be railroad engineers? I wanted to be a railroad conductor.

Why? Maybe it was the idea of donning that blue uniform or walking down the aisle of a coach in a hat bearing a brass conductor's badge. Possibly it was the thought of climbing aboard the rear sleeper of the Silver Meteor, closing the bottom half of the Dutch door, leaning out over the top half to scan a busy passenger station platform at night through the cloud of escaping steam heat vapor, tugging twice on the communicating cord, and speaking into a portable radio, "Okay No. 83, let's highball."

It probably had more to do with the perspective of railroading I gained as the grandson of conductor J. E. Beazley. As we all tend to do, I remember much more of the good times—the early years my grandfather spent in passenger service as the "captain" of the Tidewater Virginia section of the George Washington, Sportsman, and FFV—than his final years.

Thinking back to those good times, I can almost smell the baking pan of piping hot biscuits escaping the oven at my grandparent's northside Richmond home as the rays of the early morning sun battled the thick branches of gigantic oaks that edged the curbing along Edgewood Avenue. I never met a railroad wife of that generation who couldn't cook excellent made-from-scratch biscuits. While most fast-food restaurants offer biscuits topped with sausage, ham, and cheese, true southerners know how the Good Lord intended biscuits to be eaten. They were created for the express purpose of sopping up dark Brer Rabbit sorghum molasses, or being covered with fresh honey—the kind that came packed in a Ball Mason jar with a handwritten label on the outside and a big comb of bee's wax on the inside. Grandpa used to purchase ours at his barber's shop on Fairmount Avenue, fresh from the country, kept chilled in a refrigerator in the back room along with dozens of eggs, hand-churned butter, and pounds of smokehouse bacon.

I remember standing at the bottom of the staircase as my grandfather came down, white shirt starched, shoes shined, and buttons glowing. Kept in a porcelain container on his dresser were his uniform buttons and hat badges. Depending on whether he was the conductor or the flagman that particular trip, the dark navy blue suit would either be trimmed in gold or silver, respectively. A gold name tag with blue lettering identified him as J. E. Beasley. (The name was actually spelled with a "z" instead of an "s," but his railroad records and retirement information were filed under the "s" spelling because some clerk thought it should be that way. In the end, it was a moot point, because he died the day his first Railroad Retirement check arrived. He never got to cash it, and the family had to return it.)

From his vest pocket he would pull his gold Hamilton Railway Special, shake his head, and call out, "Eva, it's 7:15. I've got to go away from here."

I always sensed a great deal of pride in my grandfather when he was about to make a passenger run, especially as the conductor. Being in charge of a trainload of people is a tremendous responsibility, and he worried about it—not that he could not do the job properly, but about little things like counting tickets and filling out delay reports. As was expected of the son of a Carolina County, Virginia, farmer, Everett Beazley spent more time in the fields learning to plant and harvest tobacco than he spent in the classroom learning to read and write—something that haunted him all of his adult life. No one values a good education more than the person who has never had one, and few take it for granted more than those upon whom it is freely bestowed. Grandpa never went beyond the second grade and hardly developed his penmanship beyond that level. When he received the booklet to fill out in order to become a conductor, he was so self-conscious of his handwriting that he dictated the answers to my grandmother.

"Am I going with you, grandpa?" I'd always ask as he left for the station.

More often that not, the answer was "no," simply because someone had to look after me while he was conducting the train. Still, I probably made more trips on a passenger train than most little boys my age. When grandma could come along to keep an eye on me, and later when I was old enough to be entrusted to the care of porter Luther Goode, I made the trip over the Peninsula Subdivision of the Chesapeake & Ohio, frequently.

I studied every move my grandfather made. Standing on the rear platform with him, I learned that two tugs on the whistle cord when the train was standing meant the engineer would be opening up on the throttle of the big blue, gray, and yellow E8s. Likewise, I knew that two tugs on the same cord when the train was moving was a signal to stop the train. This proved useful one afternoon at Williamsburg, Virginia, when my grandfather got down off the rear car of No. 41, the westbound George Washington, to speak with Blackie Moore, the baggage man on No. 46, the eastbound Sportsman, on parallel tracks (when the road was still double track) at about 3:50 p.m.

The steam escaping from the connecting pipe on the rear car made just enough gurgling and hissing noises to mask the sound of our lightweight Pullman Standard consist beginning to move. Since whistles were (and to this day are) banned inside the corporate limits of the colonial capital (presumably to keep from spooking horses which pull carts and carriages up and down Duke of Gloucester Street, laden with tourists), my grandfather did not know his train was picking up speed, heading west toward Richmond, until my grandmother screamed out his name. It became readily apparent that the train would arrive at Richmond's Main Street Station minus one flagman unless it could be stopped. The ultimate consequence would be the loss of grandpa's job.

"Pick me up, grandma!" I cried. "Quick! Pick me up. I can't reach the cord." I must have been all of four or five years old at the time. Without hesitating, she was able to hoist me above her shoulders, where I grabbed the communicating cord, pulled it twice, and felt great relief as engineer Tom Rowe brought the seven-car train to a stop. Scrambling aboard, my grandfather picked me up, hugged me, and allowed me to give the cord another two tugs so the George Washington could proceed west again.

When I finally got my chance to work for the railroad, I had one thing in mind: someday to reach into the vest pocket of my own passenger conductor's uniform, pull out that same gold Hamilton Railway Special and look out over my own train as a passenger conductor. I had been in the cab of an E8 at speed and had sat in the lap of the engineer on the small, uncomfortable, fold-up seat of a Budd RDC (Chessieliner, thank you), but it was smelly, dirty, and loud. I'd much rather pace the gracefully curved aisles of the coaches of C&O's post-World War II passenger fleet than be on an engine.

In 1972, the railroad unions in conference with national railroad management agreed to what was called the Manning/Training Agreement, which gave preference to brakemen and conductors who wished to go into engine service. It also set up a framework for classroom and on-the-job training as a fireman and later as an engineer. Vacancies for the craft of fireman had to be advertised, and as retirement began to thin the ranks of engine service personnel hired following the war in Europe or the Pacific, blocks of five, 10, or as many as 15 firemen were hired. I noticed the advertisements but felt that they were for someone else.

One of the most knowledgeable and respected men ever to work in railroad management anywhere was Kenneth Kermit Kitts. Fresh out of the Navy after World War II, he was accepted into management training with former Atlantic Coast Line, at that time headquartered in Wilmington, North Carolina. For Ken Kitts and his wife Nancy, home was wherever ACL, later Seaboard Coast Line, and finally CSX told them it was to be: Jacksonville, Rocky Mount, Waycross. They are the only people I know who kept a set of blueprints and built the same house in three different cities. Fortunately for me, following the merger with rival Seaboard Air Line in the early to mid-1970s, the Kitts' home was in Richmond. To this day, they, now living in retirement near Charlotte, North Carolina, remain good family friends.

It was through Ken Kitts' urging and at his invitation that I finally got the break for which I had waited 27 years—a job interview with SCL that led to my employment as a switchman. His keen awareness and judicial employment of trends in the railroad industry caused his stock to rise in value with the folks at SCL. He retired as an assistant to the chief transportation officer at CSX's Jacksonville headquarters (only to be hired as an operating practices inspector for the Federal Railway Administration, retir-

98

ing from his second career in 1996).

Kitts is living proof that nice guys don't always finish last. I can't ever remember hearing a syllable of profanity coming from his mouth, nor seldom recall his temper getting the best of him. He was the consummate gentleman in a profession where such considerations are often totally absent in the savage stampede to reach the top. No matter what you had done, if you told Mr. Kitts the truth, he would go to bat for you—and he didn't bunt. He swung away.

Early one fall morning, I arrived at the Rocky Mount roundhouse to find a big, 20-cylinder SD45 laying on its side on the switching lead of the hostling yard in near proximity to a lowly GP7. It was readily apparent that sometime during the night, one of the hostlers had left the Geep fouling the lead, and it had been sideswiped by the big "Clydesdale" (as we used to refer to the popular six-axle locomotives), leaving it bleeding fuel oil like a wounded elephant. As I drew closer, I saw Road Foreman of Engines John Smith huddled with the shaken hostler, his helper, and Ken Kitts.

"Son," Kitts addressed the hostler, "Jacksonville doesn't get as upset with a torn-up boxcar or gondola as they do when one of these big, black-and-yellow engines is banged up, but I'll do what I can for you. All I ask is that you tell me the truth. What happened?"

You didn't lie to Ken Kitts. Not because you feared him, but because he gave you every reason in the world to trust him. When he said something, you could take it to the bank.

"Well, Mr. Kitts," the guilty hostler admitted, "not to try to make excuses for myself, but I've been out here all night, and when the sun starts coming up, I find it hard not to nod off—especially when it's cool and the engine heater's going. I didn't see my helper signing me down. I guess I went to sleep while we were making the move. That's all I can say, other than I'm sorry and I'm thankful that no one got hurt."

"You've always been a good employee," Kitts told him with obvious effort to console the young man. "I'm sure that's exactly what happened. I'll do what I can for you. I can't promise you anything, but I'll do my best." Needless to say, he did.

When I tell this story to my present-day Amtrak coworkers, I usually ask them what kind of discipline their former employing freight railroad would have handed out. Most guess that the hostler was dismissed, while others insist he served six months in the street, or at least 90 days. They all shake their heads in disbelief when I tell them that in this case, the hostler was only out of work for 10 days.

Once during a downturn in business that resulted in a series of furloughs, hardly a day passed when a cut off brakeman didn't ride the head end of the passenger trains I was firing between Richmond and Rocky Mount. In this way, they could qualify to mark up and work far away from home, rather than rely on a small unemployment check. Seaboard Coast Line had few women in train service, and all were laid off at this particular time. One day, just as my engineer and I prepared to walk out to the platform to run the Palmetto, Amtrak No. 90, a freckled-faced, red-haired Tar Heel farm girl walked into the crew room at Rocky Mount. She had been on the rails for less than a year. With a grip in her hands, she asked if she could ride the engine with us.

"Do you have something to ride on?" asked my retirement-aged hogger.

"Yeh," she responded. "Would you like to see it?"

"Well, that's not necessary right now," he answered. "I know who you are, but when you get up on the cab of a passenger train, it all has to be official." (The usual practice was for an employee to obtain a headend permit from his or her trainmaster or road foreman, which would be filled in and signed by the engineer after the trip was completed, to attest to the fact that the trip had been made.)

As we prepared to leave Rocky Mount, our new road foreman (a fellow with whom I had been hostling only three months before) walked out of the station toward the train. He spoke with the conductor, then boarded the coaches, and we received the highball to leave town.

"I thought you were going to have to get off the engine and either go back in the coaches or ride another time," I told the young woman. "The road foreman would have been the third person in the cab had he come up here, and only three are allowed. You'd have been the odd man out," I laughed, realizing what I had just said.

"Our old conductor won't honor those headend passes most of the time," my engineer added, blowing for the crossing at Grand Avenue. "You'd have been out of luck, I'm afraid."

"He wouldn't have honored my ticket?" she asked.

"Why would you have a ticket?" I countered. "You're up here to learn the road, aren't you?"

"No," she said. "I'm cut off. I'm just going to visit my brother in Baltimore."

The old engineer and I looked at each other in total astonishment. We took for granted that "something to ride on," to which we referred in the crew room, was a headend pass. We had an unauthorized person on the engine. We were dead meat. We'd be fired for sure. We knew it. Both of us: him with 40 years of service behind him and me with 40 years ahead of me. Our next stop was Petersburg, 100 miles and over one hour away. Once there, after having her duck each time we passed a train, I led her down the side of the engine away from the platform, sent her back to the coaches, and prayed that no one was the wiser.

The following day, I caught the job as engineer, and I was met by the road foreman as I got down from the cab in Rocky Mount.

"Did that woman get off the engine at Petersburg, or did you let her ride all the way to Richmond?" he asked me.

"Look," I attempted to explain, "We didn't know she ..."

"That kind of stuff will cost you your job," he interrupted. "Don't let it happen again." That made two officials I have grown to respect. He could have had my job. (Today, he's a top official with CSX in Jacksonville, a well-deserved post.)

About three weeks later, Ken Kitts and John Smith scurried around the corner of the old brick passenger station at Rocky Mount and met me in the crew room. Both looked as if something awful had just occurred.

Kitts, without asking about the family, looked me sternly in the eyes. "Tell me that you didn't have a woman up on the engine of No. 90, please."

"Well, Mr. Kitts," I swallowed hard and said, "I could, but I'd be lying, and I'm not going to lie to you or anyone. You know me better than that."

"What's your explanation?" asked John Smith, the road foreman who put me on the engine my first day as a fireman.

I then proceeded to spell out the details of the event in question.

"That's exactly what her statement said," Kitts nodded. "I'll go to Mr. Strange [the superintendent] and see what I can do for you, but in the future, ask to see a person's headend pass first. Don't assume anything."

As it turned out, the Rocky Mount-based engineer we had relieved that day (an official in the union, no less) had turned us in. Unfortunately, to some people, brotherhood is a totally meaningless term.

True to Ken Kitts' word, I never heard anything else about the incident.

After hired by SCL, I often ran into Mr. Kitts. While our conversations usually began with inquiries about mom and dad, or my Aunt Chris and Uncle Cliff, the subject usually gravitated toward railfanning or photography.

During a layover in Rocky Mount in 1979, where Kitts was then assistant superintendent, on his way to his daily afternoon workout, Kitts spotted me on the steps of the YMCA dorm, where our crews were then lodged. Even though he asked about the family, I could tell there was something else he wanted to address. Out of the blue, he asked if I had ever considered entering engine service.

"Not really," I answered. "I'm waiting to be promoted to conductor. They're using men junior to me in emergency. Although I'll retain my place on the seniority roster as long as I accept promotion the first time it's offered to me, I'm missing a lot of work because I've been passed over."

"Doug," he said with a Tennessee accent, "someday they're going to be running trains with no cabooses. There'll be only an engineer, a brakeman, and a conductor. You may see it, though I'll probably be long gone, but trains are going to be run with only two people in the cab of a locomotive—and you can bet that one of them is going to be an engineer. If you're going to make a career out of the railroad, you ought to consider taking a firing job. Take up the craft of engineer. With all due respect to our conductors and brakemen, over time most people can learn to swing a lantern or sort waybills; not everyone can run a train. They're going to be hiring a block of firemen in Raleigh and in Rocky Mount."

"What about Richmond?" I asked. "I'm engaged to be married, and my future wife has her own career teaching school in Henrico County [just outside of Richmond]."

"We don't need men there right now as badly as in North Carolina," he noted, "but once you establish yourself after 18 months, you can go wherever your seniority will permit."

"I'll give it some thought," I assured him, still not totally convinced that this was what I really wanted to do.

For the next few weeks, I thought about Kitts' words. But I wanted to take promotion first, even if I went into engine service later. Seaboard Coast Line had a policy of promoting brakemen with two years of service to the rank of conductor in the month of January each year, I learned from Richmond Trainmaster J. W. Benz.

"No exceptions," he stated, when I asked him repeatedly about becoming a conductor during a visit to the old SAL freight building, where SCL's Richmond Terminal offices were then located.

"But I'll have almost three years service next January, and there are people out there junior to me who are being used as conductors in Rocky Mount and Hamlet," I reasoned.

"Can't do it," he said, leaning back in his chair, across the office he shared with Road Foreman Bob McDougald.

"That's your final word?" I asked.

"That's final," he responded.

Reaching into my coat pocket, I pulled out a letter I had typed in anticipation of this situation and handed it to McDougald. "Here, put me in engine service!"

"You can't do that!" yelled Benz. "We need you."

"That's not what you've been telling me for the last 15 minutes," I reminded him.

"I've got all kinds of brakemen who have passed up promotion time and time again. They'll never be promoted to conductor," he said with his voice softening. "You'll go ahead of all of them in seniority if you wait until next year when promotion is offered to you."

"That's not good enough," I shrugged. "I'm not ready to be a conductor, but I could have been in engine service, running trains months ago? That doesn't make a lot of sense. No, I'll go into engine service."

Within a week, I received a letter from Bob McDougald, acknowledging my application for engine service and informing me that I would be notified of the first available opening. Not one to hold a grudge, Jim Benz never walked past me again without shaking his head, laughing, and reminding me that if I had only waited, I could have been a conductor. So I never took promotion to conductor.

The call I had been waiting for came soon thereafter. A lot of the old heads not only calculated their Railroad Retirement checks to the penny, but optimized their final paychecks by working just enough time to earn their vacations for the following year, for which they gladly accepted cash payment. The 120 days credit necessary to do this meant that they "pulled the pin" at the end of April or May. So Bob McDougald, whose dad coincidentally retired as an engineer the day I entered engine service, rang the phone at my new apartment, two blocks from the Richmond Amtrak Station, on the morning of April 27, 1979.

"You ready to be a fireman?" he asked. "They've opened up two blocks: five men in Raleigh and 10 in Rocky Mount."

"I'll take Raleigh," I said without a moment's hesitation. I had lived there once and loved it, and I had spent the past two years laying over in Rocky Mount and hated it.

"I don't know if you'll have the seniority to hold Raleigh," he answered. "Remember, you have to bid your brakeman's seniority, and there are a lot of older men in Raleigh than you."

"Look, Bob," I pleaded. "[Raleigh Road Foreman] Carl Wicker knows me,

[Superintendent] Joe Winfrey knows me, [Trainmaster and former Chief Dispatcher] Chester Gillespie knows me—everyone in Raleigh knows me! How about making a call to see if I can hold a job there?"

"If not, would you consider Rocky Mount?" Bob asked. "After 18 months, once you establish your seniority, you can go to Raleigh if you can hold a job there."

"I don't know, Bob," I said. "My fiancée can probably get a job teaching in Raleigh or go to one of the colleges there. There's good shopping, good housing, and I think we'd be happier there. The only thing going on in Rocky Mount is when Jesse Helms shows up once a year when all the farmers bring their tobacco to market."

"I'll call Carl and see how you'd stand in Raleigh, but they're going to hire more people in the weeks and months ahead. Passing up this chance could mean losing a lot of seniority, and that could hurt you badly down the road," McDougald warned.

"When would I have to go?" I asked.

"This afternoon," Bob answered.

"This afternoon?" I exclaimed. "Sandy's at school. We're getting married June 14. What am I supposed to do? Just show up and say, 'Guess what? We're moving to Raleigh or Rocky Mount this afternoon.'"

As it turned out, that's basically what happened.

McDougald's call to Carl Wicker in Raleigh turned out to be a dead end. Carl's territory was from Raleigh to Richmond and from Raleigh to Portsmouth. As luck would have it, he was on his way to Franklin, Virginia, on the Portsmouth Subdivision, and could not be reached. That one unanswered phone call had an immense effect on my life. With no assurance that I would be awarded a job in Raleigh, I had to make a decision to go to Rocky Mount or to stay in train service.

"What's it going to be, Doug?" Bob asked. "John Smith will wait for you in Rocky Mount until 4 p.m., then it's someone else's job."

"I guess it's Rocky Mount," I moaned.

I packed my bags with what I figured would suffice for a couple of days, stopped by the bank, and then drove to Varina Elementary School, where my fiancée taught a fourth grade class. I called first, to make sure I could have a few minutes with her—alone. Although we had talked about the possibility of my entering engine service, we believed it would be in Richmond. Standing outside her room in the ancient school-house, in a hallway in which the terrazzo floors, high ceilings, and transoms over each door allowed no spoken words to remain secret, I broke the news to her.

"I'm going to Rocky Mount," I said.

"On what train?" she asked. "When is it going to put you back? I need your help addressing the wedding invitations. We need to cut down the list a bit."

"I'm going into engine service," I shyly confessed. "I've got to stay for 18 months, then I can come back to Richmond."

The dam broke. With a shrill cry of helplessness, she fell against me and began sobbing. Doors opened down the hall, heads popped out, and puzzled faces stared at the two of us.

"Does this mean the wedding is off, or what?" she managed to ask.

"No," I said. "I was planning on us moving there after the wedding."

The tears flowed harder and the sobbing became louder. "Rocky Mount?" she asked. "You've told me so much about laying over there, and it's all been terrible. Now you want me to pack up, give up my career, and follow you to a place you've described as a place you hate."

Trying to make the best of a bad situation, I suggested that I might have been too harsh in my descriptions of the small railroad town, because when I was there, I was lonely. I didn't really consider myself to be lying, just using positive thought to convince her (as well as myself) that there was some redeeming quality of the eastern North Carolina crossroads.

"They have some nice neighborhoods and good schools, and the cost of living is cheap," I suggested. "Besides, the pay is considerably more, and they don't lay off engineers. Most importantly, look how much safer I'll be in the cab of a locomotive than riding the side of some boxcar.

"Sandra, it's not going to be easy, but it's going to pay off for us in the long run. Nothing that's worth anything comes easily," I preached. "We'll be better off the rest of our lives for doing this now. You'll see."

With that said, she agreed not to terminate our engagement and placed her trust in my judgment. "We'll have to wait for the right time to tell my folks," she said, clearing her throat. "I don't know how they'll react."

I knew.

Although almost 20 years have now passed, and even though Sandy's parents came to accept me as their daughter's husband, when we first started dating, I was clearly not their first choice for a son-in-law. No one would have been, least of all me. I worked for the railroad, which meant unpredictable hours and days off. When we announced our engagement, they responded by saying they didn't believe it would last six months.

"I've got to be in Rocky Mount by 4 p.m.," I said softly. "I've got to go. Wish me luck." Saying nothing further, we embraced. As I held her, I looked up and saw dozens of pairs of eyes staring at us. Knowing that they had been spotted, they darted back inside their classrooms, closing the doors in unison, like some jack-in-the-box in reverse.

As the Rocky Mount exit from I-95 appeared in the distance, I cursed Carl Wicker for not being in his office, I cursed the railroad for not having a fireman's vacancy in Richmond for me, and I cursed Rocky Mount for not being Raleigh. Realizing this attitude would only make my 18 months in Rocky Mount worse, I resolved to accept what I could not change and make the best of it.

"Besides," I reasoned to myself as I drove past the deteriorating blocks upon blocks of tobacco warehouses, "this town is not just buildings, but people—good people." I could do a lot worse than Rocky Mount.

Crossing the mainline tracks at Bassett Street, I was introduced to a part of town into which I had not previously ventured. The area which surrounds the shops and yards in Rocky Mount, as in most company towns, is a proliferation of small cottages thrown up quickly and inexpensively, or larger, older homes partitioned hastily into $20-per-week boarding rooms using sheet rock and impromptu doorways. Therein were housed laborers and their families, conveniently within walking distance of the railroad. As the large shops closed, employment dwindled to mere hundreds where thousands had once toiled. The area decayed. The streets were strewn with old cars, old bottles, and old men too feeble to work or young men too high to care. I hoped that Sandy would not have to see this part of town.

Road Foreman John Smith met me as I opened my car door, welcomed me to Rocky Mount, and introduced me to Larry Hull, who had given up 12 years as a conductor at Collier Yard to enter engine service this same day. I had worked with Larry on occasion but didn't know him very well.

After boarding an old idling former ACL GP7 in the hostling yard, Smith showed us the automatic brake, the engine brake, the throttle, and various other features on the locomotive.

"You'll most likely end up hostling for a few months until a school is set up for you to attend to become engineers," he informed us. "If you stand for it, you might mark up on the fireman's extra board, where you'll be called to protect firemen's jobs on passenger trains as well as hostling jobs here. I'm going to mark you up right now as firemen in the Rocky Mount to Florence through freight pool. You'll be bumped as soon as you get back in, but it'll give you a chance to see the road and make a few bucks. Since Mr. Riddell has been to Florence as a brakeman in freight and passenger service, I'll put him with Mr. Gardner, who is due out on the Piggyback Special, No. 175. Since Mr. Hull has never been south of Rocky Mount, I'll put him with Mr. Lee, due out on No. 111. It makes some local stops and will give him a chance to familiarize himself with what's out there."

With that, we were introduced to the crew clerks at CO (the initials for the telegraph operator's office at South Rocky Mount Yard), marked up, and called for our trains. Unfortunately, things didn't go as planned. Number 175 was running late, so we swapped trains. I ended up on No. 111 with Harvard Gardner; Hull fired his first trip on No. 175.

Number 111 was the junk train. Every division on every railroad has one. If there was something dirty or boring to do, a wide load that had to be nursed down the road at 10 mph while everything else passed it at 60 or 70 mph, 111 was the candidate of choice. That night, it had two GP7s to ferry to Florence for 90-day inspections. Seaboard Coast Line 750 would be in the lead, and owing to its lack of alignment control couplers, SCL 761 would be third out. Second, fourth, and fifth slots were filled by ancient GE U25Cs in the 2100 series. With an engine consist like that, the trip was sure to be a long, drawn-out affair, if not a total disaster.

Harvard Gardner was a former road foreman and arguably one of the best engineers ever to run a train. With his pinstriped railroad hat and gold pocket watch, Harv looked every bit the classic railroad engineer of every young boy's dreams. Lard Bryant, an east end (Portsmouth) ACL trainman, was our head brakeman that night.

We left Rocky Mount at about 6 p.m., and after picking up and setting off at Fayetteville's Milan Yard, we settled down for the remainder of the run to Florence. The 750 ran hot a couple of times after we had closed the radiator shutters to cut the chill that prevailed in the cab, despite the use of tape and newspapers to seal the cracks around the cab's front door. Harv showed me how to manually cut on the number one cooling fan and open the shutters to alleviate the problem, thus silencing the clanging alarm bell.

At Dillon, the bell rang again. It was not the 750, but apparently the 761 which was running hot.

"We've got to slow down to 50 mph going through Latta," Harv noted. "Just go back to the other Geep and do the same thing: Open the shutters and cut the fan on. Be careful; don't fall off."

That turned out to be the least of my problems. What saved me from being killed in the ensuing accident was that I stopped for a moment to see if the second engine, 2111, was loading, as indicated by its control stand ammeter. When I crossed over from the rear of the 2111 to the rear of the 761 and started by the cooling water tank, just shy of the engine block itself, the old GP7 exploded.

Blinded by the eruption of the crankcase, I thought I was in heaven. It was only the pain I experienced as I was thrown against the handrail (which kept me from being thrown overboard and killed) that made me realize, "I'm still alive! For how long I don't know, but I'm still alive!" I felt something wet and burning on my face. I was sure it was my flesh burning. Screaming, I fell to the running board and passed out.

"The fireman's dead! The fireman's got to be dead!" Harvard Gardner yelled at Lard Bryant above the din of the bells that now sang their deafening alarm as the burning locomotive illuminated the small South Carolina community of Latta. He put out an emergency radio transmission and within seconds had the Rocky Mount train dispatcher on the air.

Suddenly, I opened the rear door of the cab; and on my hands and knees, looking like a badly butchered carcass that had fallen from a meat hook, I let out a blood-curdling scream that could have been heard in Florence, 40 miles away.

Sitting on the floor of the engine, the bells still ringing madly, I realized that Lard was holding my head up, my arms draped over his knees as he sat in his seat. He attempted conversation with me to keep me conscious.

"Where did you find me?" I asked deliriously.

"Find you?" he responded. "You crawled in here, don't you remember?"

I ventured into and out of consciousness until I saw people in white. These were surely the angels, but they had no wings or halos. There were red lights flashing, and soon I was in an ambulance, and then a hospital operating room—but where?

"Dillon, South Carolina," the doctor told me. "You know, the last guy this happened to died. You're lucky you didn't bleed to death. You've got a few broken bones, a concussion, and we're going to have to watch you for a while, but I think you're going to live. You married?"

"Married?" I writhed in pain as I remembered Sandy. "I'm supposed to be getting married, but I don't know if she'll have me like this. What does my face look like?"

"Would you like to call her?" he asked.

"Would you please dial the number for me?" I responded.

The railroad claim agent (who had been out at a dance and showed up in a tux with his wife in an evening grown) had already called Ken Kitts at home. Kitts had called my folks to assure them that my injuries were not life threatening. When the phone rang at Sandy's parents' home, she answered and reacted in shock to the news.

"Who is that calling here at this time of night?" her mother asked.

"It's Doug," Sandy whispered, cupping the mouthpiece.

"The nerve of him calling here at 11:30 at night!" her mother responded.

"There's been an accident, and he's been hurt badly," she told her.

"Oh," was her mom's only response.

"I want you and mom to come down on the train as soon as you can get here," I begged. "I guess it's too late tonight, but please come tomorrow."

She promised she would, told me that the wedding was still on and that she loved me, then hung up.

Within a few hours I was taken to "the best medical facility available," the McCleod Infirmary in Florence. It was not today's ultra-modern regional medical center, but an old, run down, brick building with central, unisex bathrooms at the end of the hallway and an old PBX switchboard that had probably handled calls from Teddy Roosevelt—when he was with the Rough Riders.

"This man is a Seaboard Coast Line Railroad employee," the claim agent loudly announced. "See to it that he gets the very best private room available."

Apparently, the best private room available was the one nearest the restroom, because that's where I was taken.

"I understand you were in a locomotive explosion, is that right?" the nurse said as she thrust a thermometer into my mouth and told me not to speak. "You're lucky. The last time this happened, the poor man died before I could take his temperature."

With daybreak, the sun poured through the stained and dusty Venetian blinds in my room's east side window. A knock came at the door.

"They said to bring you a TV," the service man said. "You the guy who got blown up on the train last night?"

"Yes," I managed to answer, figuring that the story must have made the local news.

"Boy are you lucky," he smiled. "I don't know whether anyone has told you this or not, but the last guy that happened to died before I could get the TV into his room. I don't think they even paid me for it. You know, they should have. They ordered it. Wasn't my fault he died."

By supper time, the Palmetto arrived in Florence, and with it my fiancée and my mother. From the station, a member of the crew gave them a ride to the adjacent Holiday Inn in an old car that died in the hotel parking lot. Suitcases in hand, Sandy and mom climbed the stairs to my hospital room.

"What can we do for you?" Sandy asked.

"Get me back to Richmond," I shot back.

"That sounds good to me," she said as she reached over and kissed me. "Now, tell me all about how being in engine service is going to be better for us, and so much safer for you."

We all laughed.

Chapter 10: A Twist on the Newlywed Game

I've always been amused by the way those TV quiz show hosts break the ice by asking contestants how they got to know their spouses, or if there was anything unusual about their wedding or honeymoon. A popular daytime game show was even created where recently married couples could win cash and prizes for predicting their spouse's responses to questions often yielding comical tales or unbelievable stories of chance meetings and near-disastrous courtships.

While there was hardly anything out of the ordinary about two high school classmates getting together some 10 years after receiving their diplomas, how Sandy's and my wedding occurred, or almost didn't, rivals even the best stories of the game show's guests.

At this point, I'll explain exactly what a "crankcase explosion" is, since I didn't even know what had caused the blast that very nearly took my life. Exhaust from a diesel locomotive is mechanically forced from the stack of the engine by the turbocharger (on older or non-turbocharged units, by Roots Rotoblowers). If this is not accomplished properly, fumes accumulate in the sump or crankcase of the locomotive, contaminating the pure lubricating oil and causing it to become a highly flammable mixture. When the temperature reaches its flash point, the liquid explodes. To prevent damage to the engine or injury to employees, a pressure sensor, which should indicate whether the turbocharger or the rotoblower is doing its job, is mounted on the side of the engine block. When the stainless steel plunger protrudes out from the device so that a red ring is visible, it is a sign that instead of the normal "vacuum" condition existing inside the crankcase to suck dangerous exhaust out, positive pressure (and very likely, dangerous fumes) is building up. When this "crankcase over pressure" device activates, it automatically shuts down the engine. When the engine shuts down, however, its cooling system ceases to work, and the temperature rises. When the "hot engine" alarm bell began ringing on former ACL GP7 No. 761 that night, it was a warning with consequences I was not aware of as a first-day engine service employee.

As it turned out, I was a mere five feet short of the engine block itself when, at 40 mph, the old GP7 blew. The heavy steel door—one of several that formed the exterior of the engine compartment, all of which were nearly ripped from their hinges—actually protected me from the flaming, lava-like debris that erupted from the bowels of the 16-cylinder motor-turned-explosive device. The force of the blast was of such magnitude that the locomotive's number boards disintegrated and its handrails were

108

bent enough to necessitate their removal with a cutting torch before any other trains could pass on parallel track.

Knowing nothing about a diesel locomotive, my dad's first question was, "What did you do wrong? You must have done something wrong, touched something, messed with a switch or a button of some kind. Locomotives just don't explode." After calling my cousin Jack Stecklein in Philadelphia, a retired Pennsylvania Railroad/Penn Central engineer, dad learned that crankcase explosions, while not everyday occurrences, are not uncommon, and that I indeed had nothing to do with causing it.

In fairness to the City of Florence, today McCleod is one of the finest regional medical centers in the country. However, in 1979, with the new hospital facility under construction, the old pre-World War II building was sorely lacking, both in amenities and basic cleanliness. When my mom returned from a trip to the rest room at the end of the hall (even my private room lacked plumbing), she appeared shaken.

"There were cigarette butts on the floor," she said, "and the wash basin looked like the ones you'd expect to see in a filling station." She wanted the best care possible for her injured son, and this just wasn't cutting it. She got a hand towel and some soap and began cleaning the room.

I was just glad to be alive. Were it not for the skill of engineer Harvard Gardner, I would have bled to death. As I explained to my two guests, Harv spotted a 200-car train on a 20-foot-wide unpaved crossing, which allowed an ambulance driver to reach me quickly and transfer me to the small, new Catholic hospital in Dillon, where the bleeding was stopped and my injuries were termed non-life threatening.

Some 10 years later, I would hit a van on that same crossing at the throttle of the 79 mph northbound Palmetto, sending its driver 250 feet through the air and depositing him in a mud puddle. Though his vehicle was totally destroyed, the driver was able to walk over to U.S. 301 and flag down a car, which took him to that same hospital in Dillon, where a South Carolina Highway Patrolman arrived soon after and charged the barely scratched motorist with public drunkenness. Traveling nearly a mile past the point of impact, the Palmetto's engine stopped in the heart of Latta, right in front of the sheriff's office. When I explained I had hit a car, he asked where the accident had occurred. When I told him the crossing, he shrugged his shoulders, shook his head, and said, "That's not in my jurisdiction." A lot of memories flood my mind every time I pass that spot.

Since both my mother and my fiancée had to be at work Monday, they made arrangements to return to Richmond on Sunday. I made plans to accompany them. When the Palmetto halted at the Amtrak station in Richmond on Sunday, my future mother-in-law was waiting at the gate for the three of us. After satisfying herself that I was indeed going to be okay, she asked, "What were you doing all the way down there in South Carolina?"

"Well," I struggled, "I'm going into engine service at Rocky Mount."

"You mean you're going to have to relocate there?" she asked.

"Well, it's only for 18 months," I assured her. "Then we can come back to Richmond."

"We?" my fiancée's mother questioned. "Are you suggesting that my daughter is going to move to North Carolina?"

"That's what we're planning on doing," I said.

"Well," she announced, "we simply won't send out the invitations. The wedding's off! Come on, Sandra. We're going home!" With that, she grabbed my fiancée's suitcase with one hand, her arm with the other, marched out the door to the parking lot, and drove off. (The nuptials did take place as scheduled. But with only six weeks to recover from my injuries and the effects of some minor plastic surgery on my face, the wedding pictures could have passed for publicity shots for the film THE BRIDE OF FRANKENSTEIN.)

I was back in a Richmond hospital within hours of returning home. The full scope of a concussion's effects are not always readily apparent. In my haste to get back to familiar surroundings, I had assured myself and the doctors in Florence that I was well on the road to recovery. Actually, the road had a few more U-turns and potholes in it than I first realized, and I spent a week in Henrico Doctor's Hospital—in a private room that had its own bathroom and a clean sink.

On June 1, 1979, five weeks later (two weeks shy of our wedding day), I was certified okay to return to work, so Sandy and I traveled to Rocky Mount and found an apartment on the western fringes of town, where we could quickly access Interstate 95 to get back to Richmond in less than two hours. When we moved into our new home after returning from the honeymoon, she applied for employment with the school systems in the area. The week before the fall semester was to begin, she landed a job teaching at Bassett Elementary School, a block from the roundhouse. I could actually blow the horn and wave to her in the classroom when I turned engines on the wye.

Lest you think of North Carolina exclusively as the land of Barney Fife and Gomer Pyle, the educational system is a far cry from the backwoods schoolhouses depicted by The Andy Griffith Show. Years earlier, when I sold radio advertising for a station in the Raleigh-Durham-Chapel Hill area, I proudly informed prospective clients that, largely because of the renowned Research Triangle Park and the campuses of NC State, Duke, and the University of North Carolina, there were more PhDs per capita in the Triangle than anywhere else in the United States. The cost of living in the Raleigh suburb of Cary was listed as one of the country's most expensive.

But this wasn't Raleigh. It was Rocky Mount. And while the people there were some of the most friendly and down to earth anywhere, for us it wasn't Richmond either. By the time Thanksgiving rolled around, we were both miserable. When school let out for Christmas, Sandy quit her job. With a small settlement from the railroad stemming from my injuries, we were able to make a down payment on a house in the Richmond suburb of Mechanicsville. Henrico County's public school system received Sandy back into its classrooms, while I found a $40-per-week room with kitchen and bathroom privileges just two blocks from the Rocky Mount passenger station in which to live for the remaining 10 months before I could exercise my seniority to Richmond. Larry Hull, the fireman with whom I had swapped trains that fatal night, had also found lodging in the rooming house previously mentioned.

Until I could attend school and be promoted to the rank of engineer, I was a fireman, luckily drawing full fireman's pay, a minimum of $63.54 per day, with time-and-a-half for working on scheduled days off or a second tour of duty on the same day. Once school started, I was paid the student rate, $58, and worked five days a week, with no overtime, no mileage, and no meal allowance.

For those who think being a fireman entails sitting in a locomotive cab across from the engineer and drawing a paycheck for doing nothing (as the railroads have tried to suggest ever since diesels first appeared on the property), they're completely mistaken. It's probably the term "fireman" itself—a throwback to the days when men shoveled coal into the firebox of a steam locomotive—that did the most to convince the public that big labor was forcing the railroads to maintain men on the engine, "firemen with no fires to tend." The term lingered on until the United Transportation Union (of which the Brotherhood of Locomotive Firemen & Enginemen was a founding party) officially retired the title.

Had this been done earlier, and the name "assistant engineer" adopted (as has now been done), it would have more realistically reflected the true role of the second person in the cab. In fact, "student engineer" might have been more appropriate, because what we were doing was learning our craft from a skilled hogger, who was passing along a knowledge of train handling and locomotive operating that had been proudly handed down from generation to generation of railroad engineers.

As a locomotive fireman, I was a hostler, a hostler helper, and a passenger train fireman, depending on which assignment I was called to fill. It was the job of a hostler to move engines wherever they were needed within the terminal. We set up engine consists for through freight trains, locals, and yard jobs. Along with a helper to throw switches and guide backing moves, we spotted locomotives for fuel and water, climbed atop of Geeps and U-boats to fill their bunkers with sand for traction, and moved engines into and out of the roundhouse for the shop forces to inspect and repair.

On rare occasions when a passenger fireman marked off, we were called to be the second man in the cab of: the Silver Meteor, No. 83/84; the Palmetto, No. 89/90; or the Auto Train, No. 3/4, between Rocky Mount and Florence. While the Palmetto was powered by P30CHs or F40PHs with electric heating and air conditioning, the Meteor still had SDP40Fs and E9s or E8s in A or B configurations in 1979. The Auto Train (before it ceased to operate as a private entity) had its own steam generator cars, although at the very end it employed a number of dangerously old and worn-out retired Amtrak E9s, with steam generators I once refused to start because the inspection date had lapsed by more than a year.

On July 9, 1979, on the return leg of my very first trip as a passenger fireman on the Meteor while working with engineer Ray Pate, we had F40 No. 301 in the lead, followed by E9Bs 470 and 472. Ray had a case of stomach flu.

"You ever run a passenger train, son?" he said, wearing his black Cromer railroad engineer's hat as we climbed aboard the 301 at Florence.

"No, sir," I answered. (I'd only been back at work two weeks since being injured. I'd hardly moved a light engine in the yard.)

"Well, you're going to run one tonight," he added, heading down into the nose of the diesel, where he stayed until we arrived in Fayetteville. Now there was a man who knew every inch of track, every crossing, every milepost.

"You should be looking at the signal at the south end of Latta," he shouted above the roar of the engines as the 18-car train sped through the night. "Get 15 pounds of brake, bail off the independent, and reduce to number five throttle. When you pass the southbound signal, knock them off, and you should be running 60 mph. When you pass the second road crossing, open up to number eight." It was like that the whole way. My hands may have been on the throttle, but Ray was running the train. You can't learn that from a simulator. You've got to know what you're doing.

It was on passenger trains that the fireman's title still applied. We had to keep the balky Vapor-Clarkson steam generators going, even in the summer, because of the need for hot water in the dining cars and the restrooms of the coaches and sleepers.

I was sent on a qualifying trip on No. 89 to Florence, returning on No. 84 with Tom Edwards. A black man, Tom followed in the footsteps of his father, Tom Edwards Sr., as a "colored" fireman. In a world were the term "colored" is considered offensive, it should be noted that this was an official job designation employed by many railroads that segregated their work forces until the practice was ended in the late 1940s. The difference between "white" firemen and "colored" firemen was an understanding that "colored" firemen were not promotable to engineers. Once steam engines began to disappear, so did the "colored" firemen. Railroads sought to rid the cab of all firemen, especially those they did not wish to promote. Tom was one of the last "colored" firemen on SCL. As fate would have it, I was the man who relieved him when he made his final trip in 1981. I would later write about his life in an article that appeared in the winter 1997 issue of VINTAGE RAILS. But before he could hold a copy of it in his hands, he passed away on the night of December 29, 1996, only hours before I arrived at his home to deliver copies of the magazine and return some personal photos he had loaned to me for publication. I graciously accepted his family's invitation to speak of his love for trains before the crowd of hundreds at his funeral in Rocky Mount on January 2, 1997.

Tom had helped me regain my confidence. I was so afraid of another crankcase explosion that when it was necessary to pass by the engine block of a locomotive, I ran. Unfortunately, a fireman in passenger service in those days spent most of his time nursing a sick engine or steam generator in the black hole of Calcutta, as we used to refer to the dimly lit confines of the engine room of the old E units with their portholes covered over. Even today, I cringe when restarting the motor of a locomotive that has shut down, and I thank heavens for headend power—no more steam generators. Following my injury, a sticker was given to each engineer on the railroad, to be placed in their operating manual. Where it once stated that it was permissible to attempt resetting and restarting an engine whose crankcase protection device had tripped, the sticker cautioned employees to keep a safe distance from the engine and make no attempt to restart it.

Though they rode like Cadillacs, in their last days Amtrak's secondhand E units were cantankerous and dangerous. Were it not for people like Tom Edwards, who kept them running with the use of clothespins, matchbook covers, string, and bailing wire, many trains would have died on the road, many passengers would have caught their death of pneumonia for the lack of steam heat, and far more would have been served cold meals for want of hot water.

While firing for Maddox Marshburn on the northbound Meteor (with SCL President Tom Rice's business car attached at the end), both of the steam generators on SDP40F No. 646 failed. F40PH No. 305 was on the point, but it was not equipped for steam heat. I tried twice to get them started but was successful with only the one on the engineer's side of the unit. As I watched and listened, the pressure built up and kept going. I back blew it and also blew it down, but it was clear that its pressure limiting device was not working, so I shut it down.

"Son," Marshburn told me. "They'll need hot water in the diner soon for breakfast. Give it one more try, but don't get yourself hurt again. If it won't top off, shut it down."

"What about Mr. Rice?" I asked.

"It won't be the first time he's had cold orange juice with his ham and eggs instead of hot coffee," Marshburn chuckled.

Today, railroads recruit engine service candidates off the street, as we refer to non-railroaders, and send them to school before they've held a throttle in their hands and, in some cases, before they've been on the railroad itself, as a brakeman, for more than a few months. By comparison, when our formal classroom education began in spring 1980, I felt fairly comfortable moving engines about Rocky Mount and operating Amtrak passenger trains to Florence under the watchful eyes of veteran engineers. When I entered the classroom of "Choo Choo U," as it was called by some of the old heads, I had almost a year of on-the-job training and hands-on experience behind me at the side of engineers like Geep Johnson, Johnnie Barnes, and Herman Overman, in addition to those previously mentioned. Those names probably mean little or nothing to most people, but to those of us who aspired to be even half as good as those engineers, the names were legendary.

Not to dismiss the importance of modern teaching methodology, but I once sat at the throttle of a simulator programed to provide the conditions that I would encounter while running a 150-car freight train between Richmond and Rocky Mount. The object was to improve the way I handled such a train. At Petersburg, Virginia, according to the simulator, I repeatedly caused a train separation as I approached the north side of the Appomattox River Bridge.

"There's a dip just before you get to the river," the instructor said.

"There's no dip there," I argued. "I run trains over that route every day, and I tell you, there's no dip, and I've never gotten a knuckle or draw head there or anywhere so far, the way I handle a train."

Checking the profile against which the data was entered into the simulator, the instructor showed me the paperwork, "See! Right there!"

"See right here," I pointed to the milepost location on the chart. "It has an 's' prefix, meaning this is the former SAL route, which has been abandoned for years. We use the old ACL route. You've mistakenly entered a piece of one railroad into the data base profile of another. No wonder I'm getting knuckles according to your fancy electronic toy. I know where I am, but your machine doesn't."

Computers are only as good as what humans feed into them. I'm not knocking technology, but I don't believe I could have understood much of what was taught to me in engineer's school without the knowledge I gained in actual engine service during the year prior to my formal classroom training.

I had to continue firing in Rocky Mount after graduation from engineer's school, because I didn't stand for an engineer's job. But when my 18 months were up, I exercised my seniority to Richmond and was immediately placed on the engineer's extra board, because they were actually short of engineers as a result of the recent merger with the Chessie System that formed CSX. I was one of the very few engineers qualified to operate to Portsmouth, Virginia, so trains were often held until I could get eight hours rest before being called to pilot another C&O grain train to the docks of Hampton Roads for export.

I'll never forget that last night in Rocky Mount, though. Along with Larry Hull, I stood outside the window at the crew clerk's office at CO, South Rocky Mount Yard, and counted down the seconds until the clock on the wall said midnight.

"Five, four, three, two, one," we chanted in unison. "Happy New Year! Notify the crew clerk at Acca that we're coming home!"

Chapter 11: The Homecoming

In a way, I never left Richmond because I never allowed myself to refer to Rocky Mount as home. When my obligation to stay in that small, southern railroading and tobacco town ended at 12:01 a.m., October 27, 1980, I walked out of the yard office at South Rocky Mount feeling a bit like a released prisoner. Instead of a saw buck in the pocket of a new suit of clothes, I had a diploma identifying me as a qualified locomotive engineer. My departure went largely unnoticed, although the crusty old, cigar chomp'n, former Atlantic Coast Line road foreman of engines, to whom I had announced my intentions earlier that day, offered his thoughts. "Go on back to Richmond! See if I give a damn! There's only one thing I hate more than a Seaboard sonofabitch, and that's a Richmond sonofabitch."

No tunnel or escape plan was necessary. I was a free man.

In all fairness, few places are more friendly or tightly knit than Rocky Mount. Its residents consider themselves to be living in the middle of God's green acre. They didn't understand anyone wanting to leave, and regarded those who spurned their generous southern hospitality and warm invitations to stay as being little more than heretics, atheists, or damn Yankees. It was a pretty town. I wondered sometimes if its Main Street, bisected by the double high iron of the former ACL, might not have been viewed through the window of a Florida-bound Pullman by Walt Disney himself many years ago, and served as the inspiration for Disney World's Main Street USA.

Had my wife and I permitted ourselves to indulge in the priceless luxuries of small town life instead of fleeing home to Richmond or shopping in Raleigh whenever the opportunity presented itself, we probably would have felt differently about our time in Rocky Mount. I doubt that we would have chosen to remain there past the period for which I had contracted, but at least the memories of our first year as newlyweds would have been less bitter and more sweet.

Not everyone who came down from Richmond to take those precious firing positions returned home right at the end of a year and a half. One Richmonder who accepted the invitation to go into engine service in Rocky Mount on the same day as I did in 1979 was taken house hunting by an anxious real estate agent his first night in town. He proceeded to sign a contract on a house, in the dark, in the wee hours, without first asking the opinion of his pregnant wife. When he brought his expectant spouse to town the following week, they were both stunned. Seeing it for the first time in the light of day, they discovered to their dismay, that located across the street, was a city playground complex that erupted in deafening grandstand cheers from the crack of dawn, until the lights were turned off at midnight, throughout the year, during baseball, football, and basketball seasons—hardly an atmosphere conducive to the needs of a new mother and sleeping infant.

Trying to put the best possible face on a hastily made decision, my friend sat on the front porch of his new home, fired up a big El Producto cigar (from which the pink, "it's a girl" wrapper had just been removed), and said to me, "Look, where we came from, a railroad engineer doesn't amount to a pimple on a gnat's ass. He's just another blue collar worker. Down here, he's respected. He's considered to be a highly paid professional. He not only belongs to the country club, he's a trustee. He is somebody! We don't have any intention of going back. We like it here." (At the end of our tenure there in 1980, a few days after I had left town and marked up as an engineer back home in Richmond, my friend put his house in Rocky Mount up for sale, packed up his family, and came home too, although it took him forever to sell that house.)

I don't remember much about the drive home in the early morning hours of October 27, 1980, because all I could think of was the fact that I was going home. The settlement for my injuries in the locomotive crankcase explosion enabled us to make a down payment on a modest brick ranch home in the Richmond suburb of Mechanicsville. Sandy, teaching in Henrico County again and living there by herself for the last year, had not only transformed it into a beautiful home, but she had prepared two welcome home gifts for me that will remain in our home forever.

Entering the front door, she greeted me passionately, stepped back, and asked, "Notice anything special?"

My first instinct, of course, was to stare at her, thinking that maybe I had missed a change in her personal appearance.

"No, dummy," she frowned, obviously disappointed that I had not taken immediate notice of the large object sitting against the living room wall, "Not me. Look around the room."

There, with a blue ribbon around it and a brass lamp on top, was my grandfather's writing desk. It took me a moment to realize what it was, although I had sat at it and gone through his railroad paraphernalia almost daily as a child. Opening it, I found another brightly wrapped gift. Upon lifting it, I remarked, "What's in here, a brick?"

It was a brick—one with an embroidered cover, intended as a door stop, which read, "Doug Riddell, Engineer."

"Don't get too used to that job as a fireman on passenger trains," Richmond Road Foreman of Engines Bob McDougald warned me. "This merger with the Chessie System means there's going to be more work here than we can handle. There's talk about moving unit trains of coal and grain to Portsmouth, and you're going to have to pilot a lot of Chesapeake & Ohio crews. We need to get you qualified in through freight right away. Are you ready?"

Ready? I thought firemen spent some time as firemen before being promoted to engineer. All of those old heads used to complain and gripe because they served 10 or 15 years on the left hand side of the cab, where the old codger they fired for wouldn't even let them touch the throttle. I was being thrown right into the water as a newborn babe to sink or swim. Don't get me wrong, I felt I was ready to be an engineer. I wanted to occupy that vaunted throne on the right hand side of the locomotive and draw the big bucks that came with the territory, but after whetting my appetite 18 months for a full three course meal, I at least expected to be able to sit down and enjoy the salad and entree before being handed the dessert, the bill, and being told to leave. Unfortunately, circumstances dictated otherwise, and not only did I not get the chance to taste the delights of being a fireman for more than a few weeks—I figuratively found myself receiving my dinner at the "drive-thru" window.

At Bob's insistence, I marked up in the Richmond-Rocky Mount through freight pool firing for W. G. "Chuck" Dunn, instead of the much easier Amtrak passenger pool. One of the more senior former ACL engineers, Chuck was glad to have a fireman, and took me under his wing. The old ACL's relatively flat, directionally signaled, double-track main line from Richmond to Rocky Mount allowed much longer trains to be operated than on the more rugged, singletrack, CTC dispatched Seaboard Air Line main from Richmond to Raleigh. If you didn't know what you were doing, you could get into trouble on either route.

I immediately understood why McDougald recommended I mark up with Dunn. From day one, Chuck put me in the seat and let me run. This took a great deal of trust on his part, and gave me a tremendous shot of confidence. When I would arrive at Acca's Bryan Park engine terminal to sign the register sheet, check the board to see which engines we would be assigned, and where they were located, I would find Chuck already in the cab, no matter how early I got there. No matter who I fired for, no matter what the assignment, and no matter how well I got to know the engineer, out of respect for him, I always asked if he would like for me to run for him. Chuck always looked up at me and surrendered his seat without saying a word. As luck would have it, when I marked off one trip, he derailed just south of the Virginia-North Carolina state line. No one was hurt, and it was determined that his handling of the train had nothing to do with the incident. The 20 or so cars that left the track did so after an overheated journal gave out, but when I showed up for work the next trip, Chuck looked at me and laughed, "Would you kindly arrange to let me know when you're going to take a trip off so that I can mark off too, and we can both miss out on the next derailment?"

As a promoted engineer, protecting an engineer's job always took precedent over working a regular firing assignment, and four days after returning to Richmond, I made my very first day as an engineer filling an emergency vacancy on October 31, deadheading to Collier Yard in Petersburg to work a midnight yard engine at the throttle of former SAL GP7 No. 907. Two weeks later, on Sunday night, November 16, I was again called in emergency, this time for my first freight train—a unit coal train delivered to an electric power generating plant at Wheelwright, Virginia, on the Bellwood Subdivision—with brand new SD40-2s 8048/8060/8093. At daybreak, as we cut the caboose off in the cab track at Acca Yard and took the signal to move the engines to the roundhouse, I asked a crew member to photograph me leaning out the cab window. I had it framed with the notation that it was my first freight run as an engineer.

Having graduated from engineer's training school on August 7, having moved back from Rocky Mount on October 27, and having fired for Chuck Dunn for just five weeks, on Monday, December 5, 1980, I was officially marked up on the Richmond engineer's extra board. I was no longer a fireman.

My Grandfather's railroad, the C&O (in Virginia, at least), was a bulk commodities carrier. Other than solid trains of steam coal destined for the bellies of huge colliers at the road's Newport News, Virginia, piers, or export grain for the land of the Czars, which was barged across Hampton Roads for loading at Portsmouth or Norfolk, only carloads of steel for Newport News Shipbuilding and Drydock Company or shipments to and from the huge Anheuser Busch brewery near Williamsburg even warranted the scheduling of a single, daily "manifest" freight over its Peninsula Subdivision.

The savings from end-to-end mergers, such as the Chessie/Seaboard one, are realized more from service and route coordination than from elimination of duplicate facilities and the abandonment of overlapping lines. Moving export grain via an all-rail route to Portsmouth in lieu of the expensive, cumbersome, and good weather dependent barge crossing of Hampton Roads from Newport News, resulted in an immediate and substantial economy of operation.

Rather than a costly, full-fledged merger of operating forces (which would come later), CSX opted for "coordinated service." The marriage of the roads that formed CSX not only joined two geographically opposed carriers, but operationally mated two Olympic gold medal winners which were, unfortunately, competitors in far different sports—a fleet footed sprinter and a slow moving weight lifter. The logic of employing as many as six, seven, or even eight four-axle locomotives in high-speed merchandise freight service (which was fairly commonplace on the Seaboard System) seemed totally foreign to Chessie officials. They were used to moving a 200-car coal train down the steady descending grade from the hills and hollows of West Virginia to the Port of Hampton Roads at 35 mph using a GP40 and a GP9. At the same time, Seaboard officials suffered anxiety attacks waiting for the arrival of several carloads of high priority, time sensitive automotive factory parts, which lazily meandered down the tow path of the James River Canal behind one of those 200-car coal trains. The responsibility fell upon them to do whatever was necessary to get those cars to Portsmouth before the deadline. Otherwise, the Ford truck plant in Norfolk, to which the shipments were destined, would have to be shut down for lack of parts and material.

From their office windows at James Center, CSX officials could see Rivanna Junction (site of the world famous triple railroad crossing), where C&O's Rivanna, Piedmont, and Peninsula Subdivisions came together high atop a long steel viaduct skirting the waterfront in the heart of downtown Richmond. Unfortunately, it too often served as a hold out point for trains entering C&O's congested Fulton Yard, just to the east. His curiosity piqued by the sight of a merchandise freight train that had been sitting at the junction since early morning, a very high ranking CSX official made a lunchtime call to the yardmaster at Fulton, inquiring as to the identity of the train and the reason it sat there. When told that there was no room for it in the yard, and that the train was the one that included those delivery penalty auto parts, the phone lines nearly melted from the heat that ensued. It was thereafter forbidden for that train to be held out of Fulton Yard. And thereafter it wasn't. It was simply tucked in a siding, out of sight of the company's top brass west of town at Sabot or Westham.

Seaboard System train and engine crews did not ordinarily operate from Richmond, south and east to Portsmouth. While stationed in North Carolina, however, I got to know that territory well. When I returned to Richmond, I was one of only a handful of engineers qualified over the non-signaled Portsmouth Subdivision. When coordinated service began in earnest in 1982, Chessie's car float service was abandoned, and as they say on Wall Street, my stock went through the roof. I could hardly get my rest before being called back on duty to pilot another C&O crew from Fulton Yard to Portsmouth. Since no connecting track existed initially that allowed a southbound train to go east at Weldon, North Carolina, all C&O trains were cabbed at both ends, and the motive power ran around them south of Weldon.

While the holding company's top brass had good reason to toast their good fortune, employees at the new railroad's various yards and offices across town began eyeing each other with suspicion and anticipation as to which railroad's management would emerge dominant, and where the inevitable job cuts would come.

The agreement to coordinate service between workers of each respective railroad at Richmond was reached in late 1981, but it was not implemented until January 1982. At that time, with few engineers scheduled to be on vacation, I had actually been cut back to firing, temporarily, so I marked up on the Richmond to Portsmouth train known as No. 890, returning the following day as 891. (The train ran every day. Seaboard crews only got to run it every third trip.) It was considered an eastbound C&O train, but departed Fulton westbound. Once on the SBD, it was a southbound movement, at least to Weldon, where it became a northbound train.

Confused?

Just how dizzying this is can best be exemplified by an incident that happened shortly after the first coordinated trains began rolling. Veteran Seaboard special agent Red Currie was called by our crew to meet our train upon arrival at Portsmouth to remove a vagrant spotted en route. As we slowly pulled by the yard office, Red signed us down to a stop and coaxed the illegal traveler out of a boxcar. From my perch in the window of the lead Chessie U23B, I could see that the man, who was quite understandably upset, became totally enraged after Red pointed toward the waterfront and said something to him. The would-be hobo had to be restrained by newly arrived members of the local police force, who handcuffed him, and took him away.

"What on earth did you say to him to make him so mad at you, Red?" I asked as I entered the yard office, before heading to our motel.

"Oh," the agent laughed, "he wasn't mad at me. He was terribly upset with himself. Turns out that he jumped bail at a court hearing, right across the Elizabeth River, in Norfolk early this morning. He must have thumbed a ride across the Hampton Roads Bridge Tunnel, where he hopped a westbound C&O freight train at Newport News. When the train arrived in Richmond, he was spotted by their police, so he scampered around Fulton Yard for an hour or so to elude them. He grabbed up on the first thing smoking westbound, only it turned out to be your westbound train. Satisfied that he'd be in West Virginia or Ohio in the morning, he went to sleep."

Stopping to mop the sweat from his brow with a handkerchief, Currie shook his head and laughed, "When we woke him up, he said he didn't mind being thrown around in that dirty old boxcar, and he didn't really fear being locked up, 'cause no matter what happened to him here—wherever he was—it sure had to be a long, long way away from the jail from which he had escaped back in Norfolk, Virginia."

Red went on to tell us that the errant jailbird then looked up and saw the sign over the yard office door that read "Portsmouth."

"This Portsmouth, Ohio?" he squinted. "I must have really slept good."

"No," Red Currie informed him. "Portsmouth, Virginia, right across the river from Norfolk, where you're going to be in about five minutes after these kind gentlemen put you in their police cruiser and take you through the mid-town tunnel to jail."

"No. 890 or No. 891. So, what's in a number?" most non-railroaders would ask. As it so happens, a great deal is at stake.

A train's number identifies it in the timetable, and helps everyone to determine who has the right-of-way when two trains meet or pass each other. Superiority of trains is determined by right, class, and direction. A sound knowledge of those three elements is the mortar that holds the bricks together when trains are operated without an electronic signal system of some kind. Traditionally, even-numbered north- and eastbound trains of the same class are superior to odd-numbered south- and westbound schedules. Thus, with all of the different directions in which it traveled, No. 890/891 was a train with a glaring identity crisis. Since the method of operation on the now very busy Portsmouth Subdivision depended on the use of a railroad approved watch, a timetable, and a set of train orders to prevent two different trains from being in the same place at the same time, everyone had to know what they were doing.

Almost all of C&O's trackage in Virginia was signaled, much of it CTC dispatched from Chessie's modern offices in Richmond. Life aboard its freight trains consisted of ambling along at 35 or 40 mph, knocking down block signal after block signal, and easing to a stop in the receiving yard at Newport News. When the speedometer of the old six-axle C&O, Baltimore & Ohio, and Western Maryland locomotives began pegging 50 and 60 mph on the former ACL raceway south of Richmond, there was naturally a bit of apprehension among men who had never even run a passenger train faster than 65 mph. When the headlights of those same engines illuminated the darkness of the deer-filled peanut fields of southeastern Virginia on the former SAL's single track at 49 mph—with no signals to guide them, heightened apprehension quickly turned to outright fear. All of this was remedied within a few months of the commencement of coordination when a system of DTC, or Direct Traffic Control blocks were established, and the time honored system of timetable schedules, clearance cards, and train orders became just another chapter in railroad history.

Called for 3:30 p.m. to pilot a C&O crew from Fulton to Portsmouth, I was told that we would have only 17 loads of automobile parts in our train. Those cars had to be in Portsmouth by 9 p.m., or the plant would not be able to operate past the 11 p.m. shift change. Since the regular crew had already departed as scheduled, earlier in the day, I drew a C&O freight pool crew, who were in no small measure displeased that they were going to Portsmouth instead of Newport News.

"I got Raleigh on the phone," said the Rocky Mount dispatcher, who would line me up all the way to Weldon, run me around the train in the center siding, and then hand me over to the Raleigh dispatcher for the remaining 76 miles to Portsmouth. "He wants to know who's gonna be running, you or the C&O man. If it's you, we'll put everything in the hole and give you nothing but green, 'cause we figure we've got a chance to make the market. If it's the C&O man, forget it."

"I'll do the best I can," I told him.

"You're on," the dispatcher said. "The chief says, 'Put it in number eight, and don't be late.'"

When I showed up at Fulton, the power listed for the run was an old WM SD40 and a C&O GP9, but Chessie GP40-2 No. 4444, which had just come in on a manifest freight, was substituted for the elderly Geep at the last minute. At 4:30 p.m., we began picking our way through the crossovers beneath the tall tower and within minutes started the assault on Hermitage Hill. True to the dispatcher's word, we got the best signals possible, and with only 17 cars and two cabooses, no helper was required to shove us. Still, it would require four hours and 30 minutes of judicious running and a lot of luck to get our precious shipment to the loading docks at the Ford plant.

Clearing the wye at Acca Yard, I moved the throttle all the way to number eight with one motion. The trailing 4444 immediately kicked us in the rear while the old Western Maryland six axle (still in back with gold speed lettering) belched black smoke, heaved, and abruptly responded.

"What's wrong with this thing?" I asked the Chessie hogger.

"They had this thing on the pushers all day," noted the C&O engineer.

Within minutes, we blasted over the James River on the high-arched viaduct, and dropped down hill toward the 60 mph curve at FA Tower. At this point, the old ACL main line originally headed straight for downtown Richmond, interchanging with Southern Railway predecessor Richmond & Danville Railroad before crossing the James to connect with C&O and RF&P at Byrd Street Station.

"Hot damn!" the brakeman howled. "Look at this bad boy go. Now this is railroad'n!"

Braking hard, we leaned into the super elevated curve, as the alarm bell began ringing and the old WM warrior shut down completely. While the 4444 simultaneously shoved us and pulled the train, the C&O engineer went back to investigate. "Ain't even out of Richmond, but we're out of fuel," he shouted as he closed the door. "Guess they got in such a hot hurry that they forgot to service it. When we went around that curve, what was left in the tank shifted and the pump started picking up mud from the bottom."

"Let's hope that the other unit has enough to get us there," I responded. It did, but it ran dry 10 miles out of Portsmouth on the return trip.

Everything else went like clockwork. We headed into the pass track at Weldon, ran around our train, coupled to the other end, and took the signal to go north. Switching to the former SAL radio channel, I was greeted by the Raleigh eastend dispatcher, "Got power problems, Douglas?"

"Yeh," I chuckled. "One down, one to go, but we should be all right."

"You let me know if you need help. I've got switchers at Franklin and Suffolk that can come rescue you if anything happens. They've told me that you're hauling gold tonight, brother. The railroad's yours. Run'em!"

Typical of the old Seaboard, even though it was non signaled, the railroad to Portsmouth was impeccably kept. And just as typical was the old Seaboard philosophy of getting the freight to market before the competition. That night however, other than tip-toeing through the yard limits at Boykins, Franklin, Suffolk, and Portsmouth, we "flew low." We didn't stop at Franklin, Virginia, as was customary, to have our lunch bags filled with hot peanuts, salted in the shell or fresh from the roaster at Sach's, for just a quarter, although they sure would have tasted good.

Ducking under Norfolk & Western at Kilby, we ran parallel to the old abandoned Virginian right-of-way with its big, concrete whistle posts, by the joint Suffolk station. Virginian Railway and SAL engineers used to race each other through the Great Dismal Swamp to see who would hit the signal circuit for the diamond at Algren first. There, the Virginian once bore to the east, crossed the Seaboard at grade, and headed for the piers at Sewell's Point in Norfolk. Now, with the exception of black bear and other wildlife, the VGN right-of-way was untraveled by anyone or anything.

"Bring'em on, C&O extra," exhorted Portsmouth yardmaster Johnnie Harrell. "The yard engine is in the clear at the Beltline connection switch. As soon as you stop, cut your engines off and blank the angle cock so that the yard crew can couple up to your rear and deliver those hot cars. You made a good run."

Passing the yellow high signal at the Norfolk-Portsmouth Beltline doubletrack main line, we entered Shops Yard and were routed straight down the main line, where a team of car inspectors, the listing clerk, Bonnie, and Johnnie anxiously awaited us. Dumping the air after I stopped, I finally allowed myself the luxury of glancing down at my watch. It read 8:59 p.m.

It would seem that the return trip the following day would have to be a compara-tive breeze. We didn't really need five engines, so the fact that two of them were out of fuel just added a little more tonnage to the 50 or so cars we had in tow. Trouble was, we were no longer the hottest thing on the railroad. It was payback time, as they say. It took us forever to get across the Portsmouth Subdivision to Weldon. We had to wait our turn to even get out on the old ACL high iron. By the time we were ready to leave Petersburg's Collier Yard, dispatcher Lloyd Boone called me and asked if I could make Richmond in the 59 minutes left before the federal 12-hour "hog law" got us. I assured him I could make Acca, but beyond that, we would probably tie up.

"If you can make it to Acca and get your train on the east route [the SAL line downhill from Hermitage Yard toward Fulton], I'll take you. If not, tie your train down right there and I'll call a taxi cab for you. You've got to clear the main line. Eighty-two [the northbound Silver Star] will be right on your tail all the way, and you've got to clear the main line at Acca, or you'll stick him."

"Light'em up, Lloyd," I told him. "I'm already rolling."

I saw nothing but green all the way to Richmond. We ate up the 35 miles to AY interlocking with time to spare. Veering east toward Fulton, I stopped at Hermitage Road where a yard crew took over for the remaining six miles to the C&O yard.

"You did fine," Boone chimed in over the radio as No. 82's two F40s whined by us and threaded the double slip switches at Acca, on its way to the passenger station at Greendale. "C&O says they've got two grain trains called out of Clifton Forge. You'll be on the first one, called on your rest."

Filling out my time card at the yard office at Fulton where I spent my childhood watching little Alco S-2s kicking cars while my grandfather went upstairs to get his paycheck, I heard the screen door slam hard as my C&O conductor brushed past me.

"Take my [assigned] cab and put it on the Hampton Branch Local," he angrily ordered the crew clerk. "Don't you ever call me for another one of those Seaboard trains—never! Those sonofabitches are crazy! They run a hundred miles an hour [a great exaggeration to be sure] on the main line, and damn near as fast on that non signaled branch line."

Noticing me out of the corner of his eye, he couldn't hold it back. "Son," he huffed, seeming almost apologetic by comparison, after he took a deep breath, "You're a good engineer, but that old cab has been following coal trains down east for 30 years at 35 mph. I don't know how fast you were going on the way up here from Petersburg, because I couldn't get a bead on a milepost—everything was a big blur. The axle generator sounded like a dynamo gone crazy. I was sure at one point it was playing 'Nearer My God to Thee' for a chorus of angels. Every time I heard the radio speaker, I listened carefully to see if it was the Good Lord announcing our arrival in heaven."

True to his word, the old man retired working the Hampton Local in Newport News, and even in a pinch, the crew clerks knew better than to call him for a train for Portsmouth.

Walking to my car, I looked out across the empty fields that had once been a thick expanse of urban slums until the federal government concurred with hurricanes Agnes and Camille to proclaim one of Richmond's oldest neighborhoods to be a flood prone disaster area. No longer lined with tenements, stick ball playing children, or horse drawn wagons laden with refuse, now bulldozed clean, the streets of Fulton Bottom hardly resembled the cobblestone thoroughfares my grandfather and I navigated after leaving the railroad yard. Nonetheless, just like 20 years ago, I was very much at home.

Chapter 12: Like No Other Train

Question: What's purple, white, and red all over? Answer: The balance sheet from the original Auto Train. Toward the end it was not only purple, red, and white, but blue and gray, black and yellow, aluminum mist with red-and-blue stripes, plus every other color combination that adorned the assorted U-boats, E9s, Geeps, SDP40Fs, and on one occasion even a flexicoil-trucked SW1500 borrowed to lead the terminally ill Auto Train over the Richmond, Fredericksburg & Potomac and Seaboard System main lines from Lorton, Virginia, to Sanford, Florida. It was a railfan's dream. You could go home after shooting only one train and brag of having bagged engines from Louisville & Nashville, Family Lines, Seaboard Coast Line, RF&P, Seaboard System, and Amtrak as well as the Auto Train itself.

The final rites for Eugene Garfield's revolutionary experiment were conducted on May 1, 1981, although the diagnosis was pronounced and the epitaph written many months before. Despite a credit line of Swiss francs and attempts to generate its own capital by assembling freight cars and overhauling passenger cars through subsidiary Railway Services Inc. (even chartering its own office car), the Auto Train was mortally wounded by devastating derailments and the inability to make essential repairs to locomotives and rolling stock. Toward the end, prepayment was required before the dispatchers would allow movement onto the high iron of RF&P and Seaboard System. Even fuel was delivered on a cash only basis.

With engineer W. G. "Chuck" Dunn at the throttle of RF&P GP35 No. 136, trailed by SCL GP40-2 No. 6611 and Amtrak E9 No. 417, the last northbound run screamed by my work train at Collier, Virginia, at 9:15 a.m. "Save me your orders," I begged conductor "Red" Hunnicutt over the radio. "Sure thing, Douglas," he responded in his polite North Carolina drawl.

I climbed down from the cab of SCL NW2 No. 20 (a former 1940 Electro-Motive Division demonstrator, Atlantic Coast Line No. 600) to capture No. 4 on Kodachrome with my ancient Canon FTb. The late-morning Virginia sun poured through the stand of tall pines on the eastern right-of-way, evoking a cathedral-like aura for this mournful occasion. Seemingly within a moment, the anything-and-everything diesel consist, the steam generator car, sleepers, coaches, dining cars, and auto carriers passed, and the top-heavy cab roared by. As I returned a highball from flagman Richard Stankeiweicz, the engine's horn sadly invited those stopped at the Halifax Road crossing to pay their last respects. The tall, three-aspect wayside signal dropped from green to red, the crossing gates rose, and an eerie silence settled in, interrupted only by the sounds of the automobile tires bounding indifferently across the steel rails of the old, doubletrack, ACL main line. The last Auto Train rounded the curve, passed over the Norfolk & Western belt line, and faded into history.

Returning to our assigned task of distributing lengths of welded rail, I found myself a bit embarrassed as my conductor questioned my swollen, red eyes. "Hell man, it's just a train!"

But what a train. I was lucky enough to have worked both the head and rear ends as its brakeman, and I later took the throttle as its engineer. I can assure you, it was like no other train. Even today's AMD103-led Superliner II Amtrak Auto Train, and before it, the aging P30s and vintage heritage fleet consists had their own idiosyncrasies. While demanding the same meticulous train handling, neither evokes quite the same emotion in me as recalling the cachunk-cachunk exhaust building to a steady, thunderous roar as the tandem U36Bs accelerated the 44-car consist south out of Richmond's Acca Yard, racing rush-hour commuters on the parallel Beltline Expressway. From atop the arched viaduct spanning the falls of the James River, we viewed the sun setting over the distant Blue Ridge Mountains.

Reviewing my notes and photos, I was amazed by how much railroading in general has changed since I hired out as a SCL switchman in Richmond. Much of what we did and what was then expected of us is grounds for dismissal by today's operating and safety regulations—not to mention being dangerous. At the Rocky Mount passenger station, for instance, Auto Train engine and train crews swapped out on the fly, with the train usually moving five to 10 mph. Everyone was required to be able to get on and off moving equipment at 15 mph. Today's railroaders are taught how to dismount safely, but are admonished to do it only in an emergency in deference to hefty judgments against railroads under the Federal Employer's Liability Act.

Steam. The old Auto Train was a slave to steam heat. In its later reincarnation, Amtrak fortunately avoided reliance on the product of the temperamental steam generator. Don't bemoan its disappearance as part of the lost romance of railroading. To a young railfan fireman thirsting to know every detail of engineers' lives aboard the legendary ACL R1 4-8-4 1800s and Seaboard Air Line R1 and R2 2-6-6-4 2500 series Mallets, the old heads would respond, "The only people who thought there was anything romantic about steam engines were those who never had to fire one."

The same holds true for steam generators. Forget the Hollywood trainside farewells filmed through a veil of hissing vapor. In the steam generator's later days, when the alarm bell rang and the pressure gauge dropped, the last thing on anyone's mind was passion. You never knew quite what to expect. Somewhere around 70 mph, you defied common sense and dutifully headed into the "black hole of Calcutta." With lube oil sloshing over the tops of your shoes, armed with a flashlight, string, clothespins, and matchbook covers, you prayed that while attempting to get the thing running there wouldn't be a fire, crankcase explosion, or main generator flashover.

"Plug" Stegall, the second trick crew clerk at Acca Yard, called me to fire No. 3 on January 11, 1981. As was customary, he told me the on-duty time and gave me the engine numbers. "I know what the 4002 is," I said, "but what are the 433, 430, and 669?"

"Look here," impatiently snapped the disabled former SAL brakeman-turned-clerk, "I got the rest of your crew to call. Mrs. Riddell didn't marry no dummy. You can figure out how to run whatever they are. You can always work the rock train if that don't suit you." I didn't relish the thought of nursing three old broken down GP7s and 60 loads of quarry rock in and out of every hole between Richmond and Portsmouth. I would rather make the roundtrip to Rocky Mount on Auto Train and be back at home in my own bed at sunrise than greet the new day in the back seat of a taxi cab headed for an interminable layover at the Midtown Quality Inn. "No thank you, Plug. I'm sure they'll do just fine."

Even at idle, an E unit's 24 cylinders create a music that is truly indescribable. As the throttle is opened, the throaty exhaust resonates off the cavernous passenger shed, its presence rivaling that of the mighty pipe organ at Radio City Music Hall. The very ground shakes. The main generator's low whine builds, shudders, and steadies with each further advance as its charge is gently coaxed into motion.

Quintessential newlyweds, Sandy and I sat in our car while the RF&P crew brought No. 3 to a stop in front of the yard office at Acca. I immediately leaped from the car when I recognized the deep chanting of the two Amtrak E9s, amplified many times over as they stood beneath the I-195 overpass which straddles AY interlocking. In the darkness, the oily gray hearts of the aged workhorses showed through the open mid-body doors. Grabbing my grip, I kissed my bride on the cheek and clamored over the rails to the lead unit. "I know the magic isn't supposed to last forever," yelled my wife, "but I never figured on being tossed aside for a locomotive!"

As I hurriedly returned to attempt to make amends, engineer Rob Yancey came out the crew room door. "Plenty of time for that in the morning when we get back," he grinned. "The electrician wants you to meet him on the second unit to try and get both motors running."

I left my grip in the U36B's cramped cab and headed for the 433. In addition to their inherently slow throttle response, the reason General Electric U-boats were generally hated by crews is that, while squeezing between their filthy radiator grills and walkway handrails, everything you wore was sucked into the safety screens by the huge cooling fan and ruined. I found maneuvering from the high rear platform into the small, Mars light-equipped nose door of former Union Pacific E9 No. 433 to be no easier a task. The classic A1A-A1A speedster was painted in the early cigar band scheme, though the 430 remained in its original "bloody red nose" livery. Both had the notation "Owned by Amtrak, Operated by Auto Train" hastily stenciled on the flank. While both retained their 24L brake, to my surprise, the 433 was equipped with a modified AAR control stand. Until three days prior, it had been stored at New Orleans, according to its Federal Railroad Administration blue sheet, and it showed.

Assured that the B-end 567 V12 had been barred over to drain condensation from its cylinder cocks, I gripped the lay shaft and engaged the starter. It rallied to the call. Forgetting that we were in high throttle demand as Rob accelerated the train, I flipped the isolation switch to "run," and the old E9's main generator responded angrily. It flashed over, and I was chased from the engine room and into the cab by a huge ball of fire. I didn't repeat that mistake again with the 433 or with the 430. After a little coaxing and a lot of cursing,

I brought their second motors back to life.

The 669 turned out to be a heater car—an E9B shell containing two steam generators and water storage tanks that seemed in relatively good shape. Not satisfied with his ample steam source, the electrician was bent on lighting up the remaining four boilers on the 430 and 433 but decided against it when their tags revealed inspections that had long since expired.

Extreme cold, even down in Dixie, played havoc with steam heating lines. At each stop, it was the duty of the flagman on a passenger train to open the rear valve, blow the steam line out, and leave the valve cracked enough to allow some steam to escape. The Auto Train's extreme length, plus the fact that it did not stop except at Florence, South Carolina, for en route servicing, greatly exacerbated this problem.

It was also inadvisable to sever the steam line in sub-freezing temperatures, thus risking a total freeze-up. Once during the winter of 1980-1981, despite the protestations of veteran conductor Red Hunnicutt, the Auto Train onboard service director made the decision to stop at old FA Tower, just south of Richmond, to switch a car with electrical problems to the rear, requiring the steam line to be broken. As a result, at 8:30 a.m. the following morning, No. 3 was parked on the main line at Rocky Mount with smudge pots burning beneath it in an attempt to thaw the steam line. That very same hour it was scheduled to have arrived in sunny Sanford.

Heating for Auto Train's cabooses left even more to be desired. Former Florida East Coast cabs, which were converted boxcars mounted on express car trucks, had their bay windows had been replaced by extended-width cupolas. They were so tall, in fact, that the cupola was reached by ascending a 12-step metal staircase with railings. They were equipped with a standard kerosene caboose stove, which kept SCL's cozy M-5 cabs comfortable, but was woefully inadequate for heating this rolling skyscraper. Thus, in winter, the flagman was provided a Pullman blanket to keep warm while in the cupola.

The battery-powered lighting was governed by a timer located next to the cab's rear door, and had to be reset hourly. Rather than risk being thrown down the stairs or out the oversized cupola windows at 70 mph, I often sat in the dark, radio in hand, seat belt tightly drawn across the blanket in my lap until time to detrain. The roller coasters at nearby Busch Gardens held no thrill for me after a night on the Auto Train caboose.

I'd love to swap stories with Santa Fe engineers who operated those red warbonnet U28Cs in high-speed passenger service across the desert southwest. They'd no doubt verify the need to carry a roll of duct tape with which to seal the front cab door and number board access hatches to prevent the cab from filling with rain, snow, dirt, and feathers. Feathers? Locomotive headlights unfortunately blind hapless deer and attract some varieties of fowl at night. Birds are most often the reason locomotives are seen with missing or mismatched number boards. Beginning with the Dash-7 model, heavier, reinforced cab doors and number boards accessible solely from the outside were incorporated into the standard GE cab design.

Because the train caters largely to senior citizens fleeing the arctic Northeast for the more appealing climates of Henry Flagler's winter playground, conductors Silas Snow, E. B. Clark, Dick Waymack, Henry Whitmore, and finally Red Hunnicutt would often find themselves ordering the engineer to contact the dispatcher (then at Rocky Mount) to obtain help for passengers, who despite repeated pre-boarding advisories left their medication in the trunk of their automobiles, inaccessible until arrival and unloading the following morning.

Walt Smith, today a retired Miami Tri-Rail commuter engineer, fondly recalls his years with Auto Train, assembling consists of full-length domes and auto carriers at the throttle of the ancient Baldwin VO1000 switcher in Sanford. Previously he worked as an onboard attendant and remembers the near disastrous result of an attempt to economize by serving complimentary leftover chicken and tuna salad finger sandwiches on the return leg of a trip. During the night there was an outbreak of dysentery, especially among the diet-sensitive senior citizens. Needless to say, that was never tried again.

Auto Train alumnus, good friend, and current Amtrak conductor Jerry Reed proudly carries on the legacy of his dad, the late Red Hunnicutt. "I remember when we served Marriott food but once tried to use china. When they realized that the Auto Train had no facilities for washing dishes, all that Correll dinnerware went right into the trash."

He recounts that crew members tried to grant every reasonable request, but just couldn't accommodate the elderly lady whose husband passed away near Savannah. "Couldn't we just let him rest there until we get to Florida?"

Amtrak ticket agent and former Auto Train employee Bill Jaworski was quick to point out that their compassion even extended to passengers' pets. "We once made a makeshift oxygen tent utilizing a plastic trash bag to revive a dog." Bill, jack-of-all-trades and master of mechanical miracles who kept many Auto Trains warm, lit, and running, had a personality and dedication that exemplified the onboard camaraderie that made the train's outstanding service famous. Once as Bill kneeled in the aisle before an open electrical cabinet, attempting to repair a hot car filled with parishioners destined for a religious retreat, the onboard chief pointed to Bill and exclaimed, "We're doing everything possible to fix the air conditioning. Look, our electrician is even praying for divine intervention."

Intermural practical jokes became legendary. They ran the gambit from collegiate dormitory gags to adorning the yellow nose of "Killer" (the nickname applied to engine 4004 because of its penchant for being involved in grade crossing accidents) with a smiling face and red bow tie, reportedly for an employee birthday. Surrendering to superstition, Auto Train finally relegated the 4004 for use as a trailing unit only, whereupon it was promptly broadsided by a truck. It was later wrecked and burned.

Following the last Auto Train arrival, customers received the same proud, professional, courteous attention for which the service will be eternally remembered. After the last guests departed Lorton and Sanford, friendships that had endured countless hardships and thousands of miles also ended. With bags packed, employees tearfully embraced each other and bade farewell, heading for the highways to get on with their lives, scattering to the four corners the earth. Were an Auto Train reunion held today, the turnout would likely be large, because when the subject arises among railroaders, there is always at least one person who proudly proclaims, "I used to work the Auto Train."

Chapter 13: Read'n, Writ'n, and Railroad'n

Just as inevitable as Daylight Savings Time or the April 15 deadline for filing income taxes comes an invitation to participate in career day at my son's elementary school. Every year, I join an assemblage of farmers, mechanics, accountants, sales clerks, and homemakers, each awaiting his or her cue to perform.

I don a genuine Lee hat, a pair of pinstriped bibs, matching jacket, red riverboat driver's shirt, and patterned bandana—hardly the everyday working clothes of an Amtrak locomotive engineer—for the benefit of Ryan's classmates. Anything else would be like Howard Johnson's without the orange roof. They really want to know what it's like to be an Amtrak engineer, so I bring along my slide projector, souvenir hats, and coloring books and indulge myself in their queries. Either railroading is still intrinsically fascinating, or after listening to a CPA's dissertation on tax law changes, they are ready for anything.

"Mr. Riddell," asked one 10 year old, "You usually bring Ryan to school in the morning and pick him up every afternoon. When do you go to work?" I have neighbors who wonder the same thing. "Weekends when your family goes to the river, in the middle of the night when you're tucked into bed, and holidays when most families are grilling burgers over charcoal or opening Christmas presents," I replied. "That's when I go to work."

Electric or diesel, passenger or freight, a 3 a.m. wakeup call is still a 3 a.m. wakeup call. Human beings come factory programed to yawn incessantly between the hours of midnight and 6 a.m. as a nagging reminder that normal people are supposed to be at home, in bed, giving Rip Van Winkle a run for his money.

The solitude of the commute to work from my suburban home at that hour of the morning is in stark contrast to the jangled nerves and crumpled fenders endured by most nine-to-fivers. Maybe the occasional startled deer, the unspoiled moonlit snow, the time to stop and exchange pleasantries with the newspaper carrier and the waitress at the all-night Dunkin Doughnuts are my rewards for having to kiss my sleeping wife and son on the cheek, adjust their covers, and steal off into the night.

"Your wife may get your love and affection, but you are married to the railroad," Trainmaster W. W. Robertson advised me as he showed me how to unlock and manually operate a dual control power turnout in preparation for my first day as a Seaboard Coast Line brakeman. "It never rains on the railroad; the sun always shines. There's no Santa Claus or Easter Bunny. Hell, there's no Christmas or Easter out here. There are seven days in a week and 24 hours in a day—you will work every one of them."

For better or worse, modern technology has made a vast difference in the way railroads do business. Whereas it once took a natural disaster, a derailment, or a labor stoppage to halt traffic on a busy main line, today a simple mainframe computer glitch at a centralized dispatching center can simultaneously leave Amtrak's 79-mph Silver Meteor standing for hours at Auburndale, Florida; render a busy industrial switcher motionless outside of Barr Yard, Chicago; and, throw the afternoon rush-hour commuter schedule into total disarray in suburban Washington, D.C. Now that's progress. While we may live in the age of the Pentium chip and have the ability to receive our movement directives from a faceless source hundreds of miles away by teleprinter or fax, until railroads can capture daylight in a bottle and dispense it as needed, there will always be the phone that rings in the middle of the night to summon the faithful to rail yards and passenger stations across the slumbering nation.

Mother Nature and Father Time continually thin the roster of those who can still recall shoveling coal into the hungry mouth of a Norfolk & Western M class 4-8-0 on the Jefferson Branch Local winding through the isolated coal fields of southwestern Virginia and North Carolina. Fewer and fewer corridor engineers remember the 22-notch throttle of the Pennsy's classic GG1. While often cursed for their cold, drafty cabs and poor visibility, to hear some of these guys reminisce about those Raymond Lowey classics, you would swear that they were speaking of their very first love or the car in which they learned to drive. I am captivated by the wondrous Irish brogue of corridor engineers Marty Burke and Eddie Hamilton, spinning their "keystone" tales in the crew lounge at Washington Union Station, of how as young men they, along with my cousin Jack Stecklein, Bill Tucker, and others, assembled the Broadway at Sunnyside Yard, Long Island, or accelerated Clockers across the Jersey Meadowlands toward 30th Street Station in Philadelphia after exiting the Hudson River tunnel.

I treasure my autographed copy of THE VIRGINIAN RAILWAY. H. Reid didn't just sign his name; he filled the title page with a drawing, the railroad's logo, and an inscription about our common bond of journalism. We shared that urgent calling, not only to report what we saw, but to preserve it. I also owe the late railroad photographer, author, and friend Wiley Bryan more than I could ever repay him for his encouragement. "Take your camera with you," he urged me. "Take pictures of everything, no matter how ordinary." He personally preferred firing steam engines, but while filling the tender of his rugged Seaboard Air Line Q3 Mike, he captured images such as a brand-new A-B-A set of "Citrus" liveried E4s blasting through quaint McKinney, Virginia, during World War II with the Sun Queen in tow.

I noticed his classic green Rambler sedan (the bumper sticker proudly proclaiming "I've been to Alaska") as I brought the Carolinian to an on-time stop at the former Southern Railway, Raleigh, North Carolina, Amtrak station a few years ago. "You working this regular now?" he asked.

"It's the best I stand for. A round trip out of Richmond to Charlotte on 79, to Southern Pines on 81, the Silver Star, and two quick turnarounds to Washington each week on the Virginian," I complained.

"How old are you?" Wiley asked. When I said I had just hit 40, he laughed. "Forty years old and holding a regular passenger job. If I had stayed out here, I might have stood for a hold down in the freight pool before I took the pension, but never a passenger job." Although he had retired after living quite comfortably as a successful investment banker, the dimming blue eyes betrayed his regret at having laid down his shovel and relinquishing his seniority on the old Seaboard.

"Come ride with me some time, Wiley. Please," I begged. While cab rides are simply no longer permitted, his friendship with then-Amtrak President Graham Claytor would surely have cut through any red tape required to secure a headend pass.

"I'll look forward to it, Doug," he replied.

Weeks later, I received an envelope containing a message from him on Richmond, Fredericksburg & Potomac stationery. He wanted more than anything to work for them but never got the opportunity. Reflecting on his 70 years of life, he let me know that cancer might postpone that cab ride. Shortly thereafter, as I passed the barn and silos of the Veterinary School of North Carolina State University, approaching Raleigh on the Silver Star, I returned the wave of that familiar white-haired gentleman standing beside the green Rambler with his camera. As I entered the station to copy the Norfolk Southern track warrant allowing us to proceed to Selma, I told baggage handler Vernon Johnson that I was expecting Wiley, and to let me know when he showed up. Apparently dumbfounded, Vernon sat me down and said, "Doug, Wiley died last week."

Later that day, after I related the story to my wife, she put her hand on my shoulder and said, "Maybe you did see him."

The cab of the Broadway or Century was once the exclusive domain of bespeckled, silver-haired gentlemen, holding down the right-hand seatbox for a brief time while contemplating a monthly Railroad Retirement check. The majority of Amtrak's engineers, however, are a long way from collecting that legendary gold Hamilton pocket watch. With rare exception, when Amtrak assumed direct responsibility for operation of its trains from the contracting freight railroads, many senior engineers, not desiring to be paid by the hour nor wishing to forgo lucrative arbitraries for such things as turning their engine or for terminal delay, opted for high mileage, interdivisional freight runs, like CSX's Orange Blossom Special.

Don't draw the conclusion that the man or woman piloting the City of New Orleans through thick, Mississippi River fog is some inexperienced kid. They probably spend more hours and run off more miles at the throttle of a passenger train in a few short years than the old-timers did in their entire career. This is because the allowable mileage for passenger engineers was recorded and regulated. (It still is on railroads other than Amtrak.) Once they reached 4,400 miles, they were "held off" and not allowed to work again until the beginning of a new month. Last year alone I logged nearly 100,000 miles running passenger trains exclusively. Corridor engineers between New York and Washington average 3,000 miles weekly—roughly 150,000 miles annually—the same mileage it would have taken an engineer three years to accumulate under the old regulated mileage formula.

Regrettably, some junior engineers have never run a freight train, having been hired from the ranks of trainmen who previously worked as coach attendants and dining car waiters, and before that as everything from plumbers to homemakers to airline pilots.

This is not to say that they aren't proficient or knowledgeable. It's just that to hear them complain about their job, you wonder how they would ever have survived a career at the throttle of a 250-car junk train, pulled by five or six broken-down, smoking, slippery U25Cs with brakes sticking in sub-freezing ice and snow. Believe me, there have been nights on conductor Henry Whitmore's SCL Bellwood Switcher cab when I dined on Spam, pork'n beans, and coffee that tasted every bit as delicious as T-bone, truffles, and champagne. I still keep sardines and saltines in my grip out of habit.

Noted one old engineer I once fired for, "All you have on the railroad is your seniority and a few friends." Depending on how you exercise your seniority, you could end up with even fewer friends. Seniority determines which job you work, which day(s) you have off, and when you take vacation. Not intending to be curt when my mother-in-law asked how many years it would be before I could take vacation at Christmas, I simply answered, "Never." The gap-tooth smiles and joyful squeals of a young child racing down the stairs in the predawn darkness of Christmas morning to discover Santa's bounty are experiences reserved for railroaders to enjoy with their grandchildren.

Only six months after having vowed to love, honor, and obey a beautiful young school teacher, I secured a promise from my road foreman in Rocky Mount that I would be allowed off for our first Christmas together. This pact with the devil meant that the preceding week I could not attend the wedding of my new bride's brother—a choice her family has never truly forgiven me for making. When I called the crew clerk to mark off on Christmas Eve, I was told that no such promise was ever recorded, and that under no circumstances could I be off. The tearful plane-side farewell between Ingrid Bergman and Humphrey Bogart in CASABLANCA was not nearly as heart wrenching as the Christmas Eve goodbye we shared as I climbed aboard Auto Train No. 3 at Richmond. I would not return until the arrival of the northbound Palmetto late Christmas Day.

I was allowed to deadhead to Rocky Mount that night for the trip to Florence, South Carolina, on my train, instead of having to fight traffic on I-95. Equally "excited" about being torn away from his new bride, engineer Barry Kennedy caught up on the fly at Rocky Mount, oblivious to the revelers in the full-length red, white, and purple dome cars who gathered around the piano, sang carols, and toasted the season with egg nog. The cold December rain that quickly froze on the U36B's windshield and seeped through the windy crack around its front door formed misty halos on the colorful lights, illuminated Santas, and candle-lit manger scenes in the windows of isolated homes in the pine woods and shuttered businesses in the small hamlets we streaked through.

Even the empty vending machines at the Heart of Downtown Motel and the Florence Amtrak station mimicked Scrooge on Christmas morning. Since no restaurants or convenience stores were open, when the Palmetto pulled through track four, we held the train captive, refusing to move it until we could be served something to eat. That night at Richmond, my wife's embrace, reheated ham biscuits, and a few gaily wrapped packages were all that remained of the sumptuous feast and the mountain of presents my family had excitedly torn into that day. More or less confirming Pavlov's theory of learned reaction, after 22 years of heightened and dashed hopes, "Jingle Bells" sadly elicits a more cynical than joyous response from me.

As you may now have guessed, railroad marriages—truly successful ones, that is—

are as rare as operative E units in the 1990s. There are few spouses with the perseverance to accept the constant absence of their mate, the almost single-handed raising of a family, and the inability to commit to even the simplest of social obligations, usually scheduled on weekends. On our second date, my future wife and I stood on the steps of the Richmond Coliseum, attempting to sell two front row tickets for a Billy Joel concert we could not attend. When my beeper sounded as we parked our car, I called the crew clerk and was told that I risked the loss of my job should I refuse to work the Silver Meteor as the flagman. Many times since, I have attempted to purchase Billy Joel tickets and fly to the concert site, if necessary, to atone for my sin that night, but obtaining those tickets is almost as difficult as maintaining a railroad marriage. Like most spouses, my wife hates the railroad but loves the paycheck.

Because Amtrak trains run on an advertised schedule as opposed to the anytime, any-day nature of most freight assignments, it might be reasonably assumed that those of us who work exclusively in passenger service should be able to enjoy some degree of predictability in scheduling our private life. Quite often, however, we do not. Purchasing a new suit for my son and a blazer for myself to wear to church Easter Sunday, for instance, proved to be a jinx. I spent 20 minutes replacing a sealed beam headlight and attempting to restore the loss of headend electrical power on the Silver Star at Southern Pines, North Carolina. Added to the 20 minutes lost by the Jacksonville crew that delivered the train to me 45 minutes late after stopping to work on the same problem at Hamlet, left just enough time for me to pop into the rear pew just as our pastor pronounced the benediction.

While my life is not as overtly dangerous as the life of a law enforcement officer or circus acrobat, when the closing garage door announces that I have left for work, my wife stirs, no matter how soundly she has been sleeping. Although we involuntarily avoid discussing the possibilities, we recognize that for all of the safety slogans and reassurances, one thing has not changed about railroad employment since the first flanged wheel rolled on strap iron covered stringers: Death and injury come hand-in-hand with the territory.

The front page of the September 22, 1987, McKeesport, Pennsylvania, DAILY NEWS features a picture of grips being handed down to fireman Dave Simms and me from the cab of the Capitol Limited's lead F40, No. 355, by CSX engineer pilot Norm Spall after we had derailed on Pittsburgh & Lake Erie, at Portvue, Pennsylvania, the previous night. What is not immediately evident is that the engine is buried up to the coupler in what had been a parallel road, less than 100 yards from our Youghiogheny River crossing and less than 50 feet from a gas main. Nor is it visible that on the far side of our derailed train is a loaded CSX ore train we averted striking head-on by luckily and uncontrollably rolling over on the opposite side of the right-of-way.

As a large brick warehouse rushed closer and closer toward us, Dave kept shouting, "We're going to hit the building! We're going to hit it!"

"Better that than the train coming at us on number two track!" I yelled. "Shoot'em! CSX freight train, shoot'em!" I screamed into the radio handset. "This is Amtrak 29, and we've derailed." Up north, they say you've "upset" the train—an oddly polite reference, it would seem, for such a traumatic experience. Down south, we're less formal. "Shoot'em" is a desperate cry uttered only in the most extreme of situations, calling for an emergency application of the brakes, yielding an unnerving boom, and thus the term. The ore train's engineer later told me that he had no idea what "Shoot'em" meant, but that when he determined that our engine was floundering, noticed sparks flying, and saw the red emergency strobe flashing, he had a pretty good idea of what I was trying to say. He put his train into emergency and also hit the deck.

Earlier, on August 15, about 10 miles west, with the fog-veiled morning skyline of Pittsburgh in the background, everything but the lead truck of my three-engine, 14-car eastbound Capitol Limited came to rest between the spread rails. Passengers in the dining car had to be informed that we had derailed, since the headend power, air hoses, and cars remained coupled and upright. A few months later, westbound near Connellsville, Pennsylvania, in the dark and drizzle that hid the roaring whitewater rapids of the Youghiogheny, racing far below the ledge which carried the former Baltimore & Ohio doubletracked main line around treacherous outcroppings of Allegheny Mountain slate and shale, we struck a Volkswagen-sized boulder. While it did not derail the train, lead unit 383 was disabled, and the dining car was left spotted pre-cariously beneath the source of the original slide, which continued to shower us with chunks of rock until emergency repairs were made and the train moved to Connellsville. When I meet Dave these days, now an experienced corridor engineer in Washington, we can laugh about it. But each time we uncork the vial from which escape the memories of those terrifying moments, we recall more of the details that were otherwise repressed, and we consider ourselves even more fortunate.

There is no way to truthfully describe the eruption of human emotion that is set off by the deafening exhaust of the emergency air brake valve. The slack runs in and you sit there in utter and total helplessness, witnessing a light show of sparks that illu-minates the darkness. The acrid odor of steel upon steel permeates the cab. Your heart races. Your stomach empties. You violently attempt to scream, as if your protestations will prevent the thousands of tons of locomotives, coaches, and human cargo from altering its inevitable course. With the specter of death a millisecond away, the instinct for self preservation takes hold, and you hurl yourself to the floor, hoping that the weight of the engine will be enough to keep that flange on the rail, that the structural integrity of the cab will sustain a rollover, and that God will be merciful to you, your passengers, and your crew.

Impact. The locomotive heaves and lurches. As it returns to earth, the ballast thunders and shakes the cab floor. Your engine has left the rails in an erratic stampede and is plowing up the roadbed and right-of-way in search of something to halt it. Objects never thought capable of movement take flight throughout the cab as if weightless. For what seems an eternity, you are tossed about, striking the console, the walls, the seat. Inside this shuddering, tilting pinball machine, as lights flash and bells ring, both the atheist and the believer beseech a Supreme Being for intercession.

Just as suddenly, the silence becomes deafening. In the dust and dirt, you realize you're still alive. Aching and bleeding, you pull yourself up onto your elbows, then your knees. Not sensing the odor of fuel oil from the locomotive, you pray as you search for a light and fusees among the debris to protect your train from being hit by another. Still terrified, with radio in hand, you try to remember who you are, where you are, and what you want to say. With luck you reach the dispatcher and help arrives.

Not your typical day at the office. Not the typical day on the railroad. But when it happens, whether or not it occurs on your division or even on your railroad, there is a shared feeling for what the man or woman at the throttle has gone through.

Focusing again on the young schoolgirl, before all of these thoughts spill out into a class of 10 and 11 year olds, the tongue is restrained and the memories tempered. At this point in their young lives, the passing train means a friendly wave and a special toot on the horn from the man in the cab. Their imagination is stimulated as they wonder where all of those people are going, how fast the train is traveling—a thousand questions for each clang of the crossing bell. Finally, in answering her, you simply say, "It's a very hard job with a lot of challenges and demands on you and your family, not a lot different from your mommy or daddy's job." The innocent, satisfied smile tells you that you've said the right thing.

Chapter 14: Why Don't They Learn?

In America, we traditionally mark the transition from adolescence to adulthood using the family automobile as a reference point—more specifically, the age at which one learns to drive it. Crossing the bridge into the land of maturity would not be possible without the indoctrination received in Driver Education. At the tender age of 15 years, I ambled into a large classroom located in the gymnasium at Henrico High School to begin a week of instruction on the rules of the road—a prerequisite for actual behind-the-wheel tutoring, which would follow during the long, hot summer of 1965.

As the bell rang to signal the beginning of my sixth period class, word quickly spread throughout the crowd of 30 rowdy teenage boys that we would be viewing SIGNAL 30, a frightening film primer intended to alert us to the dire consequences should we fail to take serious this important new privilege of motor vehicle operation. Produced to counter the intoxicating TV commercials depicting life in the fast lane, SIGNAL 30 and other equally horrifying driver education movies injected stark, shocking realism into those idyllic teenage fantasies. Considered too violent, insensitive, or at least politically incorrect by today's standards, these films are no longer shown. Judging from the paled complexions, lowered eyes, and quiet voices of those who exited the classroom then, they served their purpose.

Entering the room, Coach Wayne Lowry looked strangely out of his element dressed in a jacket and tie, rather than his customary green-and-yellow Henrico Warrior sweatshirt and shorts.

"No," Lowry growled. "You're not going to see SIGNAL 30, not today. What you are going to see is more important. There are a lot of railroad tracks around here, and a lot of people get themselves killed ignoring the warning signals that a train is coming. I don't care what you've got under the hood. You may be able to beat everyone else drag racing across Broaddus's Flats on Saturday night, but you can't win against a train at a railroad crossing. Even if you tie, you lose."

Blinds drawn, lights out, the thin strip of celluloid began winding through the chattering gears of the projector, casting its flickering image onto the screen. The familiar C&O herald appeared on the screen, accompanied by an ensemble of trumpets and percussion and the words, "Presented in the public interest by the Chesapeake & Ohio Railway."

The image of two men—one a uniformed passenger conductor, the other an engi-

neer clad in the full regalia of pinstriped bibs and hat, gauntlet gloves, and red bandana—
took form in contrast to the backdrop of Armour yellow, silver, and the reflections of
flashing red emergency lights. The scream of sirens and a stream of static-laced radio
transmissions punctuated the surrounding darkness and occasionally overrode the
throaty, shuddering rumble I immediately recognized as the unmistakable signature of a
twin engined Union Pacific E8 at idle. Panning slowly to the left, the camera revealed
the crumpled remains of an automobile, its doorpost held firmly in the fist-like death grip
of the locomotive's front coupler.

As if reading from a cue card, a mechanically paced, deadpan, monotone, obviously "real life" engineer asked his equally emotionless conductor, "Why don't they learn,
Ralph? Why don't they learn?"

Thirty years later, I can't even recall its title, only its story line. A popular high
school athlete, late for his graduation, tried to beat the train and lost. When motorists
risk their lives and gamble those of their passengers in front of my onrushing train,
Ralph and his engineer appear on my mind's center stage, and I join them in asking,
"Why don't they learn?"

Raised national consciousness regarding highway/rail crossing safety has prompted a lot of people to ask: How can a society possess the ability to place the entire contents of a library on a computer chip and not be able to prevent such an awful occur-
rence? Sadly, the technology does exist, but, unfortunately, there has to be a commitment—not only in terms of money and manpower—but a personal commitment on
behalf of government, industry, and the motoring public to eradicate this non-biologi-
cal plague on our land.

Ideally, the answer is to eliminate every opportunity for such collisions by closing
thousands of existing crossings in favor of bridges or underpasses. Future highway planning should prohibit grade crossings entirely. Either remedy is costly, as is the cost of
erecting elaborate warning systems at the remaining crossings where grade separation
would not be feasible or practical.

All of the flashing lights, lowered gates, as well as public awareness generated by
Operation Lifesaver and other safety agencies are totally useless if the lights are ignored
and the gates are run around. Amazingly, almost one-half of all incidents take place at a
crossing where gates and/or flashing lights are already in place.

Survivors of a crossing accident always offer a good excuse; the dead can't argue.

The first crossing accident in which I was involved as an engineer occurred near
Richmond on Christmas Eve many years ago, in a storm of mixed snow and sleet. While
this might have created a festive wonderland for tykes awaiting Saint Nick, it posed a dangerous, wintry hazard for those on their way home. Through the windshield I could see what
I thought were crossing flashers ahead in the darkness, but it struck me that they were
steadily lit, not flashing. I had spied instead the rear brake lights of a station wagon hung
on the track, its tires wedged tightly between crossing and rail. I put the five-engine, 150-
car freight train into emergency, grabbed my radio, and alerted a southbound freight
approaching on the opposite track to likewise put his brakes in emergency. "Shoot'em 109,"
I pleaded. "This is 110. We've hit a car blocking both tracks."

Around the next curve, the reflection of a red oscillating headlight on the wet rail and crossties between us appeared. An obviously excited engineer, J. T. McGuire, blurted out, "Damn, fella, you called this one close." We stopped, facing each other, less than a quarter mile apart, the station wagon—what was left of it—under my engine, blocking both tracks.

"There were three women in that car coming home from the office Christmas party," came a voice from the darkness. Grabbing my flashlight, I began searching the wreckage, expecting to find the worst. The tailgate lay on the hood of the car, and I discovered that I could put my hands on the headlights and taillights simultaneously, but I found no evidence of victims.

"Oh, they got out when the gates came down and the bell started ringing," the man volunteered drawing closer. Thank God. Most people are frozen in fear or die attempting to move their car. Few have the presence of mind to get out and save themselves, while nearly everyone has auto insurance.

"This is going to be a horrible Christmas," he added shaking his head. "That's my car. My wife was driving it."

"Your wife is alive, and you're upset about the car?" I raged. "Tell her the train's engineer thinks she's an exceptionally alert woman in a crisis, but a poor judge of character to have married such a sorry, dumb ass as you."

On average, nationally, there are 15 collisions daily between trains and motor vehicles. Two people die. Twice as many are injured. Add the staggering number of trespassers who are killed or maimed, and you can understand why railroaders shun strangers on or near the tracks.

As a working locomotive engineer, crossing safety is a primary concern, because with the increased size and weight of highway vehicles and the dangerous commodities they carry, trains are derailed, locomotives are engulfed in flames, and railroaders die far too often.

I am frequently called upon as a spokesperson for the Brotherhood of Locomotive Engineers and Operation Lifesaver. Returning home from my trip at the throttle of the New England Express on the same day as an Illinois collision between a school bus and a Metra commuter train, I received a call from Ray McAllister, a columnist for the Richmond TIMES-DISPATCH. In the past, I have been very vocal about school bus safety at railroad crossings and have been personally responsible for the firing of three drivers. The laws in our state are very specific: Every bus must stop clear of the tracks, open the door, and not proceed if a train is seen or heard to be approaching, or if there is doubt that the entire bus can safely clear the right-of-way. As an engineer, I react to each violation as if my own son were aboard. However, not knowing the specifics of that accident, I deemed it then (as I do now) inappropriate for me to comment, but I did offer him insight as to what the engineer might be going through. What appeared in the following day's edition was an excellent piece on a seldom broached aspect of grade crossing tragedies: The effect on the man at the throttle, not only in that split second just before impact, but in the minutes, days, and years following a fatality.

Since the tragedy, I have scanned hundreds of publications and read of the grief of loved ones, the outpouring of sympathy from the community, the outrage of the American public, and the assigning of blame; but little is said about the engineer. Before I'm branded as an insensitive opportunist, let me tell you that I know my Uncle Ashby only from his brass memorial plaque in the shade of a giant oak tree at Forest Lawn Cemetery and faded black and white photographs. A J Class Norfolk & Western steam locomotive ended his life at a crossing near Crew, Virginia, before I was old enough to appreciate his kindness. When I think of him, again I ask, "Why?"

If I had a dollar for every time someone has offered to figuratively trade his or her firstborn child for the opportunity to sit in my seat at the throttle of a speeding passenger locomotive, I'd be able to retire tomorrow and live comfortably off of the interest until I reached the age of 100. If I were given a quarter for each one of those same people who could climb back into the cab of my locomotive once exposed to the abject horror of seeing human remains hosed down off the front of an F40, I wouldn't have sufficient funds to buy a cup of coffee.

How do you live with it? Some people do better than others. Some sit back down in the seat and take their train into the next terminal. Others never come back. I guess the rest of us fall into the middle somewhere. In the middle of the night, I've awakened from nightmares screaming and crying. I still do at times.

I was at the throttle of the Silver Star when I was involved in my first accident that resulted in a fatality. Corky Price Sr. was my fireman. As I blew for a crossing on the fringe of a large North Carolina city, a cream-colored sedan streaked across the horizon.

"Oh, God!" I screamed, "He's not even slowing down." I put the 18-car Florida streamliner's brakes into emergency. I pulled the horn handle, as if by doing so I could somehow guide my train and its passengers out of harm's way. I awaited the crash I knew was inevitable. Even the massive tonnage of the EMD F40 could not totally absorb the impact. Not knowing whether the locomotive had merely caught a front or rear bumper, or whether it had delivered a severe blow to the car's midsection, I looked in vain at my side mirror to see if the errant motorist has made it all the way across. He had not.

"We've hit a car! We've hit a car! Emergency! Emergency! Emergency!" I shouted into the radio handset, giving the exact milepost location. Slowing from the impact speed of 43 mph, the dining car, midway in the train, stopped in the center of the crossing. Patrons looked up from their meals to behold a car, crushed like an eggshell, with smoke and steam pouring from where its engine had been.

"Norfolk Southern dispatcher to No. 81, I've got the location. How bad is it?" responded the voice.

Grabbing the radio, Corky answered, "Send rescue units. Possible fatalities." Looking at me with understanding, he said, "We're stopped now. You can let go of the horn. You don't want to go back there. I will." I could only nod.

After a few minutes, he returned. "There's one fatality, a man. The police want you to come back there and give them some information."

"I'm not getting off this engine," I responded. "As long as I don't have to look at it, as long as I can separate myself from it, it just didn't happen. I can live with it, I think, I hope."

I was ordered off the engine by the local authorities and made to fill out the accident report on (what was left of) the hood of the car, inches away from the covered remains of the victim wedged between the windshield and the dashboard. Totally numb, I struggled to answer what seemed like a million questions from the police and railroad authorities—simple ones like my own name, birth date, phone number, and address—and hard ones like what speed I was traveling at impact, and the year and make of my vehicle. Railroad officials boarded my engine, removed the speed tapes from the event recorders, and replaced them with fresh ones. Drug tests are not required following a crossing accident except, when in the opinion of the investigating authorities, there is reason to believe that an employee is impaired.

Satisfied that I would subject no one to liability, we were allowed to depart the scene. I've never been able to adequately thank him for doing so, but Corky ran the train to Hamlet, North Carolina, while I sat there in the fireman's seat, barely able to keep my composure. The following morning, we deadheaded home. The following New Year's Day, when he himself hit a small child standing on the edge of the crossties, I was there to offer some degree of comfort and understanding, although, once again, he held up better than I.

My working agreement allows for me to use one day of my vacation following a fatality, and Amtrak, as well as most other railroads, has employee assistance programs, where counselors are available to help employees cope with emotionally crippling occurrences. But then it's back in the saddle.

Section 3

What Track Are We On? Amtrak!

Chapter 15: Right Track, Wrong Train

The merger that created CSX meant a lot of changes for me as a Seaboard Coast Line locomotive engineer in the years following my return from Rocky Mount after being promoted. Eighteen months had passed and Richmond was not the same place.

While I was away, a large number of senior employees I had worked with my first months on the railroad had left. A few had passed away, some had gone by normal attrition, and still others had been "bought out" by SCL, in order to free the railroad from the constraints placed upon it by guarantees of employment (or compensation in lieu of work) to railroaders adversely affected by the 1967 merger. Seaboard Coast Line eagerly offered incentives for early retirement or voluntary separation, which were willingly accepted by many former Atlantic Coast Line and Seaboard Air Line employees.

"Did you hear the news?" one very excited engineer shouted as he entered the lobby of the Rocky Mount YMCA one humid summer afternoon in 1982.

"What news is that, Frank?" I responded, looking up from the color TV screen showing *Family Feud*.

"The railroad is going to offer $10,000 to any engineer who is willing to quit!" he said as he signed the register book and slipped his room key into the pocket of his faded Levis.

"Oh, that news," I feigned, reeling in another foil for one of my practical jokes. "Yes, indeed. Your conductor and flagman just told me about it."

Astonished, he dropped his bags and walked over to me. "What did they have to say about it? Is it really true?"

"Of course it is. They even said that if you would take the $10,000 the company was offering, they'd match it just to get rid of you!" I roared, no longer able to keep a straight face.

"You sonofabitch!" he retorted, slamming the door to the dormitory's first-floor hallway, prompting a few half-asleep heads to poke out from their rooms to investigate the ruckus. "You and your damn disc jockey humor. Funny! Real funny!"

Although the ranks of those ahead of me on the seniority roster began to thin substantially, changes in traffic patterns, now feasible because of previously cost-prohibitive abandonments and consolidations, meant I was taking one step forward but two steps backward. While I crept closer to the top of the pecking order, I was still one of the most junior employees. Instead of being No. 498 on a list of 500 engineers, I was soon No. 398

on a list of 400 engineers, and later 298 out of 300.

Employment gains associated with CSX's export grain traffic, diverted across Hampton Roads harbor from Newport News on Chesapeake & Ohio to Portsmouth on SAL, were offset by the loss of much of SCL's Portsmouth to Rocky Mount through freight business. Once the heart of SAL's northern region, Raleigh was stripped of its division headquarters; the once busy CTC dispatched main line began seeing more weeds than trains; and rumors were circulating that most of the route of the *Silver Meteor* would soon be abandoned from Richmond to Savannah, and the rails would be taken up. The smaller yards and yard assignments at most terminals on the system evaporated into thin air.

Employees not covered by the "orange" book (those who hired out after the ACL/SAL merger at points slated for abandonment or reduced service) gravitated to terminals that were expected to see an increase in business. Initially, commuting hundreds of miles to work or living in temporary lodging, then putting their homes up for sale and preparing to move themselves and their families to places like Richmond and Rocky Mount, where they would displace workers with less service.

For those with respectable seniority, it was merely an inconvenience. For others, who had little or no accumulated time on the railroad, it became a hardship. With only so many jobs to be filled by a like number of employees, it was similar to the child's game of musical chairs: some people were left with no place to go when the tune stopped.

As a large contracting carrier, SCL was also greatly affected by increases and reductions in Amtrak's schedules. As a trainman, I had worked the two-car, Boston-Cattletsburg, Kentucky, *Hilltopper* when it plied the rails between Richmond and Petersburg daily after its inception in June 1977. It was probably Amtrak's most unusual looking train. Owing to the lack of a wye track where it took to the former Norfolk & Western interchange track at Collier Yard, south of Petersburg, it initially ran with a steam generator-equipped Richmond, Fredericksburg & Potomac GP7 hauling a P30CH and two Amfleet coaches "backwards" in both directions for the 35 miles between the two Virginia cigarette-manufacturing cities. In 1978, Amtrak rebuilt the three-mile-long Pocahontas connection and wye—with a westward quadrant—accessing N&W at the venerable old joint ACL/N&W downtown Petersburg passenger station (last used by the Norfolk-Chicago *Mountaineer* in 1977), thereby negating the need for the second locomotive. The train, however, did not use the historic station, but instead stopped two blocks west of it on the road crossing at Fleet Street, under the old SAL Appomattox River Bridge. It was just as well, because a short time later, Congress, in one of its spastic reactions to Amtrak funding, tightened its purse strings, lopping the *Hilltopper* off, along with the *Floridian*, *Champion*, *Cardinal*, *National Limited*, and *North Coast Hiawatha* in October 1979. Having just entered engine service in April that year, I narrowly dodged the old unemployment bullet once again.

I found work for a short period beginning in October 1984 as an engineer on Amtrak's New York-Charlotte *Carolinian*, which originally ran over SAL's now abandoned Norlina Subdivision between Richmond and Raleigh; but it was terminated less than a year later. The train was unfortunately promoted as a "North Carolina" train. While it ran packed within the Tar Heel state, most of its riders weren't even aware that they could continue to Washington and New York and make connections at other Northeast Corridor points for destinations across the country. The present *Carolinian*'s tremendous success is indicative of what can be done with rail passenger service when insightful marketing, thorough planning, and jurisdictional cooperation are properly orchestrated.

One of the biggest blows was the slow death of the original *Auto Train* in 1981. Paralyzed by a series of costly and debilitating derailments, it was unable to perform essential maintenance on its General Electric U36Bs. Toward the very end, the engine consists were totally devoid of anything even resembling purple, red, and white diesels. It was only after daily prepayment had been received by SCL in Jacksonville and by RF&P in Richmond that the long mixed train (herded along the Eastern Seaboard by an assortment of Amtrak E9s, SCL GP40s, Family Lines GP38s, and even a cab signal-equipped RF&P SW1500 yard engine) was permitted access to the main line.

Amtrak's announcement that it had acquired rights to operate the two-year dormant *Auto Train* received mixed reactions, because the newly refurbished train would be operated by hourly-paid Amtrak employees, not traditional mileage-compensated contracting freight carrier crews. Congress mandated that Amtrak hire its own train and engine service personnel, after negotiating revolutionary, cost-cutting working agreements with the operating unions, which it did in the Northeast Corridor beginning January 1, 1983.

Amtrak owned its own tracks between Washington and Boston, but the unions balked at the idea that it would be legal for Amtrak to use its own engineers and trainmen outside of that corridor. On October 30, 1983, Amtrak's *Auto Train* began tri-weekly service between Lorton, Virginia, and Sanford, Florida, manned by Amtrak's own crews. Those crews had familiar faces, however, because Amtrak wisely agreed to hire from mileage apportioned application pools of RF&P and SCL employees in seniority order, all entitled to work over the route the *Auto Train* would take.

Those who rejected the invitation to work in *Auto Train* service, and those of us too junior for initial consideration, watched with great apprehension as the big P30CHs glided through Acca Yard at Richmond and past the passenger station at Rocky Mount, without the traditional crew change. Except to pick up pilot engineers and conductors until Amtrak's own people could be fully qualified, a single crew change at Florence was now made, instead of the previously required seven swaps. Even more disturbing was the thought that if Amtrak could do this with the *Auto Train*, what would prevent it from doing it with all of its other trains?

On November 3, 1983, I was deadheaded to Rocky Mount on the *Silver Meteor* to be the pilot engineer for the train's second northbound trip. Instructed to go to the Rocky Mount YMCA to get my rest and await my call, I sat in the lobby with some of my fellow freight crew members, where a heated discussion about the use of non-SCL employees on Amtrak trains ensued.

"I never worked passenger service, even though I stood for it," one fellow said, "but they ought to shoot the rotten sonofabitches who went over to *Auto Train* to scab!"

"How can you call them scabs?" I asked. "They're people we've worked side by side with for years, and besides, our unions signed the agreement."

"Hell," he roared, "before they shoot the scabs, they ought to use the union offi-cials for target practice!"

As a local union official, I frowned and took exception to his remark. I knew that despite all of the bad press unions receive, Congress has a propensity for stepping in at the threat of a strike and appointing a Presidential Emergency Board (PEB) under provi-sions of the Railway Labor Act. The PEB—after much consideration—had a history of doing little more than rubber stamping rail management's wish list. Given Congress's desire to put a tourniquet on NRPC's red balance sheet, though it made a ripe subject for sand house discussion, what Amtrak was doing was probably very legal. What was even worse, it probably wouldn't end with the *Auto Train*.

It seemed that I had just closed the door, cut out the light, and put my head down on the wafer-thin pillow at the head of the small, narrow bed in the cramped cubical at the Y, when a knock came, followed by a familiar, raspy whisper—the voice of the call boy nicknamed "Preacher."

"Ry-dell, you're called to pilot the *Auto Train*, on duty at 5:10 a.m. to leave at 5:40, but the dispatcher says he's running so good that he might get here at 5:15."

"What time is it now?" I managed to mutter while yawning.

"5 a.m.!" he responded. "Your orders are next to the register book at the station."

"Thanks for the short call," I laughed. "I need the extra sleep."

Still clad in my shirt and trousers, I slipped on my shoes, joined the conductor pilot downstairs, poured a cup of coffee, signed out, and walked across the grass plot separating the Rocky Mount Family YMCA from the old ACL passenger station. Nearing the reg-ister room, I heard a horn blowing for Bassett Street. I had just enough time to sign the register, confirm that the numbers on the clearance card correctly corresponded to those orders stapled to it, read them over, and amble outside to the waiting train.

No. 52, the northbound *Auto Train*, was led by F40PH 277, trailed by P30CHs 707, 705, and some 40 coaches and car carriers. Amtrak *Auto Train* engineer Mike Childress, with whom I had worked as a brakeman and for whom I had fired on the Bellwood Switcher, greeted me at the door. Along with his assistant engineer (they never called them firemen on the *Auto Train*), there was Road Foreman of Engines Howard Godwin and Amtrak Trainmaster Al Scala, who would later become my boss, when I came to work at Amtrak.

"What am I, the chaperone?" I said, nodding to Mike. "You're most certainly qual-ified from here to Richmond. You need me like a hole in the head."

"We'll be using pilots until each engineer is fully qualified all the way," someone answered from a dark corner of the packed locomotive cab. "It's much simpler to have them called and waiting than to have to find one in a pinch."

With quite ample power, we accelerated out of the sleepy railroad town in the blink of an eye. I was used to the sluggish U36Bs on the old *Auto Train*. This was a treat. Later, I felt a bit awkward with so many people in the cab as the rising sun glistened on the falls of the Appomattox River at Petersburg. The trip went well, except for the times the radio crackled with taunts of "scab" and "traitor" when we passed some yard engines and a standing freight train at Collier, and when someone tripped the wrong circuit breaker in our locomotive cab's control cabinet as we passed FA Tower nearing

Richmond. This caused a penalty application of the brakes, which stopped the train dead.

"We'll probably start operating this train daily next year," Scala said. "Have you got your application in yet?"

"Oh," I nodded in the affirmative, "I've got my name in the hat."

At Acca Yard, the RF&P pilot met me at the bottom rung of the ladder, traded engine data, and asked, "They your scabs or ours?"

I entered the crew clerk's office, registered off, and was informed that I had been cut back to being a fireman. I marked up on the joint C&O/SCL train from Richmond to Portsmouth, Virginia, and by the end of the following week, I didn't even stand for that job.

On November 20, I fired for Si Cottrell on the Richmond-Rocky Mount local freight, which diverted off the old doubletrack ACL main line at Pender, North Carolina, to make the last trip ever over the Kinston Subdivision to Scotland Neck, picking up any cars located on sidings before the track was torn up and carried away. At Tillery, a small town with a post office, a gas station, and a couple of sleeping hound dogs, I recorded the sad event on film, as I spotted SCL GP38 554, U36B 1828, and GP40-2 1636 at the dilapidated clapboard freight depot. Glancing at the crossing, I thought for a moment about the hundreds of trains of potatoes, cotton, peanuts, and farm machinery that had traversed those rails. Watching two small urchins walking along the highway that crossed the tracks, I wondered, "Is this the last train they will ever see?"

For the next year or so (1984), and from week to week, I bounced back and forth between being the oldest passenger fireman and the youngest extra board engineer. Two significant things happened that year. First, while I held a 4 p.m. to midnight engineer's job at Acca Yard on RF&P (we were given a share of their jobs after our own Hermitage Yard closed and the work was consolidated there), my wife gave birth to our son, Ryan, on June 8. Secondly, true to Al Scala's prediction, Amtrak decided that there was sufficient business to warrant daily *Auto Train* operation.

"We're interviewing applicants for jobs on the *Auto Train*, Mr. Riddell," the caller informed me. "Please arrange to come to Union Station in Washington to take a physical examination and meet Superintendent Stan Bagley."

As the two-hour-late *Silver Meteor* headed north from Richmond's suburban Greendale Station, I noticed a familiar face in the dining car, where I prepared to devour French toast for breakfast. Buddy Rogers had entered engine service at Rocky Mount right after I did, and we had hostled together. A Rocky Mount native, Buddy remained there after the rest of us transplanted Virginians went home at the conclusion of our 18-month contractual obligation. There were also some applicants from Florida, who would be hired to work out of Sanford.

As it turned out, there was only one position on the north end. It was going to be Buddy or me. Since I was senior to him, the job would be offered to me first. Stan Bagley, now acting vice president of Amtrak's Northeast Corridor Business Unit, was cordial and informative. After explaining where and how we would work, what we would be paid, and what was expected of us, he opened the floor for questions.

"Will I be restricted to *Auto Train* if Amtrak assumes direct operation of all other passenger trains?" I asked.

"I personally would like to think that as pioneer Amtrak employees you would be placed at the top of any seniority roster," he smiled, but added, "The decision, however, is up to your labor union. Mr. Riddell, you have 48 hours to accept our offer of employment. Then Mr. Rogers will be given the opportunity to bid for the job."

I thanked him and said good-bye to Buddy, who had to wait for the *Meteor* to get to Rocky Mount, while I took the *Star* to Richmond.

"Let me know what you decide as soon as you make up your mind," Buddy urged me. "With things drying up like they are, I know what my answer is: Yes!"

I was not so certain. I wanted to work the *Auto Train*, but I didn't want to relocate to northern Virginia. More importantly, I didn't want to be limited to working the *Auto Train* exclusively forever, even if Amtrak later offered employment to SCL employees, if it took over the *Meteor*, the *Star*, and the *Palmetto*. Two days later, I called Buddy and told him that the job was his if he wanted it.

As it turned out, I made the right decision—for me, at least, because when Amtrak exercised its option to hire employees to man its trains outside the Northeast Corridor in 1986, *Auto Train* employees were not given the right to work anywhere else but on the *Auto Train*. They were kept on a separate seniority roster until 1988, when they were placed at the bottom of the roster of engineers that operate Amtrak trains between Washington, points in the Southeast, and Pittsburgh (work zone 5), although they retain first priority on *Auto Train* assignments. Needless to say, there were strained relationships for many years between the persons hired for the *Auto Train* and those who were hired by Amtrak to staff its other southeastern trains.

My day was coming. Two years later, the phone would ring again, and I would again be asked to work for Amtrak. This time I would accept, and it would be the right decision.

Chapter 16: Amtrak—A View from the Cab

Like the knowledgeable quiz show contestant who has given all of the right answers so far, Amtrak has repeatedly been invited back to appear on the Congressional version of *Jeopardy*. But the network has changed hands, the budget has been slashed, and the sponsors are demanding more for their money. Despite its popularity with the audiences, this Supertrain may end up syndicated in select markets only or canceled entirely.

For many Amtrak employees, coming to terms with what we have learned about our own frail condition is as frightening as falling from a cliff and waiting to hit bottom. Former Amtrak President Claytor said Amtrak was growing stronger and would be able to walk on its own by 2000. But when Thomas Downs took over the practice, he diagnosed the condition as terminal, if not immediately treated.

I discussed the Northeast Corridor Improvement Act over dinner in 1984 with Charlie Luna, past president of the United Transportation Union and former Amtrak Board member, now deceased. To justify continued funding, Congress mandated that Amtrak reduce its losses by negotiating better terms with its unions and hiring its own operating employees. Firing up one of his trademark green cigars, Charlie said, "We either get those jobs for our members under Amtrak's conditions or face massive layoffs when they employ their own people. They have the power to do it. Look what they've already done on the Corridor and with *Auto Train*."

Later, as an officer in the Brotherhood of Locomotive Engineers, I was instrumental in securing seniority rights that entitled *Auto Train* engineers to work anywhere on the system and hold prior rights on the Washington Division.

Less than a year after my conversation with Charlie, Amtrak did serve notice that it intended to exercise its prerogative by hiring its own train and engine service employees outside the Northeast Corridor, modifying in-place agreements that provided for hourly pay and the virtual elimination of arbitrary payments, among other things. In doing so, Amtrak rewrote rail labor history and left its older freight counterparts envious. Though a few problems cropped up during implementation, the savings were substantial and immediate.

In return for an experienced, qualified work force, the unions negotiated, the freight railroads concurred with, Amtrak agreed to, and Congress passed into law protection for those of us who took the giant step into the unknown, should Amtrak fail. While technically on leave of absence, our freight railroad seniority was retained and accrued.

Thus, we could return to freight if we no longer stood for passenger work and could be recalled to Amtrak upon a reversal of fortunes. We were also allowed a one-time, one-way return to our home road at the end of a six-month trial period, or if a hardship arose, such as the death or serious illness of a family member. Amtrak employees remained covered by the prevailing industry-wide health and welfare package, the Federal Employer's Liability Act, and the Railroad Retirement System.

We were told that what we did probably saved Amtrak. That provided some degree of consolation to those of us who were called scabs and traitors by many of our former friends and coworkers who stayed in freight. Opting for passenger service, even under those unconventional working conditions, proved to be a wise decision when the freight railroads later won even more drastic work rule and benefit concessions from their employees. Nearly nine years later, there are some freight employees who still refuse to acknowledge radio transmissions in passing. Most, however, accept the reality that rail labor, faced with some tough and unpopular decisions, acted to preserve jobs that would otherwise have been lost.

Passenger work still accounted for about 25 percent of the Seaboard Coast Line jobs at Richmond on August 20, 1986. Fearing I would be force assigned hundreds of miles away from home for many years because of the loss of those jobs, I bid on a position with Amtrak. As engineer on the *Silver Meteor* to Rocky Mount, my job had been abolished at midnight as a result of the Amtrak takeover. Deadheading on the northbound *Meteor*, I arrived home about 5 a.m. Shortly after, the phone rang.

"It's Amtrak!" said my wife as she handed me the receiver.

"Mr. Riddell, John Stafford here. You've been awarded the Florence, South Carolina, fireman's extra board. We need to have your decision immediately, because if you accept, you'll be on No. 88 from Florence to Washington tonight. Can you be the pilot engineer? You'll need to hop on No. 89 this afternoon to get there."

"Florence, fireman's extra board," I whispered to my wife.

"Fireman? You're an engineer! We live in Richmond!" She began crying.

"Mr. Riddell, is everything okay? I hear someone screaming."

"My wife. Look, Mr. Stafford, can I have 30 minutes to think this over?"

"No longer than that, Mr. Riddell. We've got to protect the train."

After explaining the alternatives to my wife and telling her that I could probably hold a job out of Washington as soon as I was allowed to exercise my seniority, she regained her composure. Our son was two years old, we had just moved into a new home, and I had spent most of the last few weeks force assigned to a yard job in Portsmouth, Virginia, a two-hour commute each way daily. "I have to try it for six months. If I don't, I'll always regret it."

She reluctantly agreed and for the next 32 straight days, handed up food, clean clothes, and money to me on the fly, since the *Meteor*'s schedule didn't allow me the opportunity to come home from either Florence or Washington. On weekends my family would climb aboard at Richmond and spend the day with me in Washington, when I wasn't asleep at the Bellevue Hotel. There were many times I blew for the crossing at Glen Allen, knowing they heard the echo of the horn across the few miles that separated us in the stillness of the early Virginia morning. I wanted to get off. I wanted to go home. But I stayed.

I was lucky enough to work with W. S. "Buddy" Pitt, one of the few who returned to his home road, Richmond, Fredericksburg & Potomac, at the end of six months. Because I was qualified over the SCL from Richmond to Florence, I taught him my territory. In return, he tutored me on the 108-mile-long railroad that links north and south. As the sunrise bathed the Capitol dome that first quiet Sunday morning, Buddy jokingly promised, "This engine will fit into the First Street tunnel. Really it will." To this day, I duck my head.

Within a few weeks I held the fireman's job on the *Silver Star* between Washington and Hamlet, North Carolina, traversing the former Seaboard Air Line Norlina Subdivision. Because of the proportional allotment of jobs, determined by the aggregate passenger train mileage of the railroads from which we came, I found myself firing for R. J. Clark, although he had been with RF&P for just a short period of time.

A boomer and railfan who had hired out on the Rock Island in the 1950s, Bob initially went to MoPac when the Rock died. We not only made the last trip over the old Richmond, Petersburg, Capitol City Route (as SAL employees called the Norlina Sub), but also made the first Amtrak run between Raleigh and Selma, North Carolina, over the route now used by both the *Star* and *Carolinian*.

Before I had the opportunity to exercise my option to return to freight, I was promoted by Amtrak to engineer in January 1987, first working the list out of Washington and ever since holding a regular job at Richmond. I don't know whether it was the realization that I would stand for work as a passenger engineer the rest of my life, witnessing the glory of the valley below as I topped the Alleghenies at Sandpatch, or beholding the beautiful domed entrance to Penn Station at Pittsburgh, but—despite the hardships—I never really considered returning to freight.

In 1999, however, the choice may not be mine to make. The hardships we endured may not be enough. The gargantuan concessions our unions made are now termed paltry. The protection agreed upon to entice us to work for Amtrak is now deemed excessive, and legislation may be introduced in Congress for its repeal. Once lauded as trailblazers, we are now characterized as unproductive. Time and politics are fickle commodities that cruelly consider no promise binding.

I sometimes reflect on my childhood as I come out on the throttle and lean the eastbound *Virginian* into the roundhouse curve at Fulton Yard, the Nathan five-chime horn wailing across the James River basin and reverberating through the canyon of tall buildings that form Richmond's financial district. For a moment, I am back on a blue, gray, and yellow Chesapeake & Ohio E8, the harmonious vibrato of twin V12s sending a chill throughout my body as they accelerate the eight-car *George Washington* up the 1 percent grade of Airport Hill. Looking back, I see my grandfather, his awestruck 10-year-old grandson at his side, snatching flimsies on the fly from the operator at old R Cabin. As we roar past the towering coal tipple in a haze of smoke, sand, and cinders, the yard brakemen and car inspectors stand as though at attention, while all other activity ceases until the noise abates and the yellow Adlake kerosene markers disappear into the reverse curve at Scott Street. I don't know where tomorrow will find me, but this is where I long to be.

Chapter 17: Isthmus Be My Lucky Day

You'll never see my name listed as a Lotto winner—I don't play. Ed McMahon won't ring my doorbell since all of those thick yellow Publisher's Clearing House envelopes immediately go into the trash. Of course, I'm thrilled when my son brings me a four-leaf clover, plucked from one of the few green spots in our backyard, and my wife and I still argue about whether it's the long or the short piece of the wishbone which supposedly endows its holder with good fortune. I have never given much credence to the notion that the future can be altered by throwing salt over one's shoulder or by overstepping cracks in the sidewalk. After all, look at a rabbit's foot. He had four of them. What kind of luck did they bring him?

As a child, I would wake at my grandparents home early on Saturday mornings, slide down the banister, and raid the ice box, which was always stocked with cold bottles of Coca-Cola, before planting myself in front of the big 12-inch screen of our old Motorola black and white console television set. Except for grabbing the bright yellow box of Kellogg's Sugar Pops from the pantry shelf during commercials and station breaks, I seldom stirred until Dizzy Dean and Pee Wee Reese officially wrapped up coverage of the CBS Baseball Game of the Week.

My day started with *The Little Rascals*. In one episode, when told by his teacher to use the word "isthmus" in a sentence, Buckwheat naively answered, "Isthmus be my lucky day."

Through the years, that phrase has stayed with me. Sometimes I've turned frustration into laughter by uttering those words. Many times—but not Friday the 13th of October 1995.

At that time, I was working between Washington and Newport News, Virginia, as engineer on Amtrak's *New England/Tidewater Express*, Nos. 95 and 94. Because two Richmonders (Carl Lichtenberger and I) worked this Washington-based job, we were able to take advantage of the step-on/step-off agreement negotiated by the Brotherhood of Locomotive Engineers. When No. 94 arrived at Richmond each morning, rather than deadheading two hours to Union Station to work No. 95 to Newport News that afternoon, we alternately relieved each other at Richmond. This allowed us to spend a little more time with our families: 24 hours at home, 24 hours away three times a week.

"Look, bub," Carl's voice warned from his Newport News motel room early that morning, "you're going to have to do a complete cab signal/train control test [to operate over the former Richmond, Fredericksburg & Potomac]." Normally, the predeparture test at the Ivy City engine terminal in Washington, good for a 24-hour period, sufficiently covers the entire round trip. But that morning, I would have to retest and reseal the system before continuing north of Richmond. While it only took a few minutes, it proved to be a precursor of worse things.

Since Amtrak trains operate over many different railroads, most of its locomotives are equipped with a universal cab signal/train control system, which, when correctly set, displays the proper cab signal indications, while compensating electronically for the varying height-above-rails of the permanently mounted pickup bars located behind the locomotive's pilot. Occasionally, because of the vibration, temperature, and humidity encountered in the nose of a bouncing F40, the electronic amplification components become loose, making poor electrical contact and interrupting signal impulses. Or sometimes, after striking debris on the track, the pickup bars are damaged, with the same result. In either case, a penalty application of the train's air brakes is initiated as a safety feature.

As it turned out, following the train's departure from Richmond on Thursday, after having left the RF&P Subdivision, where cab signals and train control are in service, the overly sensitive pickup bars on No. 95's locomotive, F40 No. 337 (note, the digits add up to 13), evidently detected some errant electrical currents. Rationalizing that they were cab signal indications unacknowledged by the train's engineer, the system began causing penalty air brake applications, stopping the train. Thus, Carl had to unseal the train control and cut it out to get to Newport News.

Allowing for the extra time which would be consumed in the test, I searched the employee parking lot in vain for a space for my white 1988 Cadillac with license plate "AMTRAK 1." Even the public lot was full. Anyone who doubts the popularity of train travel need only come to Richmond. I parked in front of Carl's pickup, hoping to grab his spot when the train arrived.

Confirming my bulletin orders and form Ds with Conrail's Harrisburg dispatcher, and after receiving the necessary paperwork by CSX Jacksonville dispatcher Larry Quinton, I donned safety shoes and glasses. I then walked out onto the platform to meet the inbound train, compare watches, and hold a job briefing with conductor Gary Williams and assistant conductor Roy Doxtater before relieving Carl and making the cab signal/train control test. Carl was handing down grips to qualifying engineer Gary Male as we attempted to communicate with each other over the jet-like roar of aging No. 337.

"I need your parking space," I shouted. "Lot's full!"

"You got bigger problems than that, bub," Carl lamentably exclaimed, shaking his head. "We had to put cooling water in it before leaving the yard this morning, and it's bone dry already. The leak is right behind the low water and crankcase buttons."

With that said, he and Gary opened the large side doors of the locomotive and began feeding the platform water hose to the parched mouth of the cooling water retention tank, while I performed the train control test. After acknowledging the series of cab signal changes and testing the system's ability to activate a penalty air brake application and power cutout function, I ducked into the nose compartment to place a numbered wire seal on the cutout cock and dutifully record its identifying digits on the prescribed form.

"Everything else is all right," Carl chirped, with a look of relief that said everything about his journey. "Try to bring me a better one Saturday morning, Doug."

Back in the cab, I had restored the headend electrical power (HEP) to the darkened train and was adjusting the seat, sun visors, mirrors, and footrest in preparation for departure, when the radio blared, "Foreman Higgs to the engineer of No. 94. Doug, let me check that problem before you leave. If you run out of water up the road, you're a dead duck."

Paul Higgs, one of Amtrak's most willing and knowledgeable troubleshooters, consulted the MAP100 inspection report, quickly dropped the HEP, put the locomotive's power plant at low idle speed, and headed into the sweltering confines of No. 337's engine room. Minutes later, he returned.

"I can't find a leak of any size, anywhere back there. I guess you'll be okay to Washington. I'll call the movement desk and alert Ivy City of the problem," the tall, red-haired foreman told me as he exited the cab.

Just as a quartet of yellow-nosed CSX diesels eased by on parallel No. 2 main line, slowing train No. 413 with their whirring dynamic brakes before leading its mixed freight consist through the maze of crossovers at North Acca, conductor Gary Williams called out, "All right, No. 94, lets go to Fredericksburg."

Checking behind us in the mirrors, illuminating the headlight and ditch lights, activating the sanders to counteract the moisture on the rail, tugging twice on the horn, and observing a "clear" indication on the ground and in the cab, I eased out on the throttle, and the 20-year graduate of LaGrange responded grudgingly, inching the six-car Amfleet I consist away from Greendale.

"Amtrak 94 running straight up three track on a clear signal." Checking my watch, I added, "Eighteen minutes late, Gary. We've got to do better."

Fifty minutes ahead lay Fredericksburg, Virginia. Across the river from the elevated platforms of the RF&P passenger station, Ferry Farm (the boyhood home of George Washington) rests beside the lazy Rappahannock River. In stark contrast, the table land of the southern shoreline, teeming with today's harvests of wheat and soybeans, belies its earlier yield of unspeakable suffering as the scene of some of the bloodiest fighting of the American Civil War.

As I rounded the 40-mph curve and blew for our stop at the brightly decorated Virginia Railway Express commuter platform on track No. 2, I could think of nothing but immediately checking the cooling water sight glass in the engine room of No. 337. By myself in the cab for the entire trip, station stops normally present the only opportunity to go back and check the engine. Having seen no gushing stream being expelled from it at Richmond, I assumed that it might drop a few inches at most, serving to warn me that I would need to take water at the *Auto Train's* Lorton facility. I had already anticipated this and requested that CSX dispatcher Quinton put our train on No. 3 track, the westward of the two former RF&P main lines. I was hardly prepared to find the glass nearly empty.

Amtrak schedules no less than six arrivals and departures at Newport News on Fridays and Sundays. Even with this added capacity, north of Richmond, aisles quickly become standing room, and lounge table areas are converted to revenue seating.

Further exacerbating the problem are legions of unreserved VRE ticket honorees, who appear at Fredericksburg, Quantico, and Woodbridge. There were few smiling faces train side and on board when it became necessary to kill the HEP and place the locomotive on low idle to forestall its total shutdown. In between attempts to reach the dispatcher to inform him of the dilemma, I even poured my small plastic bottles of drinking water into the tank to prevent the "low water" protection device from activating, stilling the engine and stranding us.

Just as I reached dispatcher Quinton and began to explain that I couldn't leave the station, the radio—at least the separate dispatcher-monitored channel—died. I had asked him to call the local fire department and request a tanker truck to be dispatched but didn't know if he received the complete transmission. When no one appeared after five minutes, I instructed conductor Williams to find a telephone.

Southbound No. 79, the *Carolinian*, was nearing the great arched Rappahannock River viaduct, when dispatcher Quinton came on the road channel and told its engineer, Clint Hues, to hold out of the station until our difficulties could be assessed. Clint chuckled, "Sounds like he needs a plumber."

Perspiring profusely and covered with engine room oil, I opened the large side door on the east side of No. 377 to find a gleaming yellow and chrome fire engine pulling into the VRE parking lot.

"You the fella that called for a fire truck?" inquired one of the two uniformed men who climbed the embankment nearing the side of the train.

"Yes," I said. "Thanks for getting here so quickly."

"Where's the fire?" the other asked.

After explaining the situation and telling them that I had done this a few times before, he scratched his head and said, "I guess it's okay. Anyway, we're here. Tell us what we need to do."

After removing the large spray nozzle from the hose, attempting to insert it into the retention tank, and being sternly warned that the pressure would be intense, I held on as the canvas snake hissed, uncoiled, and began to fill the thirsty engine with cooling water. At the very instant the tank topped off, I realized I had positioned myself out of sight of the firemen and my crew, with no way to signal them to cut off the supply as cold water splashed onto the fiery engine block, the floor, and me. The flow finally subsided, and I tossed the hose down to the two firefighters, who, with 50 or so onlookers, stared in complete bewilderment. I was covered with a smelly, oily concoction that had ruined my clothes. With nothing except a change of underwear and a shirt, I'd have to wait until I arrived home in Richmond the next day for dry shoes and slacks.

Of immediate concern was the fact that I still did not know how long this gulp of cooling water would last. "Let's get this thing rolling before we run dry again," I yelled into the radio. "Get those people on board."

"Clear signal, straight up track number two," I finally announced.

Roaring over Potomac Run, I paid little attention to the stone pillars that once supported Civil War General Herman Haupt's hastily erected railroad bridge. As bald eagles and presidential helicopters hovered overhead on the sunny, crisp fall day, we raced along the shoreline of the four-mile-wide Potomac River, nearing our next stop, the famed U.S. Marine and FBI base at Quantico. At the stop, I scrambled to see how much cooling water had been lost during the 15-minute sprint.

Down about one-fourth! A lot, but at that rate, it just might last the remaining 45 minutes into Union Station, barring any further delays.

Departing the small, unmanned station and curving onto the ill-conceived, single-track span across Quantico Creek, the cab signal jumped to green. We were routed up No. 3 main line all the way to Washington, as I had requested. However, as my conductor quickly reminded me, doing so required protection from the dispatcher to board passengers across the active No. 2 mainline track from Woodbridge's lone east side platform, spotting the train on a 10-foot-wide crosswalk. Not a big problem if your radio is working, but mine wasn't.

In desperation, I called for help from the *Auto Train* facility at Lorton. To my relief, Larry Quinton soon spoke, giving me protection and also informing me that Amtrak had help standing by, should it be needed. "Yeh," I sarcastically replied. "With the luck I'm having today, they'll probably dispatch a product line manager with a bouquet of flowers and a big smile." To my embarrassment, I learned that it was a product line manager who had heard my plea on the radio and contacted the dispatcher.

"Anything else?" Larry hurriedly asked, "I've got problems south of Richmond. A grain train has slammed into a fallen tree ... at m.p. 13."

Suddenly, the cab signal became erratic, randomly displaying red, yellow, yellow over green, and green. The accompanying thud and a hiss of escaping air announced that the train control had failed to continue working, but had not failed to stop us at m.p. 94 (again, the digits add up to 13). Still on the air with me, luckily, Quinton gave me permission to proceed by wayside signal indication according to the rules.

We made it to Washington only 30 minutes late. The train eventually arrived in Boston 13 minutes tardy.

Deadheading home to Richmond from Washington the following Monday, I overheard the conversation at the food service counter between No. 95's lead service attendant, Doris Trotta, and a gravely voiced, gray-haired lady. Sipping her coffee, the senior citizen sighed, "I hope this is better than the trip we had coming up. We kept stopping, the engine ran out of water, and the lights went out. And then there was this young man who was soaked to his toes by a fire hose," she giggled. "But then, it was Friday the 13th. I should have known better than to travel on that day."

Laughing uncontrollably, Doris turned to me and said, "Well, Doug. What do you think?"

Chapter 18: Superintendent's Bulletin North-38

It was May 12, 1995, and as the CSX dispatcher's bulletins for my portion of the evening's Amtrak *New England Express* train No. 99, between Richmond and Newport News, spewed from the printer, conductor Jerry Reed yelled out, "We're up to North-38 on the Florence Division. Will you bring it up on the screen, while I call the dispatcher and give him the crew, Doug?"

"Sure, Jerry. Three copies. You, me, and Savalas [Arnold, our flagman]," I answered. Our crew is usually a couple of bulletins behind, depending on how busy the railroad has been during our two-day, midweek "weekend."

Every three months, important special instructions—superintendent's bulletins—relative to the operation of trains on each division are issued to every employee over the signature of the division superintendent. Additional superintendent's bulletins are issued as necessary, in numerical order, with the number of the latest appearing on each train's daily dispatcher's bulletin, which has replaced the time-honored clearance card and train orders. Each member of our crew was thus required to be familiar and ready to comply with the contents of bulletin North 38. Because the Florence Division covers such a large and diverse geographic operating area, information contained often deals exclusively with freight carriage and for remote locations that last saw passenger service headed up by steam locomotives. Nonetheless, Amtrak employees must tote them all, as well as enough operating and safety rule books and bulletins to comprise a safety hazard in itself.

An Amtrak engineer and computer illiterate, I found myself entering a string of letters, numbers, and symbols on the keyboard of a computer terminal as prescribed by the plastic-covered, yellowing instruction sheet taped to the cinderblock crew room wall. Paper poured from the printer, cascading downward like a slow-motion waterfall, gushing onto the floor.

Reaching for the three hole punch so that I might store this information in the binder containing the rest of my superintendent's bulletins, the word "Woodward" caught my eye. Effective 0001 hours May 12, 1995, with reference to timetable special instructions for the South End Subdivision regarding Method of Operation, that segment of track known as the "Selma" DTC (Direct Traffic Control) block is renamed the "Woodward" DTC block. On portions of the railroad where there are no signals and operation was formerly governed by a timetable, train orders, and standard time, CSX (and other railroads) employ a system of DTC—verbal permission from a train dispatcher—to proceed through a series of defined, named blocks. It is also the method by which trains are moved in normally signaled territory in the event of signal suspension or emergency. In addition to a wayside sign clearly identifying the beginning and ending block limits, this information is also printed in the timetable special instructions.

As I looked up, I saw my reflection in the glass case bearing the red, white, and blue Brotherhood of Locomotive Engineers' circular emblem. Displayed inside it was a copy of the letter from former BLE International President Ronald P. McLaughlin, granting the request of our members to rename our division to honor the memory of our late secretary-treasurer: R. Brooks Woodward Memorial Division 14. The image blurred as I swallowed hard in a failed attempt to grapple with the emotion that the memories evoked. I had written tributes to Brooks that appeared in both the BLE's LOCOMOTIVE ENGINEERS' JOURNAL and Amtrak's employee publication AMTRAK TIES. Neither, however, could adequately begin to praise the humble man to whom brotherhood was not just an organization of which he was a member, but a tenet by which he lived his life.

Since that fateful Monday morning, May 16, 1994, I have often passed the location where Robert Brooks Woodward lost his life in the wreck of the *Silver Meteor*, just south of the Norfolk Southern diamond at Selma, North Carolina. According to the final report of investigators from the U.S. Department of Transportation, his death and the derailment were the direct result of an improperly fastened loaded cargo container slipping off a passing northbound CSX piggyback train and striking No. 87. All 16 cars derailed, and both of its F40s overturned and burned in the fog of what was supposed to have been a beautiful Carolina spring day, at about 4:45 a.m (the same moment I was climbing down from the cab of my two-hour late *Atlantic City Express* in Richmond). As if stopped by some invisible barrier, the wreckage lay strewn just shy of the signal bridge, previously called Sylvania, spanning the old Atlantic Coast Line doubletrack main behind a former electronics plant at the Selma/Pine Level interchange on I-95. The signal has since been referred to by Amtrak engineers as "Brooks in Black" when, per CSX operating rules, they announce the indication and location of wayside signals over the radio.

I had spent most of my four-hour layover the previous night in Washington doing union work with our division's Secretary-Treasurer Brooks Woodward. (The BLE has divisions—not locals). Our train was due out of Washington and into Richmond 15 minutes ahead of his, but we were reported two hours late and lost another hour setting out a car prior to leaving Union Station. Working with former Eastern Airlines pilot W. A. "Bill" Black, Brooks held the job—assistant engineer on the *Meteor* between Florence and Washington—that I first held when I came to Amtrak in 1986. It was all-night work, six days a week, but at least he lived in Laurinburg, North Carolina, only an hour's drive from work. Additionally, he had set up the jobs to allow more time at home, though it meant taking a pay cut by giving up a trip every two weeks. "But the time you get to spend with your family is worth every penny, Doug. I hope you can do the same with the jobs in Richmond," he added.

"Of course you might have to give up those fancy designer bibs and settle for the generic brand," laughed Bill Black, whose own faded bib overalls were his trademark. Normally dressed in slacks and a knit shirt—a far cry from the legendary, gauntlet-gloved hoggers as engineers are typically portrayed—I had indeed worn a green knit shirt that matched the stitching on the bibs I sported that night.

While Bill headed to the food court, Brooks and I bemoaned the merciless criticism accorded most local union officials by their members. In our case, as in most, it's a non-paying, honorary position, although many dues payers regard your willingness to serve as their right to demand your time at any time, even if it means interrupting a family meal, a quiet moment with your spouse, or the little sleep the railroad affords you. As we mused, the phone rang and rang and rang. "Riddell," yelled Bernadine, the Washington crew dispatcher, "One of your people claims Philadelphia won't let him make a seniority move. How about you taking care of it, please."

"We'll have to start calling you 'Dirty Harry,'" chuckled Brooks. "You can cover up with a blanket in a broom closet in the middle of the night, and they'd still know where to find you when they need a whipping boy."

"Who? The company or the members?" I retorted as we both roared.

Within a few minutes, Brooks and I got a proper interpretation of the contract, called the complaining member and assignment clerk, and had the problem resolved.

"Thanks for getting me involved again, Brooks," I laughed. Elected Division 14's first local chairman when it was chartered in 1987, I gave up the post three years later due to personal obligations. At his urging, I volunteered to serve as an appointed local representative in Richmond until the next elections were held, arranging assignments, attempting to mediate grievances, and acting as a labor/management liaison.

"Yeh, just wait till the first time something goes wrong, and they're looking for someone to hang," he added rather matter-of-factly. "Then see if you still want to thank me."

Brooks spoke with his wife, Chris, and their two children, a nightly ritual reaffirming the immeasurable depth of love that characterized their high school sweetheart romance, which produced a son, B. J., and daughter, Ginny. This type of devotion is rare in a vocation where loneliness, despair, and opportunity too often overcome the resistance of the weak and thoroughly test the resolve of the strong. But in the Woodwards' corner of the rural South, so often mocked for its unpretentious lifestyle, such lasting relationships are still the norm, and God is something other than just the first of syllable in an expletive.

The 16-car *Silver Meteor* had screeched to a halt on lower level track No. 26, led by one of Amtrak's increasingly less reliable E60s. Bill and Brooks were summoned to couple the two waiting F40s to the consist that would streak across a sleeping southland in darkness before greeting the dawn near Savannah, Georgia, later in the day splitting at Auburndale, Florida, and terminating at Tampa and Miami. "I've got to go, Doug," Brooks said. He stood at the newly painted crew room entrance, momentarily hesitating as if there was something left unsaid. Proudly wearing the BLE emblem on his grip and his cap, Robert Brooks Woodward Sr., age 41, smiled, turned, and walked away.

The phone rang and rang and rang. Before I could inflict my venom on the unsuspecting caller (whom I assumed would try to sell something to me), I recognized the voice as that of my mother. Wreck? *Silver Meteor*? North Carolina? "No Mom. I'm fine," I assured her. She always calls to check on me when there's an Amtrak derailment. Why did that strike me so strangely?

The train en route to Florida? Oh my God! Brooks and Bill!

The phone rang and rang and rang. On the speakerphone my transportation manager, Greg Baxter, sounded as though he had not slept well or was deeply troubled. Management positions are pie jobs until something goes wrong. Then you earn the money. "How bad is it?" I asked.

"Both engines overturned, 16 cars on the ground," he answered.

Then, the question every railroader asks with a prayer in the wings—a question I've asked so many times, and so many times let out a huge sigh of relief when the answer was in the affirmative: "Everyone's okay, aren't they?"

But this time there was silence. I started to ask again, hoping the speakerphone was just momentarily overridden by another noise in Greg's office. Before he could get the words out of his mouth, my body wrenched, my heart stopped, a wave of fire that gathered somewhere in my innermost soul rushed upward in an attempt to deny the awful truth.

"Woodward confirmed dead. Black too, we believe," Baxter whispered.

Woodward dead? Suddenly, it was as if I had crested the topmost peak of a roller coaster and begun the descent—that awful, hollow emptiness that tests the will of the heart to continue beating.

"No! God No! He was just standing there. I just saw him. No! He's not dead! He's not dead! No!" I melted to a quivering heap on the blue carpet of the second floor bedroom. There was no cavalry arriving just in time, no life preserver tossed from a rescue ship to the survivor. This was the end. Brooks was dead.

From across the room, I heard a voice. It was coming from the telephone receiver. Baxter. In my fit of temper, I had thrown the phone across the room. "Doug, you're needed here at the station. Please come in if you feel you can make it," he reverently said. Regaining some degree of composure, I managed an answer. I showered, shaved, and began to dress for the drive to Greendale.

As I gathered my thoughts, the phone rang and rang and rang. Baxter again. Prayer partially answered. Black is alive! Not by much, but nonetheless he was alive—helicoptered to Duke University Medical Center at Durham.

The phone rang and rang and rang. Steve Fitzgerald, head of public relations for the BLE in Cleveland, was on a conference call with a reporter for the Associated Press. He wanted to confirm a report of a witness observing an Amtrak employee pulling himself along through the ballast with two broken legs, dragging a fire extinguisher toward the burning lead F40 of the *Silver Meteor*. It had to be Bill Black, screaming to anyone who could hear his voice that his fireman was still in the cab. Assistant conductor Steve Bissett, risking his own life, climbed onto the burning locomotive and lowered himself into the cab in an attempt to rescue his friend and coworker. Bill now lives with his wife and family near Wilmington, North Carolina. Doctors worked hard to save his life, but were unable to prevent the eventual loss of one of his legs.

Collecting money to pay for the burial expenses and providing for the widows and orphans of members killed while working on the railroad, that's why railroad unions were formed. The media, which paint us as a featherbedding, placard-carrying band of ingrates, never manages to broadcast that part of the story. Once, one of the networks asked for permission to interview members outside one of our division meetings in the waning hours prior to a threatened strike in 1988. "We don't want anyone who looks like a union official," requested the reporter. "We want to get the story from someone who sounds like a railroader." Naturally, that evening on the NBC *Nightly News*, the face and voice of Brooks Woodward represented the BLE.

The phone rang and rang and rang. "Brotherhood of Locomotive Engineers," a somber voice answered in Cleveland, Ohio. "Mr. Riddell? Brother McLaughlin is expecting your call. I'll put you through. I'm sorry about Brooks." Along with his other duties, Brooks served on the BLE's Crash Investigation Task Force, which peered into the murky waters near Mobile, Alabama, searching for the answers behind Amtrak's worst disaster, the wreck of the *Sunset Limited*. Choked with emotion, Ron McLaughlin (like First Vice President Clarence Monin, General Secretary Treasurer Ed Dubrowski, and most of the BLE leadership) was personally touched by the loss of his friend. "Brooks stood there as that new engine was pulled from the muddy floor of that bayou and wondered aloud what those three men in that cab must have felt when they suddenly saw that damaged bridge and looked death in the face. I'm sure he knows now. We lost a good man, Doug. A very good man."

We did indeed, Brother McLaughlin.

Chapter 19: Steel Wheels, Glass Windows, and Iron Men

Amtrak has always reminded me of the character Pig Pen in the Charles Schultz' comic strip *Peanuts*, who goes about life enveloped in a cloud of dust, even while swimming under water. He can't escape it. It's his natural environment. Similarly, Amtrak's future has been clouded by uncertainty from day one, and like Pig Pen, it too seems doomed to amble on in a fog of tenuous existence as long as the editors of the Congressional Record are willing to pay for its inclusion in their publication.

Like a sickly, unwanted waif not expected to live past its third birthday, this runt of the litter was left abandoned on the steps of Congress in 1971. It was hoped that benevolent Uncle Sam would care for it and pay for its eventual burial.

Though clothed in hand-me-downs and nourished with table scraps, the waif did not die as anticipated, but grew to become an awkward, gangly adolescent. When the Arab oil embargo threatened to bring the country to a halt in the early 1970s, the value of Amtrak as a fuel-efficient alternative to highways, as well as overcrowded skies and airport runways, became clear. A nation that had never experienced the passenger train now heartily embraced it.

While it, like all railroad passenger systems, continues to rely on government assistance, Amtrak has reached adulthood. It has worn out, outgrown, and largely shed the WWII vintage motive power and rolling stock it was initially issued. It has ceased trying to apply band aids to wounds which require surgery, and has poised itself to be a contender in the transportation of the 21st century, purchasing equipment to vie with other countries of the world in the high-speed, intercity sprint competition. Even outside of the large metropolitan corridors of the Northeast, Midwest, and California, Amtrak has committed to as high a level of service and frequency as its own meager funds, and the support of individual states, will allow.

As such, it has presented its niggardly benefactor with a perplexing enigma. Sometimes, ugly ducklings survive and mature as beautiful swans. One, Conrail, even evolved into the proverbial goose which lays golden eggs. However, sometimes help is obviously necessary for that to occur.

The only eggs associated with Amtrak are goose eggs found on its statement of profitability, despite efforts that have brought it much closer to total recovery of its own costs of operation. While the simple act of earmarking a half-cent of the 18 cents derived from the sale of each gallon of gasoline for the highway trust fund would perpetually insure Amtrak's survival, the concept is a hard sell in a Congress that appears consumed with abortion, school prayer, misconduct of its own members, and challenges to Supreme Court rulings.

Working at Amtrak is a day-to-day challenge. It's like no other railroad. Its greatest asset is its people. Each month, I am amazed at the number of employees cited with 15, 20, and even 25 years of service that are listed in the corporation's employee publication; amazed that so many continue to outlast upheavals in government administration and changes in corporate management. For this company to have survived 28 years, there must indeed be a deep seated-core of the faithful, who, despite all of the assaults, have guarded its life support system and kept it going.

My association with Amtrak began as a railfan who desperately wanted a job with the new National Railroad Passenger Corporation, but I found myself repeatedly thwarted in my efforts to get a job, despite continued encouragement from insiders like Edwin Edel, John Baesch, and others. (Baesch is still at Amtrak, though Ed, after leaving to serve as one of CSX's first executives at its Richmond headquarters, is enjoying a well-deserved retirement.) I was always the odd fit at the shoe sale—the one everyone wanted to have, but for which no one could find a match.

Persistence paid off. I didn't get a job, but I did gain entrance to the company's L'Enfant Plaza headquarters in 1972, after Edel, then vice president-public relations, allowed me to take home the plastic HO scale lobby display model (a Santa Fe GP40 and some Santa Fe hi-level coaches), where I refurbished them with an Amtrak decal kit and replaced the GP40 with a matched A-B-B-A set of Athern F7s. I had spied a publicity shot of Patty Saunders, Amtrak's original passenger service representative, sitting beside it. I fired off a letter to Edel, noting that it was a shame Patty's natural charm was wasted drawing attention to a Santa Fe train. After all, Amtrak was not yet a household name. Weeks later, accompanied to Washington by my brother Damon, I got my picture taken in the same spot, with the Amtrak train set. Damon recalled that as we returned to Richmond, we noticed all flags flying at half staff.

"President Johnson has passed away," a passenger in the seat behind us explained to the Richmond, Fredericks & Potomac conductor as he punched her ticket. As good as my memory is, I had forgotten that.

As long as there is an Amtrak, there will be a John Baesch. John has done about every job, at just about every point on the system. He was working in the power bureau at L'Enfant Plaza when I first met him in 1972. When I was a guest journalist on the first run of the *Palmetto* in 1976, John was on board, coordinating festivities at stations along the way and crunching numbers the next day on the return trip from Savannah. When the Canadian LRC equipment made a promotional run on the *Palmetto*, John showed up on the platform at Richmond during a station stop, where he congratulated me on finally getting a railroad job on Seaboard Coast Line.

"Aren't you glad I didn't get to hire you, Doug?" he laughed. "You're doing what you wanted to do. You're an engineer, and you're probably making more money than I am."

I never knew where I was going to see John Baesch. I was deadheading home to Richmond from Washington on the *Meteor* one night in the late 1980s, when I found John putting away the last course of his meal in the diner.

"Where are you headed now?" I asked.

"Technology fair in Jacksonville. We're looking at ways to modernize train dispatching, crew dispatching; just about anything we can modernize to help save money."

For years he was in the transportation department in Philadelphia, and then he was running Boston's MBTA. At this writing, he is assistant general manager of Amtrak's crew management services center in Philadelphia, soon to be in Wilmington. Still, every time I get on a train, I expect to find John Baesch on the job.

Until I was finally hired by SCL, I shared the sentiments of so many railfans who are would-be railroaders: It seems totally unfair that people who want to work for the railroad so badly have such poor luck in securing a position in the industry. Washington Division Superintendent Stan Bagley and I were in Jacksonville some years ago at the conference in which Operation Redblock—the joint management/labor self-help program to combat alcohol and substance abuse on the railroad—was initiated on Amtrak. After dinner, we began talking about how we got our jobs on the railroad. After enumerating a litany of my failed attempts to get even a job interview with any railroad in the country before I was hired by SCL, Bagley laughed and said, "I don't want to make you feel any worse than you do, but I had just come out of the Air Force, was looking for a job—any job—and saw this ad in the WASHINGTON POST for a position with the Washington Terminal Company. I didn't even really know what it was, but I applied, and they hired me." I later found out that while shouldering all of the responsibility of division superintendent, he studied for his master's degree at night. Opportunity may have opened the door, but hard work kept it open.

When I first came to Amtrak in 1986, my management counterpart turned out to be one of the most interesting railroad people I've ever met. No matter what Amtrak was paying Transportation Manager Albert Scala, the company was getting a bargain. It would have been impossible for any business to pay him for all the effort he put into the job of orchestrating the direct operational takeover of Amtrak passenger trains from RF&P, Chesapeake & Ohio, Baltimore & Ohio, Southern, and SCL. If they offered him compensation time, he could probably retire.

A New Jersey native with ties to Erie Lackawanna Railroad, Al was a railfan before he became a railroader, which probably explained the mutual respect characterizing most of our dealings. With an ability to recall data that pales only in comparison to some kind of actual recording device, Scala possesses an uncanny knowledge of railroading. Not only was he familiar with routes, motive power, and equipment in the Northeast and at Amtrak, there was little he didn't know about the signaling systems and stations on roads in the Southwest, like Union Pacific and Santa Fe. If Al didn't know the answer to a specific question, he knew where to find out with just a phone call. Because he now oversees Amtrak's Washington Commuter District operations, our paths seldom cross, except in passing occasionally at Union Station; but when they do, the subject is trains—usually from the perspective of two people who enjoy them, and just happen to work for the railroad as well.

Amtrak was fortunate to have a number of excellent railroad operating men in Washington when I first came to work there, and one of the very best was Leonard Grzeskiweicz, now retired and living in Pittsburgh. A product of Pittsburgh's Polish Hill, he came to the company from the old Washington Terminal Company by way of the U.S. Marines.

As a union representative, I was summoned to Lenny's office one day with an engineer who had been working with an ankle that had been broken at home while he was house painting. Railroad engineers have no provision for any kind of paid sick leave, so when we mark off, we are not paid. Earlier that day, Lenny, then the terminal superintendent, saw the limping engineer pass his window and immediately took the man out of service. Railroad rules prohibit you from working in any state of physical impairment that could possibly interfere with the proper performance of your duties. Lenny's actions were out of honest concern for the employee's own safety and that of Amtrak's passengers and employees. "We just can't allow you to do this," he implored the young engineer in this informal, pre-hearing meeting. "It's just not safe."

Rising from his seat, the young man from North Carolina finally removed his hat, revealing a head as devoid of hair as Lenny's. With a soft southern drawl, the former Southern Railway engineer attempted to justify his actions.

"I would have removed my hat earlier," the engineer said, "but some people don't like people who are bald, and I figure I'm in enough hot water as it is."

"I can certainly relate to that," Lenny nodded affirmatively, tapping the flaky residue from a Lucky Strike into the ashtray on his desk.

"When I was in the Marines, they didn't ask me if I felt up to doing my work," the engineer said. "They ordered me to do it, and I did. Mr. Grzeskiweicz, all I'm looking for is an honest day's pay in return for an honest day's work—no more, no less."

"I can understand that too, son," Grzeskiweicz said, sitting a little straighter against the back of his chair, "I was a Marine."

"The railroad didn't cause my injury, so it shouldn't have to find someone to replace me because I was unfortunate enough to fall off a ladder at my own house," he concluded.

Impressed with his forthrightness, Grzeskiweicz took the letter of charge, turned it face down on his desk, drummed his finger tips on the worn blotter, and said, "Go on home, rest that ankle, let it heal good. Mark back up when you're able, and let's forget about this."

We were about ready to get up from our chairs when suddenly, torn between the course of action he had prescribed and what he knew needed to be done, Leonard Grzeskiweicz shook his head, crushed the half-smoked Lucky into the ashtray, turned the paper back over, and said, "No, son. I can't do it. As much as I admire your spirit, I just can't do that. What you did was wrong. Although it didn't, it could have resulted in a more serious situation with dire consequences, had an emergency arisen requiring you to climb down out of the cab and go a couple of miles down the tracks with a flag and some fusees to protect your train, for instance. But if you and your union representative will agree, we'll put a letter of reprimand in your file, and if at the end of six months you're not involved in any other rule violations, the letter will be thrown in the trash. This never happened. Do we have a deal?"

Before anyone could say another word, knowing the alternative for this young man was a long, unpaid vacation or possibly outright dismissal, depending upon his past disciplinary record, I jumped up, shook Lenny's hand, and assured him that this was certainly a wise and amicable solution to the problem. Apparently stunned by the pace of my actions, the young engineer slowly stuck out his hand to shake Lenny's. I had believed we parted as friends—Grzeskiweicz with the satisfaction that he had acted fairly but firmly; the young engineer with the assurance that he was not going to lose his job; and I with the knowledge that there was a man of honesty and integrity whom I could deal with in the future at Amtrak.

Out of earshot of the office, the young man turned to me and angrily scowled, "You sonofabitch! I'd rather he'd fired me than be humiliated like you let him do to me in there. You've got a lot of nerve. Damn union." He hobbled away and very seldom had anything to say to me before he was injured in a grade crossing accident and retired on disability before reaching the age of 40.

Being a local union official is an honorary and unpaid position, except for being reimbursed for lost wages to represent a member at a disciplinary investigation. This is true of most local railroad union representatives. Though I've been a union member all of my years on the railroad, I don't recommend local union leadership for those whose ego is easily bruised. The fact that I have been an elected local and regional union official for most of my years probably brings into question my reasons for not following my own advice.

Someone has to do it. Railroads are a lot like the Army. Both rely heavily on rules and regulations to maintain uniformity and order. Management's local labor relations officer and the union's local representative act as liaisons, both with the authority to smooth differences that crop up between the two parties they represent. Both are armed with a certain amount of implied trust when a compromise needs to be reached.

As I write this, I'm looking toward the conclusion of my tenure as president of my division of the BLE, and the end of my active involvement as a local union official. Everyone should have the opportunity to sit in the hot seat for a term or two. You look at the industry, your employer, your coworkers, and even yourself from a different perspective. But writing is becoming more of a full-time activity for me, something that hopefully will enable me to embrace my eventual retirement from Amtrak/CSX without really having to cut the umbilical cord to railroading. For as I said in my very first "From the Cab" column, "There's no other place I'd rather be."

Section 4

Keep'n Track

Chapter 20: Did You Hear the One About...

I think of myself as a locomotive engineer who writes, not an author who happens to work on the railroad. When I composed my first piece for the Chesapeake & Ohio Railroad Historical Society's magazine, I simply set out to tell a story of participants in the fascinating world of the flanged wheel whom I had come to know from being brought up around the railroad. Truly, I never pictured myself as a wordsmith.

I've met a few authors who've told me that my image of a working writer is a bit distorted. Sure, for some, expressions flow easily, but for others, every word is a struggle. For me, anything and everything to do with the railroad triggers the recollection of a memorable tale. The mere mention of a certain location, type of locomotive, or former coworker gets me reminiscing.

The people I've worked with are an endless source of stories that define the human side of railroading. Recently, upon hearing that my book was about to be published, one of my conductors predicted, "With your monthly magazine column and a book coming out, I imagine you'll quit Amtrak." Hardly. To begin with, as another rail author told me, "If you believe that you're doing this for money, you'll be bitterly disappointed." More importantly, without my link to the railroad, I'd be cut off from my source of material.

I never know what will prompt an epic tale of the rails. Ironically, one anecdote was related to me at a time of great personal sadness by good friend and fellow Amtrak employee Jack Hammill, who had just learned of my mother's death from cancer, in May 1998. Jack is a chief of onboard services for Amtrak working out of the Miami, Florida, crew base and is one of the best at his trade. Nearing the age of retirement, Jack is a ball of energy, whose career with Amtrak began in Boston during the company's infancy. Our friendship goes back to the days when I was a trainman in the late 1970s. Jack is a consummate master at damage control. His combination of enthusiasm, empathy, and humor enables him to soothe patrons when things aren't going according to plan. Jack's an effective communicator when the need arises, and during the course of his nearly four-day round trip between Miami and New York each week on one of Amtrak's three Silver Service trains (*Silver Star, Silver Meteor, Silver Palm*), seldom does everything go without a hitch.

"I was sorry to hear about your mom," Jack said recently, placing his hand on my shoulder. We met on the platform at the Richmond, Virginia, Amtrak station as I passed him on my way to the locomotive cab of that night's *Silver Star*.

"Bad thing about it, Jack, is that I was on the road when it happened," I added. "But then, the odds were that it would happen that way, because we're gone so much of the time."

"Yeah, but that doesn't make it any easier," he answered, supportively. "I know. It happened that way with me too."

For a moment, I felt a little guilty. I was only 100 miles away, departing Union Station in Washington, D.C., when I was notified that my mother had suddenly, though not unexpectedly, lost her gallant, 19-year battle with breast cancer. I was able to get home within a couple of hours on the next southbound train from Philadelphia. I assumed Jack was at the other end of the road, many hours or hundreds of miles from home when his emergency occurred.

"No," he said, "We were southbound, just a few hours out of Miami, when the ticket agent at Winter Park handed up a message. My wife would meet me with our family car at West Palm Beach to take me home. My mother was near death."

Jack went on to explain that it was necessary for him to quickly determine inventory levels and gather receipts with which to complete his paperwork. This he would entrust to the dining car steward to turn in after the train's arrival in Miami, when the equipment was taken to Hialeah Yard. The railroad, like the postal service, marches on, regardless of circumstance or consequence. The chief of onboard services is the train's business manager as well as its public relations representative.

"I sat down at a table in the empty diner and tried to complete my paperwork as best I could, torn apart emotionally, when I noticed a passenger standing in the aisle beside me," Jack remembered. "He told me that the conductor had directed him my way because the train had lurched suddenly as he was passing through a vestibule door, and he had struck his head. Removing a moist paper towel from his face, I could see that he had a big knot coming up where he had been hit by the door."

Jack Hammill smiled and offered help or compassion to the passenger, never for a moment letting on to him about his own personal grief—a class act always.

"Please sit down, sir, and let me record the details of your accident and offer you what assistance we have available on board until we can get you medical attention, should you feel you need it," Jack continued.

The man thanked him.

Hammill began filling out the multitude of required forms, noting when and where the accident had taken place, and then he inquired if any passengers had witnessed it.

"As I was finishing up the report, it just got to me," Jack Hammill explained. "While I was very much concerned about this man's injury, I couldn't keep my mind off of my mother, wondering if I'd get home in time to see her one last time. Despite all of my efforts to remain very professional and in control of myself, tears just began welling up in my eyes and started running down my cheeks. One droplet landed squarely in the middle of the report, smudging the ink and startling the injured patron. He looked up at me with this totally bewildered expression and apologetically shrugged, 'Look mister, there's no need to get so upset. It ain't all that bad. All I did was hit my head.'

"You know, I needed that," Jack Hamill laughed. "It was exactly the right prescription for what ailed me. It provided me with just enough diversion to gather my wits about me to prepare me for what was ahead."

At the other end of the spectrum, during my first year as a passenger trainman on the railroad, I also worked with one sour old conductor, who not only handled a similar situation badly, but did it in such a manner that we both could have lost our jobs, or worse.

Even though I had precious little seniority, by virtue of being passenger qualified and by taking the time to stay abreast of vacant positions that suddenly popped up, I caught a lot of passenger assignments. For a few months that first year, I was even able to hold a regular passenger flagman job between Richmond, Virginia, and Columbia, South Carolina. Depending on how the jobs were set up to work, some of the more senior employees declined to bid on assignments that didn't pay as much money as they could make in freight service, or ones with long layovers away from home.

During peak travel times, Amtrak operated its *Silver Meteor* (Nos. 83/84) and the *Champion* (Nos. 85/86) as separate trains, less than an hour apart over the parallel former Seaboard Air Line and Atlantic Coast Line railroads, all the way from New York to Jacksonville, Florida. When business was slow, an abbreviated combined train ran as far south as Jacksonville, where they were separated. The *Champion* then took the old ACL route to the Sunshine state's west coast, while the *Meteor* followed the former SAL right-of-way to Miami, just as they had done for decades prior to the 1967 merger that created Seaboard Coast Line. Both had nobly served as flagships for their respective systems. It was therefore rather ironic in February 1978, that Amtrak chose to route the *Champion* and the *Silver Star* (Nos. 81/82) over the former SAL north of Jacksonville, with the *Meteor* operating via the doubletrack main line of the former ACL. But then, what's in a name, especially when the consists of all three trains were nearly identical in their red, white, and blue Amtrak livery? None bore even a faint resemblance to their vaunted namesakes.

The assignments were set up so that the conductor, baggage master, and flagman of the southbound *Champion* (No. 85) from Richmond returned on the northbound *Silver Star* (No. 82) after a lengthy 20-hour layover in Columbia every three days— obviously not a very desirable assignment, even though we were paid by the mile for 372 miles in each direction. To my amazement, I bid on and once held that assignment for nearly a month.

The down side to this story was that I drew a prize grump for a captain. This old curmudgeon had all the personality of an open sore. He could cast a pall on a Fourth of July celebration or make honey turn sour. Thinking about it over 20 years later, he was probably the chief reason I was awarded the job. No one wanted to work with him.

The southward trip was typically uneventful. Since we left Richmond at 11:30 p.m., most patrons were asleep, the lounge car attendant had made his last call, and the majority of the local work at Petersburg, Virginia; Raleigh and Hamlet, North Carolina; and Camden, South Carolina, had been handled by the six-hour-earlier *Star*. Our 6:30 a.m. arrival in Columbia, however, often meant that we carried an extra sleeper or two filled with recruits on their way to the Army's Fort Jackson basic training base. But with luck and a fast cab ride to the ancient, crumbling, downtown residence hotel at which we were billeted, the grinding window air-conditioning unit hypnotically drowned out most of the sounds of the city, and the heavy, green roll-up window shade managed to block out enough of the light of the day to allow us to enjoy a deep, peaceful sleep.

Adapting my lifestyle to the hours that my schedule allowed, I'd usually wake about mid-afternoon and walk the quaint streets of South Carolina's capital. Since the only television set in the hotel was bolted to a stand in the lobby with a hand-scrawled note attached to it threatening mayhem to anyone other than the desk clerk daring to touch its controls, I frequently found myself ogling display models in the electronics section at Tapp's or Davison's department stores.

Old sourpuss had an automobile he kept in Columbia. Our baggage master and I never refused his invitation to dine, although we ate at the same cafeteria each trip. My parents passed along a time-tested truism: Note where truck drivers stop to eat. They know where to find good food—probably why you don't see many semis in the parking lots of major fast food chain outlets. Conversely, railroaders also have such a reputation: Railroaders know places where they get the most for their money, regardless of quality— obviously why you sometimes find the locomotive of some branchline local idling in the vicinity of a fast-food restaurant featuring a two-for-one promotion.

Although economy was probably my conductor's motivation for electing to eat at this particular establishment, I began to notice that the same waitress usually served us, and she managed to elicit a smile from the old codger. He once even broke into an outright grin when she winked at him. Her smile faded just as quickly when she got a good look at the minuscule gratuity the old tightwad left on the table.

Open 24 hours a day, Columbia's Seaboard Station Restaurant was the best bet in town for breakfast at 3:15 a.m., when our crew signed up for the trip north. Unlike our nocturnal southbound trip, things starting popping as soon as we departed town. The smell of fresh coffee and hot bacon cooking in the *Silver Star*'s diner was the only alarm clock most passengers needed. By the time we arrived in Hamlet, where the train was watered and fueled, there was usually a line forming. Making matters worse, most of the onboard crew bolted from the train to buy cartons of comparatively inexpensive cigarettes at the Terminal Hotel.

To make sure that all revenue was collected, when the train pulled away from Raleigh at about 8:30 a.m., the flagman started at the rear, and the conductor at the head, and each passenger was asked to show his or her ticket receipt. No one was allowed to pass. We even stalked the restrooms for scofflaws. One morning, as I was doing my ticket sweep, I stopped a young father nearing the vestibule of his car shouldering his toddler child. Behind my back, unknown to me, an elderly gentleman, fearing that the door would slide closed on me, lacerated his hand attempting to hold it open.

"Conductor," he yelled as I walked away from him, "I've hurt myself. I'm bleeding. I've just come out of a hospital in Florida following surgery, and I think I should at least have a tetanus shot."

I immediately walked him to the train's lounge car, grabbed the first aid kit, wrapped his fingers in sterile gauze, adding ice to stem the swelling, and applied pressure to stop the flow of blood. I sat him down at one of the small oval tables that lined the center aisle of the former U.S. Army hospital car turned Amtrak piano-lounge, offered him something to drink, and went to find old grumpy.

"Can't you do anything right?" the old conductor spouted (as if anything I did had caused the passenger's injury, or as if anything he could have done would have prevented it). "Take me to him, and let me do the talking. You've done enough."

Surprisingly, when the conductor and I arrived, the injured passenger was calm and comfortable in the care of our lounge car attendant. The bleeding had stopped, and further investigation showed it to be no more than a severely skinned knuckle. Just the same, the Philadelphia-bound senior citizen quite reasonably insisted that he be allowed to visit a doctor (at Amtrak's expense) to be examined. The sigh of relief I breathed was short-lived.

The passenger agreed to the conductor's request for him to lead us to the scene and demonstrate how he was injured.

"So instead of pushing the switch plate on the door that says PUSH, you tried to hold back the door with your bare hands?" the conductor asserted.

"Well," the injured patron explained, "I grabbed it the best way I could to try to keep it from closing on your coworker's back."

"I've seen all I need to see," the conductor said, tersely clearing his throat and nodding his head at the same time. "In other words, it was your own stupidity, and not the fault of the equipment, that caused your injury."

"Stupid! Who's stupid?" the passenger reacted as if he'd been slapped in the face.

Without hesitating, I grabbed my conductor's arm, whipped him around and forcefully whispered, "Look, captain, all he wanted to do five minutes ago was get a tetanus shot. Keep this up and he's going to want a lawyer, not a doctor."

With eyes that could have sliced through steel, the old railroader gritted his teeth, motioned for me to take my hand off of him, and told me to return to the rear of the train. "I'll deal with you later."

I figured my railroading career was over. By the time I reached the rear car, I was sure that before the next trip, I'd be the recipient of a certified letter telling me to appear for an investigation into the incident. With every curve in the track, I thought of at least one more charge that would probably be made against me. As fate would have it, I found a current copy of BROADCASTING MAGAZINE and began scanning the help wanted ads. I was sure that within a matter of days, I'd be looking for another job back behind a microphone or in front of a television camera. When I reached the crew room at the Richmond station, the old grump was waiting.

"Well," he proudly announced. "I saved your job. All that man wants now is a tetanus shot. I talked him out of suing you and having you fired."

I was so angry that no words would come out of my mouth. What could I have said anyway? I walked out the door and drove home. The phone call I got from the railroad was from the crew clerk, not the trainmaster. I'd not been fired, just displaced by a senior employee. I really didn't care that I only stood for the unpredictability of the extra board once more. I was just glad to get off of that job.

With the spring timetable change, the *Meteor* and *Champion* were again combined, assignments were reshuffled, and the conductor took a flagging job on the *Palmetto* (Nos. 89/90) between Richmond and Florence. Again, I only stood for the extra board and worked whatever the railroad called me for, and one summer day I was called for a work train between Richmond and Petersburg. Work trains mean long days of boring monotony, compared to through freight or passenger work. Their conductors, usually the most junior on the roster, are draftees, not volunteers. Since the work train is the lowest, least important thing moving, the conductor's primary function is to keep in the clear of all superior trains and beg the dispatcher for precious time on the main line in order to dump rock ballast, set out lengths of welded rail, or distribute wooden crossties. Many times, when traffic is especially heavy, it's not unusual to spend all day in a siding, making only two or three moves out on the main line before knocking off. There's a lot of time to talk and pass the time. This day in particular, I had just shared the tale of the injured passenger and old grumpy with my crew, when our own conductor returned from the block phone with news of why we were waiting so long for the overdue northbound *Palmetto*.

"They had to stop in Petersburg to take the train's flagman (the very same grumpy conductor from my past) to the hospital," he explained.

"Heart attack or something like that?" I asked.

"No," my young conductor said, shaking his head. "He was opening up the trap door to detrain passengers at Petersburg, lost his balance, and smashed his finger."

"Gee," I wondered, without thinking of how cruel it must have sounded when I blurted the words aloud, "do you think it was the fault of the equipment, or his own stupidity?"

Chapter 21: Life Imitates the Movies

Not a trip goes by that I don't encounter a father with his young son upon his shoulders, waving at me from alongside the right-of-way or examining the cars and locomotives in my train at the station. This scene is as old as railroading itself.

The photo which I'm most proud to have taken is one I shot at Dillwyn, Virginia, some years ago when the Old Dominion Chapter of the National Railroad Historical Society sponsored its annual *Fall Leaf Special* over the Buckingham Branch (the former Chesapeake & Ohio Railroad's Buckingham Subdivision). Beside the neatly kept classic C&O frame depot in this small southside Virginia hamlet was that day's power: the chapter's former Richmond, Fredericksburg & Potomac Railroad Electro-Motive Division GP7 No. 101.

I was attempting to park my car so that Ryan and I could join the other excursionists for this busman's holiday on the rails, when I caught sight of a scene that no artist could have rendered more aptly. I spied a young father about to snap a picture of the Geep, American flags fluttering from the mounting brackets on both sides of its short high hood, sunning itself on this brilliant, cloudless Saturday. Clinging affectionately to the dad's leg was a bib overall clad toddler, complete with red bandanna and engineer's hat. If one picture could define the love of trains, this would be it—no caption required. For me, it's always been the people who have made railroading special, not merely the equipment.

Because of all the time I spend away from home, were it not for his love of trains, I don't know that Ryan and I would be able to have the close, special relationship that we've developed over the years—the same kind I had with my late grandfather. Since I work for a passenger-carrying railroad, as opposed to a freight-only operation, Ryan frequently makes weekend trips with me, just as I did with grandpa Beazley. Had grandpa not taken me along as much as he did, I'd probably not have known him as well as I did during the 12 years he was a part of my life.

Now 14 years old, Ryan strides the aisles behind my conductors, handing out seat checks and making out his own delay report. He knows every inch of the railroad over which I am qualified and once, from memory, drew a map of the RF&P between Richmond and Washington that included every station, milepost, signal, and switch. Another trip, on the *Carolinian*, we even had Ryan stay close to a relatively new trainman so that my son could show him the ropes. Because having any unauthorized person in the cab of a locomotive is against the rules, I can't permit him to join me for fear of losing my job. But Ryan's decided that when old enough, he wants to hire out on the railroad. I've made it clear that I will not permit this unless he goes to college.

I'm acquainted with former CSX CEO Hays T. Watkins through our mutual involvement in the C&O Railroad Historical Society. Watkins has been extremely gracious and generous, having engineered the donation of a vintage EMD F7 freight locomotive to the society's collection and lending his support to continuing fundraising efforts. Once, when remarking how Ryan was growing, he asked what my son wanted to be when he grew up. "The president of CSX," Ryan replied, completely unrehearsed.

"Some of the top people in our organization started with that kind of ambition," the startled retired railroad executive smiled. "If I'm still around when Ryan comes of age, I'll see if I can't help get him pointed in the right direction." I appreciated the offer immensely, and Ryan was thrilled.

Current CSX CEO John Snow attended our most recent fall railroaders' barbecue and, upon seeing Ryan and me together, asked if he intended to be a railroader like his father. The Hays Watkins story was told once again, and Mr. Snow seemed pleased. "Of course," I injected, "much of his college tuition is invested in CSX stock, so we're depending on you."

"Just as we depend on you as an employee," Snow reminded me.

Not all sons of Pullman porters and engineers ride their fathers' magic carpets made of steel. Some wish to have absolutely nothing to do with the railroad. The demands of life on the high iron have sometimes done far more to cause the ruination of family relationships than to bring them together. Ryan bowls in a Saturday morning youth league with a friend whose late great grandfather worked with me in freight service on SCL. Since we discovered this connection, the youngster's mother spends the entire session asking me about the grandfather she hardly knew because he was always on the road.

When I first entered engine service at Rocky Mount, I was lucky enough to learn my craft at the side of some excellent engineers. Ned (not his real name, for reasons that will become obvious) was one particular engineer in the freight run whom I often teamed up with. He was fast, but he was good. When at the throttle, he was all business; but once we arrived in Florence for our layover, he was personable, generous, and witty. I sensed, however, that there was something missing from what I knew about Ned, something contradictory that lurked just beneath the surface.

"How's your marriage surviving the railroad so far?" he asked me as we headed for his car in the parking lot of Ryan's Steak House on South Irby Street, obviously having heard that my wife had returned to Richmond to live.

"Well, Sandy quit her job teaching third grade at Bassett Elementary School and we put a contract on a brick rancher in the Richmond suburbs right after the Christmas vacation break," I said sadly. "I'm living by myself in a rooming house not far from the passenger station. A newlywed has enough trouble adjusting to life with her new spouse, let alone adjusting in a new town where everyone is a stranger and her husband is gone all the time. When my hitch in Rocky Mount is up, that's where we'll live."

"You planning on having a family?" he asked.

"Yeah, I'd like to have at least one boy and one girl," I smiled. "More, I hope."

"Let me give you some advice," Ned went on. "If that's what you both want, put things into priority order: Your family comes first. I learned the truth the hard way, and I found it out much too late. You don't have to make the same mistake."

Without saying another word, we drove south, away from the business district, and made a left turn onto one of the loop roads that encircled the rapidly expanding town, serving as the trunks from which its meandering network of residential developments branched. Once ordained to serve as a railroad crossroads because of its locale—midway between Richmond and Jacksonville—locomotives were maintained at, and freight and passenger trains departed for destinations in all four directions from, Florence. Modern Florence, however, has weaned itself off the railroad payroll and has become more readily known as a mecca of industrial growth in the new South, just an hour's drive from Myrtle Beach.

We entered a neighborhood where the large brick Georgian homes with horseshoe-shaped driveways seemed to have been placed so as not to disturb the tall, long needle pine trees that abounded, covering the ground with their needles, or pine straw (a colloquialism attached to it by Carolinians). This was a breathtaking part of Florence that I had never seen. Strangely enough, from my experiences, I've noticed that the parts of cities and towns built next to railroad rights-of-way are usually some of the most blighted. Even on layover, railroaders are lodged along neon commercial strips not far from the tracks, places that leave the passerby with a false impression of the picturesque localities through which he or she passes. Florence was just that way.

I assumed Ned's unannounced decision to trek through this foreign section of town was spontaneous, a way to break the monotony of traveling the same worn path back to our place of lodging. Instead, it was to serve as a setting for another lesson in my continuing education as a railroad engineer.

Suddenly, we stopped with the car in gear and the motor running in front of one of those houses, silhouetted by the much too early setting winter sun. Inside the graciously appointed home, behind the flowing draperies which framed the tall shutter-accented, neocolonial styled windows, I could make out a man, his wife, and their children—the average American family—seated at the dining room table, no doubt discussing the events of the day together over the evening meal. Norman Rockwell would have been hard pressed to sketch a more idealistic scene.

"That's my son's house. That's him, his wife, and their kids," Ned nodded.

"Gosh, I guess if I wasn't with you and it wasn't dinner time, you'd be dropping in for a visit with the grandkids. I'm sorry," I said.

"No, not really," Ned said, slowly accelerating the old Chevy while looking back solemnly over his shoulder. "He'd hardly know who I am. Probably wouldn't want me in his house. What would we talk about? The only thing that ties us together is a birth certificate stating that I'm his biological father. I was never a real dad to him, not like I should have been. All those years when he was growing up, taking part in school activities, playing Little League baseball, and getting to know the young ladies, I was forced to Richmond to fire passenger trains or had to work the Stone Switcher here in

Florence, 16 hours a day, seven days a week. Even after I stood for something closer to home, I worked the highest paying job I could, so that he had the right clothes, a car when he was old enough to drive, and tuition after he was accepted at the university. I thought I was doing the right thing. He grew up right in front of my eyes, but I never got to see it. I'm as much a stranger to him as those people walking on the sidewalk. Just goes to show how dumb I am."

Ned said nothing more and drove back to the motel. I never forgot that night. I think about it every time I notice a deepening in the tone of Ryan's voice, buy him a larger pair of shoes, or purchase a longer pair of pants. As much as I love the railroad, there are those dark, lonely moments—the Ned moments—when I retreat from the world, lay my head on the pillow, and stare at the ceiling in my hotel room, asking myself if I will end up the same way. Will I someday drive past my son's home late at night, tormented by the ability to look through the open window and observe his life, but unable to reach out to him because of the cold brick walls of good intention that I have foolishly allowed to be built between us?

Unlike children, who don't know how to cope with their father's protracted absences, the spouses of railroaders learn to adjust—for better or worse, as the wedding vows say. I've often wondered why the railroad is not used as the backdrop for romance novels, soap operas, or dramatic films. The chief elements—loneliness and opportunity—are there.

One of my favorite movies, HUMAN DESIRE, stars Glenn Ford as a Korean War vet returning to his job as a midwestern locomotive engineer. It features some of the most accurate and picturesque stock footage of mid-20th century American railroading that exists, including overhead shots of the steam-powered Baltimore & Ohio *Capitol Limited* emerging from Harpers Ferry tunnel, passing sections of ACL's *Champion*, and Santa Fe F3s pulling up in front of the mission-style San Bernadino depot.

In typical Hollywood fashion, all of the clips are randomly arranged. For instance, Ford and his fireman, Edgar Buchannan, occupy the cab of a Rock Island Alco FA that crosses what is obviously the Delaware River at Trenton, New Jersey, into the Nevada desert. After the FA is, for some reason, cut off from its B-unit at the end of a run, it is twirled on a turntable. Go figure.

Romance, murder, and intrigue seem to occur with every signal as the result of a predictably doomed May-December marriage between overworked railroad official Broderick Crawford and bored housewife, Gloria Graham, who always seems to be looking for a few good men.

Frighteningly, the film's plot resembles the trials and temptations that face many real life railroad families. Crawford stays under the gun, bachelor Ford is continually on the road, and Buchannan's movie daughter, a wholesome sweet girl, competes for Ford's affection with Graham's tragic character.

Our instructor in Rocky Mount, Ralph Pharis, explained more than just the mechanics of operating a railroad locomotive. During momentary lulls in classroom activity, he would expound on the life which we were about to embark upon.

"Buckle down, study hard, and someday this railroad will reward you with the income to have a nice brick cottage in a good section of town, a paycheck to pay for the gas to drive your Cadillac back and forth to the railroad yard, and money to pay an orthodontist to straighten the teeth on all of those children you'll seldom get to see," he used to joke. Another favorite saying was, "Go out and party tonight instead of hitting the books and you'll flunk out of school and end up pumping gas at Joe's Blue Sunoco, third shift, with Tuesdays and Wednesdays off." Twenty years later, I can still remember every word—the humorous stuff as well as the things that have often helped get my train over the road when we should have been sitting somewhere broken down.

"Tend to your family just as carefully and faithfully as you do your job, or you'll end up like fireman Jones who worked the *Champion* out of Florence to Savannah," he told us. "Every night, just like clock work, the *Champion* would pull out of Florence on time, and every night Mrs. Jones would call the roundhouse to inquire if her husband's train had left town. It got to the point that I simply picked up the phone and said, 'You're safe, Mrs. Jones, his train has left town.'

"One night, because of the sudden illness of the engineer on a northbound train, Mr. Jones swapped out with him when the two trains met just south of town, and he arrived home a few hours early to find a fellow railroader in bed with his wife," Ralph said, laughing softly and shaking his head. "Mr. Jones was a good shot. He made sure neither his wife nor that conductor were never unfaithful again. Of course, he's serving time for murder at the big house in Columbia. They say he goes crazy every time he hears the whistle of a train leaving town. It only makes sense, right? And what's the moral to this story?"

"Be a faithful husband and father?" answered one bright student engineer.

"Hell no," smiled Ralph Pharis, tamping some more Benson and Hedges tobacco in the bowl of his pipe and lighting it with a single snap from his worn Zippo lighter. "The key to maintaining a good railroad marriage is to always call home first so your wife can put some food on the table and get that other man out of the house in plenty of time."

Chapter 22: Passing the Torch

Looking out the window of our rambling Virginia country home in the sprawling Richmond suburbs, the leaves are at their peak of change. A lack of rain has dimmed the brilliance of the red maples, but against the canary yellow of our neighbor's oaks and the unwavering hues of his evergreens, they still weave a fitting curtain, bringing a spectacular close to autumn.

Thinking about the changing seasons, I watch as Ryan boards his bus for school. Ryan is now a freshman at Atlee High School. Appropriately, the large campus borders the CSX/Chesapeake & Ohio Piedmont Subdivision main line that once hosted six daily passenger trains. In my youth, I stood on a spot in a vacant field, now the site of one of his classrooms, and clicked away with my ancient Canon FTb at Electro-Motive Division E8s in charge of C&O's *George Washington* and Amtrak's *James Whitcomb Riley*, GP7s and GP9s growling over the undulating terrain with the Charlottesville-Richmond local, and even Western Maryland red and white F7s occasionally pressed into service to supplement new C&O General Electric U25Bs.

While it might seem touching that Ryan should grow up so close to the places that meant so such to me, the empty grain and coal drags that rumble past his classroom window unfortunately serve to distract him from studying. While a second grade education might have been fine for my grandfather, and while I have managed to earn a comfortable living as a railroader and have been able to use the writing skills which I obtained with a mass communications degree, I constantly try to dispel any illusion my son has that he can get a job as a railroad brakeman after high school without a college education, and still enjoy a comfortable lifestyle. It won't happen for him or anyone else, not in today's world of infinite technology and competition for even menial jobs. It wouldn't surprise me if by 2004 a college degree is a prerequisite for most kinds of railroad employment. Today's major railroads require candidates to pay their own tuition and attend a post high school graduate course before they will be hired as a conductor or an engine service trainee.

Along with the gold Hamilton Railway Special that my grandfather bequeathed me, I wish I could pass to my son my grandfather's reverence for the education he never received. Don't misunderstand: Railroading provided his family with a good living when he was working. But my grandfather spent 10 of his 30 years on the railroad not working. He was furloughed at least once a year every year that his name appeared on the seniority roster, with the possible exception of World War II. It is only as I near the half-century mark with nearly 25 years of railroad service that I fully understand my grandfather's fears: that he had done me a disservice by taking me along when he went to the railroad yard on payday or to the railroad station to ride with him when he worked in passenger service.

I didn't listen to him; how can I get my own son to listen to me?

People I've met trainside or during speaking engagements often assume that my father worked for the railroad. He didn't. He had the opportunity, but has never regretted not acting on it.

My dad has always been my hero. He bagged groceries, delivered packages, and even painted the city water filtration plant in Richmond. He never gave up hope that the right job would come along, and it did. He started with AT&T shortly after I as born for $1 per hour and retired in 1986 with over 35 years service, the same year I transferred to Amtrak.

The railroad paid more (when you weren't furloughed), and my grandfather hinted that dad could get a job on C&O. But dad pointed out to grandpa once, that when you calculated what they both earned from the time they left for work until the time they returned home, there really wasn't much difference in their hourly rates. "What good is all of that money when you're sitting down in Newport News in a bunkhouse?" dad asked grandpa. "I'm at home every night, and I only work one weekend tour of duty a month. I'm at home with my family. You can't put a price on that." Grandpa never pursued the subject after that.

Not to deflate my ego when I first got my job with the railroad in 1977, but the same comparison revealed that, although it appeared that I made more than he did, the time I spent away from home lowered my actual earnings per hour to less than dad's. At the time, I was single. But as time ticked away with grandpa's Hamilton, marriage and fatherhood changed my perspective markedly.

It wasn't just the railroad. I became very active in my union. Except for full-time elected positions in the railroad's trade unions, being a union official is a non-paying, thankless task. My hat is off to anyone who can stay in the saddle of that bucking bronco until the bell sounds, allowing him or her to dismount and limp to the sidelines. I have no doubt that working railroaders would be worse off without the unions. Railroads are businesses, and profit is the sole motivation. Before the ink is dry and while the handshakes are still taking place following a contract signing, work immediately begins to test how far the envelope can be pushed. Even with all of the privileges and advantages made possible by union membership, it is the union member who is usually the most thankless and most critical of unions. It is only when he or she gets into trouble and has to rely on the savvy of the union representative to save his or her job that a member will stop to say thank you.

I feel good about the time I served as a local union official. I was very successful in terms of positive decisions when I represented members who were accused of work rule violations. I tried to be a two-way conduit for the exchange of ideas. As a result, I ended up becoming a convenient target for both sides. I knew I did a good job after I left office when my harshest critics, disenchanted with my successor, offered their undying support if I would throw my hat in the ring next time. But once I took the oath of office again, my recent supporters returned to their role as my harshest critics.

The decision to relinquish my union position came at the same time I was approached to write this book and contribute to VINTAGE RAILS magazine, while continuing to write "From the Cab" for RAILNEWS magazine. The timing was right.

Timing has always seemed to work to my advantage. I've always been in the right place at the right time. The Good Lord has always been there, like a chief dispatcher with an awfully big territory to cover. My first night as a fireman, if I had been two feet further, two seconds sooner along the walkway of Seaboard Coast Line GP7 761, I would have died when it exploded.

Things have always worked out for me. Maybe it's because of grandpa's Hamilton Railway Special. I have the same reservations my grandfather did about the future of a young man with a totally encompassing love for trains; but everything worked out okay. With that in mind, maybe the ticking of that 992b movement within that handsome gold case is grandpa's way of reassuring me that everything will be all right. Perhaps, someday, I will turn grandpa Beazley's Hamilton Railway Special over to my son, Ryan, when the time is right for him. And I'll know when it's time.